Advance Praise

More Straw Bale Building

In *More Straw Bale Building,* we see once again the combination of experience, knowledge, thoughtfulness, and friendly style that made *Straw Bale Building* such a useful book. The evolution of straw bale construction toward more widespread and dependable use will be given yet another boost by this book and from all those who will benefit from having read it.

— David Eisenberg, co-author of *The Straw Bale House,*
and director of the Development Center for Appropriate Technology

More Straw Bale Building contains a wealth of the latest information on planning and building with straw, and is an excellent guide to sustainable construction in general. Magwood and Mack are two of the most knowledgeable and experienced bale builders in North America, and it shows. Their practical treatise is a recommended must-read for anyone considering a straw bale building project.

— Mark Hoberecht, president, HarvestBuild Associates, Inc.

The "Ontario Three" have struck again — with an important contribution to the planning and completion of a straw bale home. This practical book will keep paying for itself each step of the owner-builder's way. My thanks to the authors for the extensive research and insights collected into this "must have" book for my clients!

— Habib John Gonzalez, Habib John Gonzalez, Sustainable Works; builder, educator, researcher

The straw bale movement has grown and evolved—and so has this book. In this updated and expanded second edition, the authors provide the latest understandings and techniques to build smarter, better, and more simply.

— Mark Piepkorn, co-editor of *Green Building Products*; former editor of *The Last Straw*

By weaving in comments from others along with their own, Chris, Pete and Tina provide an in-depth overview of building with straw. There is no substitute for hands-on experience, which the authors clearly demonstrate throughout the text.

— Kris J. Dick, Ph.D., P.Eng., Principal, Building Alternatives Inc.,
Adjunct Professor, Department of Biosystems Engineering, University of Manitoba

Taylor Publishing
www.dirtcheapbuilder.com
TEL: 707-441-1632
PO BOX 375
CUTTEN CA 95534 USA

Times — and everything in the straw bale world — are changing, and so are our building methods. With *More Straw Bale Building,* the authors have taken an old standard and brought it up to date by adding new sections and revising the old. This excellent book will provide guidance to a new generation wanting to build a straw bale structure. *Straw Bale Building* has long been a planning, job site and coffee table volume, and now there will be a revised companion setting there along side of the original.

— Gerald Goodman, Arctic Building Consultants,
straw bale building consultant, designer, and owner

With extensive hands-on experience backing them up, Magwood, Mack and Therrien once again share the most up-to-date information in the field of straw bale construction. By outlining lessons learned, comparing techniques, and highlighting the latest & greatest approaches, *More Straw Bale Building* will help the newcomer build a dream with more confidence, while giving the veteran straw baler new ideas, methods and techniques to chew on.

— Rachel Connor, Sustainable Building Instructor, Solar Energy International

In *More Straw Bale Building,* the authors detail with humour and clarity the challenges nd benefits of numerous straw bale systems they have explored both as owner/builders and as contracters. The fact that more than half the book addresses issues that come up before actually installing any straw provides a realistic picture of the preparation needed for the execution of a successful building — and the chapter on common mistakes is worth the price of the book in itself! As important resources like *More Straw Bale Building* become available, straw bale construction edges its way closer to being a significant mainstream alternative.

— Kim Thompson, Straw Bale Projects

More Straw Bale Building

A Complete Guide to
Designing and
Building with Straw

CHRIS MAGWOOD,
PETER MACK
AND TINA THERRIEN

ILLUSTRATIONS BY DALE BROWNSON

NEW SOCIETY PUBLISHERS

Cataloging in Publication Data:

A catalog record for this publication is available from the National Library of Canada.

Cover design by Diane McIntosh, photo courtesy of Catherine Wanek.
Book design and layout by Greg Green and Mary Jane Jessen.
Illustrations by Dale Brownson.

Printed in Canada.
First printing April 2005

New Society Publishers acknowledges the support of the Government of Canada through the Book Publishing Industry Development Program (BPIDP) for our publishing activities.

Paperback ISBN: 0-86571-518-1

Inquiries regarding requests to reprint all or part of *More Straw Bale Building* should be addressed to New Society Publishers at the address below.

To order directly from the publishers, please call toll-free (North America) 1-800-567-6772, or order online at www.newsociety.com.

Any other inquiries can be directed by mail to:

New Society Publishers
P.O. Box 189, Gabriola Island, BC V0R 1X0, Canada
1-800-567-6772

New Society Publishers' mission is to publish books that contribute in fundamental ways to building an ecologically sustainable and just society, and to do so with the least possible impact on the environment, in a manner that models this vision. We are committed to doing this not just through education, but through action. We are acting on our commitment to the world's remaining ancient forests by phasing out our paper supply from ancient forests worldwide. This book is one step toward ending global deforestation and climate change. It is printed on acid-free paper that is **100% old growth forest-free** (100% post-consumer recycled), processed chlorine free, and printed with vegetable based, low VOC-inks. For further information, or to browse our full list of books and purchase securely, visit our website at: www.newsociety.com

NEW SOCIETY PUBLISHERS   www.newsociety.com

First comes knowledge, then the doing of the job.
And much later, perhaps after you're dead,
something grows from what you've done.
—Rumi, *Mathnawi, V, 1053*

Books for Wiser Living from
Mother Earth News

Today, more than ever before, our society is seeking ways to live more conscientiously. To help bring you the very best inspiration and information about greener, more sustainable lifestyles, New Society Publishers has joined forces with *Mother Earth News*. For more than 30 years, *Mother Earth News* has been North America's "Original Guide to Living Wisely," creating books and magazines for people with a passion for self-reliance and a desire to live in harmony with nature. Across the countryside and in our cities, New Society Publishers and *Mother Earth News* are leading the way to a wiser, more sustainable world.

Contents

A Note from the Authors

In our note to the first edition of this book, we expressed our surprise at having become *professional straw bale builders*. Those are four words that would have been unthinkable together a decade ago, and yet we are now joined by many others who have the same job description. In our province alone there are numerous builders and companies specializing in straw bale structures, and around the world the number has grown so that it's no longer possible for all of us to know each other.

And yet, among the many people who now make these buildings, live in these buildings, or aspire to make and live in them, we continue to find a unique kinship and understanding. The term "straw bale movement" sometimes gets bandied about. Though it's far from an organized, cohesive movement, there is no doubt that it is growing quickly, and that many of us involved have the same goals.

Our society is heading toward a new understanding of our built environment. For centuries, people were always closely involved with, and

responsible for, the buildings they inhabited. Now we spend even more of our time in buildings, many of which are extremely unhealthy, but have lost the connection between ourselves and the places in which we live, learn, and work. As we learn ever more about how buildings work (and, just as importantly, don't work), we understand the importance of creating buildings that are healthy, unique, beautiful, and well suited to their inhabitants.

Learning about straw bales has been a motivating factor in this education, for us and for many others. But straw bales alone are not a solution; they are part of an answer that will take more than the rest of our lives to figure out. Everybody who takes a step in this direction is merely adding to a pool of knowledge that, someday, will see the widespread creation of buildings that meet high ideals of performance, aesthetics, and environmental appropriateness.

Please accept this book as part of our ongoing contribution to this wider learning.

Acknowledgments

The authors would like to thank the following people a whole bunch:

All of Pete's parents
Julie and Emma Bowen, ultimate superheroes
Andrew McKay and Andie Haltrich
Barb Bolin Val Bishop, and all at SSFC
Barb Lilker
Barry Griffith
Becky & Sherman Butler
Blackwell Engineering
Bob Platts
Camp Kawartha: Jacob, Karen, Sue, John,
    Dale et al.
Cam Todd and Canadian Classic Contractors
Catherine Wanek and Pete Fust
Cari and Russ
Cheryl, Beth and Grace
Chris and Judith Plant
Chris Walker
Dale Brownson
Dave McKey, Goldie and others
David Saunders
David and Anne-Marie Warburton
Deirdre McGahorn
Don Fugler
Don Polley, may he ride forever
Draydon Hartwig
Frank Tettemer & Cheryl Keetch

Gabrielle Justine Magwood
Gail & Brian Robins
Gary Magwood
Gary H's Clean Pants
Gavin Dandy and Everdale
Gerarda Schouten
Glen Hunter, Joanne Sokolowski and baby Gil
Grant Moorcroft and Moorcroft Hemp Farm
Grassroots Store
Great White
Gut Hung Lo
Habib Gonzalez
Hank, Anita and Melissa Carr
Helen Knibb
Ian & Marchand, the Dynamic Duo
Jack Seigel, Connie Cochrane, & Ryan Seigel
James & Crissy Swan
Jan "Concrete" Cohen
J.D. Stevens
Jeff Rupert
Jenny Madden, Peter Brackenbury &
    Charlie's smiles
Jim Gleason and company
Joe Cox
Mr. Joe Hiscott
John Marrow

John Panagapka & Karen Hunsberger
John Straube
Big Johnnie Taylor
John Wilson & Leigh Geraghty
John Wise & Anita Jansman
Jolien van der Maden
Joy Allan & Bert Weir
Joyce Coppinger and *The Last Straw Journal*
Kara & Tony Willan
Karen, Joseph and Elizabeth Soltan
KATO Construction
Ken, Kari, McKenzie and @#$#$
Kim Thompson and her hugs
Kris Dick
Lars Keller and Jo Morandin
Laura Ponti-Sgargi
Laura "Baung Lassie" Taylor
Leslie the Old, Peter the Cheater, and
    Duff the Dog
Linda and Robert Smith
Louis Theberge
Mana Vermeulen
Marianne "No Bacon" Beacon
Mark Piepkorn
Marthe & Albert Attema
Martin Liefhebber
Master Fut Yu
Michael Greenhough and co.
Mike Henry
Orville Thertell
Ontario Straw Bale Building Coalition
Patrick Marcotte & Sherri Smith
Patty Apac
Paul Longhurst

Paul Patterson & Tim Whalen
Regis Cornale
Rene Dalmeijer
Ricardo and Chris Sternberg
Ron & Donna Hunter
Ross and Patti Kembar
Russell Scott and everybody at the
Ecology Retreat Centre
Sandy Z
Scott Pegg
Sean Flanagan & Maureen Corrigan
Sean 'mind the splash' Bonham
Simon and JP at Generation Solar
Skye Faris
Sparo at Arro
Spatch Noseworthy
Squirtin' Burt Sturton
Stephen, Laurie & Malaika Collette
The Grumpy
The Putz Frau thanks the Putzmeister
The Spotted Dog (Rob & Scott)
The Straw Wolf, may he snarl forever
TOLA
Tom Rijven
Uncle Paul and Uncle Paul's Vic Lemmon
Shelly the dog, Gus the dog and all the other
great job site dogs
All our workshop "graduates"
Other contributors we may have forgotten Lego
blocks, Meccano sets, and for their inspiring,
pioneering work in straw bale construction,
David Eisenberg, Athena and Bill Steen, David
Bainbridge, Matts Myhrman and Judy Knox,
Steve MacDonald, and Bruce King.

Introduction

What to Expect from This Book

The idea of straw bale building has certainly hit a nerve in our collective thinking. An almost forgotten building style that was only ever used briefly in a small prairie region of North America has, in the past 25 years, spread to become practiced almost everywhere. Tens of thousands of people worldwide have chosen this system to build their homes, often in the face of resistance from local authorities and to the raised eyebrows of family, friends, and neighbors.

Straw bale building is certainly not the first alternative building style to be introduced and popularized, but its continuing growth and movement toward mainstream acceptance are unique among such alternatives. When we first started building with bales (nearly ten years ago!), it was a rare person indeed who knew what the heck we were talking about; today it is a rare person who hasn't at least heard of the idea; many have seen it presented on television or in print or know somebody who has worked on one.

Why this explosive growth? In part, it might be attributed to the media-friendly nature of the material — every journalist loves a Three Little Pigs headline! Almost every major newspaper and television network has by now covered straw bale building. But once the media novelty wears off, many people remain intrigued and fascinated with straw bale construction. Impressed by the high energy efficiency, the lowered environmental impact, and the beautiful simplicity of building with straw bales, many people have been willing to commit their time, effort, and money to building this way.

Straw bale building now finds itself at an important crossroads. Unlike other "new" building systems, this one does not come from within the construction industry. The incredible growth in straw bale building has been fueled entirely by a grassroots desire to build more efficiently and effectively. This means there has been no central planning or designing, no industry-wide testing or standardization. And that has been a good thing. The vast amount of experimentation that has occurred provides us with numerous examples of methods that work and methods that do not work. This grassroots movement also requires that we continually learn from one another, so that important lessons are shared and the collective experience becomes collective knowledge.

Most corners of the world have seen a surge of interest in straw bale building, including (a) Alaska, (b) Australia, (c) Belarus, (d) Belgium, (e) Chile, (f) China, (g) Germany , (h) Iraq , (i) Israel, (j) Norway , (k) Saudia Arabia , (l) South Africa and (m) the UK.

Luckily for all bale building enthusiasts, bale builders are largely an open, honest, and communicative bunch. Through formal and informal exchanges, much information trading takes place locally and internationally. The lack of standards has allowed creative thinkers to flourish and many styles of bale building to emerge.

We see our efforts in updating this book as our contribution to this growing body of knowledge. It has been exciting, since the publication of *Straw Bale Building*, to be the recipients of news, inquiries, updates, and conversations about bale building projects from all parts of the world, and nothing would please us more than to find this revised edition playing the same role as inspiration and conversation starter. We believe that experimentation and creative thinking are essential in the growth of straw bale building, and hope to encourage such thinking in these pages. But we also believe that the style has progressed to the point where there are some basic standards that apply to all bale buildings. In this book, we are attempting to help readers find creative solutions to their own building needs while staying mindful of these basic dos and don'ts of bale building.

We hope you find that balance for yourself in these pages!

This is a Book of Options and Thinking Tools

There is no such thing as "the straw bale standard." Instead of prescribing one particular methodology, we have set out to define the questions you will face during the exciting process of planning and building. It is incredibly complex, with so many competing considerations that sometimes a project can seem overwhelming. There are numerous critical moments of debate in every building project. In this book, we attempt to outline a variety of potential solutions and then give an honest appraisal of each choice according to five criteria:

- cost
- energy efficiency
- environmental implications
- building code compliance
- ease of construction

We don't want this book to lead you to build *our* dream home; we want you to have the thinking tools with which to build — or commission — your own.

Although we do our best to remain objective about our assessments of the options, you will certainly notice a bias toward "environmentally friendly" options, and for this we offer no apology. Modern building practices are extraordinarily wasteful of precious resources, and we believe wholeheartedly in doing everything possible to lighten the load our buildings place on the planet. Choosing to use straw bales as building material is an important step toward more sustainable building practices, but the ideal can — and should — be pursued more vigorously in all aspects of a project.

Helpful Resources

A book of straw bale building options must address concerns beyond the actual bale walls themselves. The straw walls — about which we present step-by-step instructions — must be integrated into a complete package. Although we attempt to address all the crucial elements of designing and creating foundations, roofing, plumbing, wiring, and all the other myriad tasks of building a structure, you will need further expertise in these areas for your own project.

To this end, we've included a resource list at the end of each chapter to direct your research. These are references that we have found useful, but by no means do they represent the full depth of information available. Use these sources as a springboard and search for the resources that speak most clearly to your intentions.

In many chapters, you will find sidebars written by people with a particular straw bale building experience to share. These are individual takes on specific areas of concern, both technical and personal. As a growing movement, straw bale building is developed and passed on by so many knowledgeable, creative people that we thought a sampling of voices from the field would prove useful to those who are just being introduced to the idea.

Come on inside!

A Note to Experienced Builders and Straw Bale Enthusiasts

The world currently contains a disproportionate number of first-time bale builders compared to those who have experience! We've written this book principally as a guide for people who are undertaking a bale structure for the first time. For builders who have a depth of experience in straw bale building or other styles of construction, there will inevitably be some redundant information. Hopefully, there will also be much that is either new or approached from a different angle. We hope you take the time to find what's useful to you. If you are a conventional building professional, we encourage you to try some bale work and then offer it to your future clients as an option. You might be surprised at the level of interest that's out there.

Bales Aren't Just for Houses

Throughout this book, we often use the word "house" to describe bale buildings, but by no means is the use of straw bales limited to single-family dwellings. From tiny garden sheds to large factories or warehouses, bales can be used in many ways to create many structures using the principles outlined here. If you find working with bales as addictive as we do, you'll start creating needs just to have an excuse to make another bale building!

Taking the First Step and Engaging Your Brain

Building your own home is a sprawling process of input, suggestion, passion, necessity, compromise, error, change, and refinement. We hope that this book inspires and assists those who wish to leap into that sprawl, immerse themselves, and emerge with a home to be proud of.

So, in the name of inspiration, it's onward we go ....

CHAPTER 1

Why Build with Straw?

Straw bale builders must repeatedly answer the question, Why?
Why bother using straw bales? There are many answers, and we'll start by addressing the most
common reasons for building with bales.

Straw as a Building Material

Not a Building Newcomer

Despite its relatively new status as a building material in North America, straw has been used in construction for as long as humans have been creating shelter for themselves. Durable, flexible, and grown close to the building site, unbaled straw is still widely used around the world in a variety of roof, wall and flooring systems.

Straw in Block Form

The horse-driven baling machine, invented and introduced into the grain-growing regions of the North American West in the 1870s, had the unintentional side effect of turning mounds of loose straw into tight, easy-to-handle building blocks. The settlers of the Nebraskan sandhills, who faced a lack of lumber and suitable sod for building their new homes, were the first to put these building blocks to use. Some of these early bale structures are still standing and occupied — a testament to the durability of straw bale walls and the community spirit. The settlers' enduring and effective homes are responsible for the bale building we do today.

DAVID EISENBERG, DCAT

1.1: *The Pilgrim Holiness Church in Nebraska is one of the oldest surviving historical straw bale buildings. It's a testament to the durability of bale buildings, and also the community spirit of this kind of construction.*

5

Straw Bales: The Waste that Rocked the World

Enough straw is currently produced every year in North America to meet *all* our residential building needs. And the same is true in many other parts of the world, since grain farming is common across most cultures and regions. This fact alone is enough reason to move toward using this abundant renewable resource for construction purposes, even if it held no particular advantage over other building materials. The fact that straw bale buildings can out-perform buildings made from other materials and lighten the load on the planet, as well as on our pocketbooks, makes it a triply effective material with which to build.

What's in an "R"

Let me offer a slightly different take on what is likely happening with the R-value of a straw bale wall. I question whether the best, most controlled scientific testing would show anything like the R-50 that we have all heard about for [three-string, 24-inch-wide] straw bales. The test used gives a fair first approximation but is widely recognized as being less accurate than ASTM236 Hot Box testing. That said, the difference between R-30 and R-50 is really not that great. It is certainly less than the difference between R-10 and R-30, an apparently equally distant pair of values. This is because R-value, a number derived from U-factor, is the ability of a substance to resist heat flow. To understand how that plays out in actual performance, we need to convert R-values back to U-factors, the measure of how much heat flows through a substance under a predefined set of conditions. U-factor is 1.0 divided by R-value and vice versa.

An R-10 wall will allow 1/10 of one Btu (0.10 Btus) through one square foot of wall in an hour if there is a one-degree Fahrenheit temperature difference between the two sides of the wall. An R-30 wall will allow 1/30 of a Btu (0.033 Btus) through under the same conditions. An R-50 wall will allow 1/50 of a Btu (0.02 Btus) through. Obviously, if your wall is R-10, you are going to make a much bigger dent by increasing the R-value to R-30, than if your wall is R-30 and you move to R-50. It's the law of diminishing returns. At some point, common sense and the pocketbook say it's good enough.

However, the tested R-value has little to do with how the wall performs in the real world. This is much truer for straw bale walls than for stud walls. Thermal bridges occur with regularity in stud walls — in fact, at every stud. Straw bale walls have fewer thermal breaks, by far. Moreover, the R-value is measured under what can be called static conditions: you can only take your readings once the wall surface temperatures have stopped changing. This takes about 20 minutes for the average window, an hour or two for a wall, and three to seven days for a straw bale wall. In other words, the conditions at the two wall surfaces must not change for days on end, or the R-value is invalid. Well, how often in the real world does that happen with one's house? The time it takes heat to travel through a straw bale wall is about 12 to 15 hours. By the time the heat has made that journey, diurnal (daily) temperature swings are driving the heat the other way in the wall. This means that a straw bale wall can give you the real-world impact of an R-50 wall, even though it is really only R-30.

— *Nehemiah Stone built his own straw bale house in Penryn, California. The explanation above is adapted from his straw building list serve and presentations on thermal performance of straw bale homes.* ∎

Efficiency Benefits

Whether it's a concern for the environment or for the bottom line of our monthly heating and cooling bills, the high level of energy efficiency achieved by straw bale homes is often the foremost reason for choosing straw bales over other building materials. The enviable energy efficiency is due to the good insulating properties of straw bales. The role of insulation is to minimize temperature loss or gain and therefore the amount of energy consumed to maintain a desired temperature. Through a combination of thickness, the amount of air they entrap, and the fairly low conductivity of straw itself, straw bales offer insulation values that can exceed those of modern, well-insulated, frame-walled homes.

Energy Consumption Comparison

The Canada Mortgage and Housing Corporation funded a study overseen by British Columbia bale builder Habib Gonzalez. Using energy consumption data from BC bale homes, they were compared to equivalent frame-walled homes via computer modeling. The following is an excerpt from that report:

While straw bale houses have a theoretical energy saving advantage over conventional houses, there is little good data on how they actually perform. This survey attempted to provide a first cut at comparing the space-heating energy consumption of straw bale homes and conventional homes.

Many straw bale homes are wholly or partially heated with wood-burning appliances. As wood consumption is difficult to measure accurately, the 11 houses in this survey used other fuel sources — gas, oil, electricity.

Most surveys of this type compare the measured houses to "control" houses of the same size, construction quality, occupancy, etc. Control houses for this study were too hard to locate, given the diversity of straw bale house design and the use of slab-on-grade foundations. Only 3 of the 11 study homes

House	Actual energy use (GJ)	Model energy use (GJ)	% SB vs. Model area	Total inside floor (m²)	Year built	Bale wall type	Comments
1	115.6	100.9	12.7	133	1996	Post and beam	30% total wall area glazed; 78% single glazing
2	52.9	48.6	8.3	108	1998	Post and beam	20% total wall area glazed; 100% single glazing; hydronic heat
3	98.6	103.5	-4.7	156	1998	Post and beam	Hydronic heat; interior work unfinished
4	24.6	31.9	-22.8	48	1997	Load bearing	Cottage apartment and store room
5	96.7	129.7	-25.4	210	2000	Log post and beam	Two storey; hydronic heat; ventilation system not used
6	104.7	129.4	-19.1	189	2001	Modified post and beam	Hydronic heat
7	56.4	81.7	-31.0	218	1999	Modified post and beam	Water source heat pump
8	152.9	249.5	-38.7	267	1998	Timber frame	Two storey; basement apartment; B & B
9	142.1	186.3	-23.7	209	2000	Timber frame	Two storey; partial hydronic heat
10	105.7	137.4	-23.1	153	1999	Post and beam	HRV in use
11	73.4	95.7	-23.3	91	1998	Load bearing	Ventilation system not used
Mean	93.1	117.7	-21	162			

had full or walkout basements. Instead of actual control houses, the energy use of the conventional houses was modeled using HOT2000 software. The measured space-heating consumption of the straw bale houses was compared to the modeled energy consumption of conventional 2001 British Columbia (BC) building code houses of the same dimensions as the straw houses. ☞

1.2 CMHC Energy Consumption Comparison.

R-What?

Insulation values are most commonly expressed as R-values, a measurement that denotes the ability of a material to resist the flow of heat. R-values for residential wall systems typically range between R-12 and R-20, depending on climatic conditions, building code regulations, and type of insulation. Plastered bale walls have R-values ranging from R-30 to R-50, depending on their width and orientation.

No Gaps, No Leaks

A well-built bale wall creates an unbroken wall of high insulation. In a traditional frame wall, the space between the studs might be insulated to R-12 or R-20, but the wooden studs themselves only offer approximately R-1 per inch, or R-5.5 for a common 2-by-6-inch stud. The thermal efficiency of the building is broken by these regular "cold bridges." Infrared photographs of frame homes taken on a cold day will show the outlines of the studs as cold strips on the interior wall surface. Problems can also arise in frame walls with settling and improper installation of various insulation materials, creating cold gaps. In a bale wall, only the window and door openings create cold bridges.

Reduce Your Heating and Cooling Bills

By significantly reducing the energy required to heat and cool your home, straw bale walls will save you a great deal of money over your home's lifetime.

Research Program. The contractor located 11 straw bale houses that used measurable fuel types. He visited the houses, measured floor areas, windows, and doors, and examined the energy bills. From the bills, he was able to extract the energy used only for house space-heating, by subtracting the energy consumption of appliances, lighting, water heating, etc. Using the measurements of these houses, he created simulated houses built to current BC building codes and having 2-by-6 walls. All interior floor dimensions, floor insulation (if any), window dimensions, attic insulation, solar exposure, etc., were the same in the actual straw bale houses and the simulated conventional houses. The simulations used reinforced vinyl double glazed-windows with a half-inch air gap and insulated spacers, according to common BC construction practice, even if the windows of the straw bale houses were of a lesser quality. When the study home included windows with high-efficiency elements, such as low-E tints and argon gas, the modeled home windows matched these details. The simulation program used (HOT2000) has had wide application in the Natural Resources Canada (NRCan) R2000 program and in the Energuide for Houses retrofit program. It has been extensively tested and is typically within ten percent of measured data on individual houses, perhaps with a small bias to over-predict energy usage. When a number of houses are averaged, the resulting mean should be close to the truth. In cases where the same hot water heater was used for space heating and domestic hot water use (dishes, showering, etc.), the modeling of these houses (and the energy usage in Figure 1.2) included simulated hot water usage as well.

One qualifier: BC building code requires some form of mechanical ventilation be installed. The occupants of the straw bale houses may or may not have used the ventilation systems. In the simulated houses, an air change rate of 0.2 air changes per hour (ACPH) was used in the simulations to reflect both the natural infiltration rate and whatever use of mechanical ventilation. This is relatively low but still may be higher than the ventilation rates actually experienced in the straw bale homes. Similarly, the modeled house air leakage was set at 4.5 air changes per hour at 50 pascals ☞

Lower Construction Costs

An entire chapter is devoted to "The Hotly Debated, Often-distorted Question of Cost," so here we will only point out that the materials used to create bale walls are less expensive than other common wall systems. By doubling as both wall structure and insulation, they play a dual role at a very reasonable cost. Whether you can translate this lower cost into a less expensive building project will be determined by your particular plans and how you realize them.

A significant cost advantage can be realized if you raise your own walls without the assistance of professional builders. It takes much less specific knowledge to build a bale wall than a wooden-framed wall, and you can save money by doing it yourself.

Cost will always be an important factor as we consider different building possibilities in this book. Our aim is to help you to build to your needs while meeting your particular budget requirements.

Design Benefits

Many alternative building systems require builders to adapt to new and often complicated construction techniques in order to achieve the benefits of the system. These same buildings can also require the occupants to adapt to new living conditions and configurations. These adaptations are not necessarily undesirable, but they are a significant factor in the decision-making process.

(Pa), typical for new BC stock. There were no air-tightness tests of the straw bale houses. The 1.5-inch thick stucco skins on the inside and outside of the straw generally provide good air barriers (and add to the thermal mass of the wall construction).

Findings. House space-heating consumptions are listed in Figure 1.2. Electrical houses had their kWh readings changed to gigaJoules (GJ) to provide an easier comparison to houses using other fuels. The energy use listed is usually for space-heating only, with some exceptions, as described above.

The straw bale houses used over 20 percent less space heating energy when compared to the modeled conventional houses. Some of this may be due to under-ventilation of the straw bale houses and a small tendency for the model to over-predict energy consumption in the conventional houses. However, the size of the savings and the consistency (9 of 11 houses) indicates that the straw bale houses in this survey require significantly less space-heating energy than comparable conventional houses.

A version of this report appeared in The Last Straw, no. 41.

Habib John Gonzalez is the owner/operator of Sustainable Works, a British Columbia-based outfit offering straw bale home building services, plaster spraying, consulting, and workshops. Contact: Sustainable Works, 615B Cedar Street, Nelson, BC, Canada V1L 2C4, tel/fax 250.352.3731, <habibg@netidea.com>.

The Canada Mortgage and Housing Corporation (CMHC) has funded a number of straw bale construction studies. The final version of this report (and others) can be downloaded at <http://www.cmhc-schl.gc.ca/publications/en/rh-pr/tech/02-115e.pdf >.

The H2K modeling software has been developed for the R-2000 housing system. It is an extensive program covering a wide variety of housing configurations. The software can be reviewed at <http://buildingsgroup.nrcan.gc.ca.html>. ∎

Straw bale construction is easily adaptable to a wide variety of design configurations — from the norms of traditional suburban homes to round, vaulted, or other unusual designs. Regardless of the design, the insulating and cost benefits of straw bale walls are always evident. Where building codes require new homes to blend with current fashions, or where home-builders prefer established designs, straw bales can be used to upgrade the performance of those homes. At the same time, bales leave the field wide open to spatial innovations of all stripes.

Beautiful, Adaptable Walls

Straw bale walls can be built to suit a variety of esthetics. From rounded and lumpy with an old world feel to straight, elegant, and modern, straw walls can take on many shapes and textures depending on how they are detailed. Finishing choices are almost unlimited, and different effects

HABIB GONZALEZ/SUSTAINABLE WORKS

1.3.a

JACK SIEGEL

1.3.b

PAUL BELANGER

1.3.c

TINA THERRIEN

1.3.d

1.3.a - d: *These four homes show that bale buildings are in no way limited in their design.*

can be applied to different walls in the same home. Especially attractive to many owners and builders are the deep window openings, which can be finished in a number of ways to provide seats, plant shelves, or decorative sills.

Bales Suit Human Dimensions

Bales are unusually well-suited to human dimensions, because the bale sizes were created for farmers to be able to lift, carry, and work with them effectively. This translates into useful construction dimensions too. A single bale makes a comfortable seat, two bales a comfortable stool, and three bales an excellent leaning post. These friendly dimensions can be incorporated into your design in unique and comfort-making ways.

Quiet and Comfortable

Straw bale walls are excellent sound barriers, making them an attractive choice in urban settings where ambient noise can be distracting and unhealthy for occupants.

Inside a straw home, the nature of the walls provide a pleasant sound qualitiy unavailable from flat, drywalled rooms. Sound and light behave very differently inside spaces that are not entirely flat and angular, resulting in a calmer, warmer, and more relaxing atmosphere.

Environmental Benefits

Straw bale construction can help to reduce the environmental impact of a building project in several ways:

- reduction of energy needed to heat and cool bale buildings
- annual renewability of straw resources
- low embodied energy

These factors combine to make a persuasive environmental argument for the use of straw bale wall systems. Reduced energy consumption for heating and cooling means less fuel is required and fewer emissions are produced from burning finite natural resources. Straw harvesting is much less energy-intensive than lumber harvesting and the manufacturing of insulation and other products used to build frame walls. The energy expended in straw production is already producing grain crops, resulting in a two-for-one energy saving. Straw is available locally in a wide variety of climatic regions; using locally produced bales saves energy that would otherwise be consumed in transportation.

Straw can be grown and harvested annually — unlike forests that take upward of 40 years to re-generate and rarely return to their former levels of production. Straw needs little processing to be used for building, and straw production is very decentralized; there are few regions that are not within a reasonable shipping distance of a straw supply.

1.4: *By bringing the straw bale walls into the living space, you can wrap yourself in the warm, comfortable contours that attract so many people to bale building.*

Using straw bales for building could also reduce the amount of straw that is burned off each year, considered waste. While many North American jurisdictions are starting to ban the burning of straw, tonnes of straw are still burned, adding un- wanted emissions and particulate to our atmosphere.

What is Embodied Energy?

Embodied energy, a term that is slowly making its way into the consciousness of the building industry, is the amount of energy used in producing a building material. In some calculations, only the energy directly used in harvesting and producing the material are included. In other

A Good Wall System for Noise Reduction

Most people who have been in a straw bale building have had the sensation that interior sounds somehow seem louder. Interior sounds are more distinct because they are not being drowned in background noise coming from outside. This is a clear indication that a straw bale wall works very well as an acoustic insulator. It does so because it is an almost perfect example of a damped cavity surrounded by two not-so-stiff membranes with sufficient mass — a far more effective method, weight for weight, than structures based on pure mass, like brick walls.

The anecdotal evidence of good sound insulation is supported by a test executed in the summer of 2003 at the acoustic lab of the Eindhoven Technical University. The test and the facility meet ISO 140-3 standards for testing the sound isolation of building aperture closures (i.e., windows). The test was done according to ISO 140-3, which determines the sound isolation of a building member between two acoustically separated chambers, with the test sample placed in an aperture between the chambers. Although we were aware of the limitations of the test facility for testing a wall system, we endeavored to make the test as accurate and as representative as possible. The size of the aperture (ISO standard) is 1.88m² (18 sq. ft.). The tested bale wall section had the following configuration:

- two-string bales laid flat (density 120-130kg/m³)
- earth/clay straw plaster between 25mm and 35mm (1–1.5 in.) thick (intentionally asymmetrical plasters)
- no reinforcing plaster netting or mesh or any form of pinning

The chosen sample structure was to be representative of a normal earth/clay plastered bale wall structure, as used by experienced builder Rob Kaptein of RAMstrobouw, who was also responsible for manufacturing the test sample. The graph and table summarize the test result.

The result can be expressed as *55 decibel (dB) A-weighting*, which approximates human hearing sensitivity. This result might seem low, but in fact it is very good. Most conventional wall systems — including a brick cavity wall with much higher mass — have a lower performance. Specifically interesting to note is the 2–3dB better performance at very low frequencies of the bale test sample when compared to conventional brick cavity walls. Heavy mass like a meter of concrete is still necessary for very low frequencies, i.e., less than 60 Hz.

A recipe for good acoustic isolation with a straw bale wall is: besides mass, low stiffness with sufficient mass, and acoustic decoupling. The relatively low stiffness of a bale wall with earthen plasters is ideal. The fact that the ☞

more thorough studies, the calculations include harvesting, production, transportation, storage, life cycle, recycling, and disposal. But no matter how you calculate embodied energy, baled straw is one of the best materials available.

Estimated embodied energy (production only) of some common materials:

- baled straw = 0.24 MegaJoules per kilogram (MJ/kg)

- fiberglass = 30.3 MJ/kg

- expanded polystyrene plastic (EPS) = 117 MJ/kg

- cement = 7.8 MJ/kg

cavity between the two outer plaster shells is filled with straw provides excellent acoustic damping. Care must be taken to fill all cavities and voids with very light straw/clay. Avoid any direct mechanical contacts between the inner and outer plaster shells, as these will seriously degrade sound-damping performance. Contrary to what you might expect, loosely packed bales will perform better than very tightly packed bales (rice straw, due to its floppy nature, is ideal). Pay a lot of attention to all openings and edge details; these are the weak points. An air leak of only 1mm² will seriously degrade performance. Door openings and windows are literally acoustic holes in the wall. These need special detailing and attention to even remotely approach the performance of the walls.

Freq.	R	
Hz	1/3 oct dB	1/1 oct dB
50	29.6	
63	33.5	30.9
80	30.5	
100	34.7	
125	37.4	36.4
160	37.8	
200	38.1	
250	34.8	36.1
315	36.1	
400	43.0	
500	47.8	46.2
630	52.4	
800	56.8	
1000	59.7	59.1
1250	62.9	
1600	66.4	
2000	68.2	67.0
2500	66.6	
3150	68.0	
4000	60.9	59.2
5000	55.8	

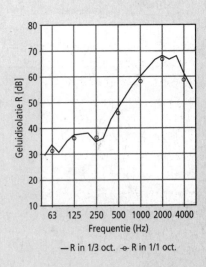

Here are some simple rules of thumb about room acoustics, depending on the type of acoustics you want to create. Soft acoustic instruments require a live room. Loud amplified sounds are better in a *dampened* room. The single most important parameter is the reverberation time and level. The harder the surfaces, the livelier the sound. A tiled bathroom is lively, hence your desire to sing (even if you can't!). Standing on top of a snowbound hillock gives the opposite effect. The bigger and harder the room, the longer the reverberation time. An oblong box approaches the ideal relative room dimensions, preferably the dimensions relate to each other at the ratio of approximately 2:3:5. This ratio will avoid the formation of predominant harmonic resonances and standing waves. The exact ratios depend on the size and acoustic reflectivity. I personally prefer rooms without parallel surfaces, thus avoiding standing waves. I think if you finish a room with earth/clay stucco on bale walls, with wooden flooring and a well-pitched ceiling, you will have quite acceptable acoustics for acoustic performances.

In conclusion, I would like to stress the following: Due to the nature of a bale wall (homogenic continuous surface), the wall itself won't be a problem acoustically, but the connections between the wall and all other structures, incorporated or surrounding, require proper detailing and careful execution. — *René Dalmeijer* ∎

- virgin steel = 32 MJ/kg
- recycled steel = 10.1 MJ/kg
- virgin aluminum = 191 MJ/kg
- recycled aluminum = 8.1 MJ/kg

(Source: Andrew Alcorn, *Embodied Energy Coefficients of Building Materials,* 2nd ed.)

As the list above shows, it can be quite an eye-opener to see the amount of energy industry expends on creating and supplying building materials. The numbers on this list show Mega-Joules of energy consumed per kilogram of material, hence the higher numbers for the lighter

1.5: *Other natural building materials, including tile and wood, can perfectly compliment the feel of plastered bale walls, and lower the potential toxicity of a home.*

materials and lower numbers for the heavier ones. But straw is both a lightweight material and it has a low embodied energy figure.

Environmental Benefits that Don't Cost More ...

Many new green building products (many are patented and proprietary) are being introduced on the market, and most of them are higher priced than their conventional competitors. Straw bales are an environmentally friendly alternative that does not require sacrifices in terms of costs, appearance, or availability. Straw bale building provides that elusive, and increasingly necessary,

alternative to wasteful, unsustainable modern practices.

... and Just Might Be Better for You

Straw bale walls offer a potential solution for those who find that the paints, chemicals, glues, and toxins embedded in manufactured building materials negatively affect their health. Organically grown straw coated with earth-based and/or lime plasters have received positive feedback from environmentally sensitive people.

Bales Aren't Magic

Although the benefits of using straw bales are many, straw is not actually a magical material. This cheap and abundant cellulose fiber just happens to get packaged into conveniently sized rigid bundles that are suitable for building. When the mystique of building with bales has been stripped away, the truth is that straw bales simply allow for the creation of very thick walls without consuming the quantity of resources that would be needed to make equally thick walls of wood, fiberglass, or other materials. Any conventional building method, if used to build walls of the same thickness as a bale wall, would provide similar levels of performance, but at a much greater financial and environmental cost. Bales work — cheaply and sustainably!

If Bales Are So Good, Why Doesn't Everybody Use Them?

The obvious advantages of building with bales gives rise to this common question. Passive resistance to bale construction comes from two sources: homeowners and the building industry.

Who Wouldn't Want a Bale Home?

Big financial commitments like the building of a house usually inspire conservatism in even the most adventurous spirits. Conventional frame houses are widely accepted as the safest financial choice. Even those who are willing to invest their money in new ideas can face significant resistance from spouses, family, friends, lenders, architects, building inspectors, building supply yard employees, and a host of other cautious types. It takes a lot of spirit and resolve to overcome such personal obstacles, and many people do not pursue their ideals in the face of such resistance.

There's No Money in Them There Straw Houses

The building industry has not yet embraced straw bale construction because it offers limited opportunities for profit. Bales cannot be patented, nor would it be immediately feasible for a building supply company to go into straw bale production. Most advances in building technology come from companies who develop products, test them, then use their testing results to obtain building code approval — or better yet, code requirement — for the product. Straw bales have little or no immediate chance of receiving the high budget testing afforded by big companies or the promotional dollars that would convince contractors to use them.

Housing contractors have no incentive to spend money retraining workers and investing in new equipment for homes that are no more costly than the ones they already make. It's just not good business to invest in a technology that does not yield a higher return than current practices.

Until consumers begin demanding highly efficient, environmentally responsible homes in sufficient quantity, straw bale construction will remain a marginal percentage of new home starts. And until consumer demand brings about widespread bale home construction, the kinds of prefabricated products that help contractors build quickly and efficiently won't be produced for straw bale buildings.

Be a Pioneer

If you decide that a straw bale home is what you want, then plunge in and do it. While you may feel like an isolated nut case at first, you will be opening doors to a whole new and lively community that will spring up around your efforts. Friends you didn't know you had will emerge to help out, and connections will be fostered with other like-minded people, both in your immediate area and around the world. Once you're settled into your house, these people will continue to make your life richer. It's an opportunity you won't want to miss.

1.6: (Above) *Crisp lines and smooth plaster compliment this built-in desk area. Even though bales offer so much aesthetic potential, it will be some time before they are part of mainstream construction.*

1.7: *Before you tackle an entire house, a small, simple building project is a good way to learn straw bale construction techniques.*

References

The Last Straw. P.O. Box 22706, Lincoln, Nebraska, 68542-2706, USA.

Email <thelaststraw@thelaststraw.org.>

Web site <www.thelaststraw.org>

The Last Straw is an international quarterly journal devoted to straw bale and natural building, and contains the most up-to-date information, as well as project reports and news of interest to bale builders. Their annual Resource Issue is an essential listing of the people, publications, and products needed by bale builders.

Books on Straw Bale Building

Bainbridge, David A., Athena Swentzell Steen, and Bill Steen. *The Straw Bale House*. Chelsea Green Publishing Company, 1994. ISBN 0-930031-71-7.

King, P. E., Bruce. *Buildings of Earth and Straw: Structural Design for Rammed Earth and Straw Bale Architecture*. Ecological Design Press, 1996. ISBN 0-9644718-1-7.

Corum, Nathaniel. *Building One House: A Handbook for Straw Bale Construction*. Red Feather Development Group, 2004. P.O. Box 907, Bozeman, MT, 59771-0907.

Gray, Alan, ed. *Strawbale Homebuilding*. Earth Garden Books, 2000. ISBN 0-9586397-4-4.

Jones, Barbara. *Building with Straw Bales: A Practical Guide for the UK and Ireland*. Green Books, 2002. ISBN 1-903998-13-1.

Lacinski, Paul and Michel Bergeron. *Serious Straw Bale*. Chelsea Green Publishers, 2000.

Lerner, Kelly and Pamela Wadsworth Goode, eds. *The Building Official's Guide to Straw-bale Construction, Version 2.1*. California Straw Building Association (CASBA), 2000. P.O. Box 1293, Angels Camp, CA, 95222-1293, USA.

Magwood, Chris and Chris Walker. *Straw Bale Details: A Manual for Designers and Builders*. New Society Publishers, 2002. ISBN 0-86571-476-2.

Myhrman, Matts and S. O. MacDonald. *Build It with Bales, Version 2*. Out on Bale, 1997. ISBN 0-9642821-1-9.

Roberts, Carolyn. *A House of Straw: An Odyssey into Natural Building*. Chelsea Green Publishing, 2002. ISBN 1-890123-30-6.

Steen, Bill and Athena Steen. *The Beauty of Straw Bale Homes*. Chelsea Green Publishing, 2000. ISBN 1-890132-77-2.

Wanek, Catherine. *The New Strawbale Home*. Gibbs Smith, 2003. ISBN 1-58685-203-5.

Videos

Building With Straw Series, Vol. 1 – 3. Black Range Films, Star Rt. 2, Box 119, Kingston New Mexico 88042. Email <resources @StrawBaleCentral.com>

Websites and Discussion Groups

The Canada Mortgage and Housing Corporation (CMHC) <http://www.cmhc-schl.gc.ca/>

The Last Straw <www.thelaststraw.org>

The International Straw Bale Registry <http://sbregistry.greenbuilder.com/>

Camel's Back Construction <www.strawhomes.ca>

Black Range Film <www.StrawBaleCentral.com>

Surfin' Strawbale <www.moxvox.com/surfsolo.html>

Straw Bale Social Club <http://groups.yahoo.com/groups/SB-r-us/>

The Strawbale Discussion List <strawbale@listserv.repp.org>

European Strawbale Building Discussion List <Strawbale@amper.ped.muni.cz>

Ontario Straw Bale Building Coalition <www.strawbalebuilding.ca>

CHAPTER 2

Other Natural Building Materials

Straw bales are only one of many natural building materials available to a home builder. While we have chosen straw bales as our favorite natural material for building exterior walls, we would by no means discourage anybody from investigating and using any number of materials and techniques. It is possible to combine many natural material options into a structure ideally suited to your needs and environment.

A Vast Palette of Materials

The same concerns that have fueled the interest in straw bale building have played a key role in the development and use of a whole array of natural and recycled building options. All of these materials and systems are viable options and worthy of investigation by anyone with an interest in straw bale building. Each choice suits a particular use, climate, budget, and level of experience. We will outline some of the most popular of these materials and methods, giving a very brief introduction to each. There are plenty of resources to help you research further, listed at the end of this chapter.

Cob

Cob is among the oldest and most time-tested building methods. Created by combining mud (soils with an adequate mixture of sand and clay) and straw fibers, cob can be used to build both exterior and interior walls, floors, ovens/fireplaces, benches, and other structural and nonstructural elements.

Environmentally sound, often free (if the site soil is suitable), practical in many

2.1a: *Cob house in the UK.*

2.1b: (Inset) *sculpting a cob fireplace,*

17

climates and conditions, easy (and fun!) to mix and build with, cob can be a wonderful medium. Thick cob walls can be load-bearing, but often cob is used as an infill with wooden framing systems. Cob does not offer a great insulation value, but it does contribute thermal mass, making it a good interior wall material in cold climates and an exterior wall material in warmer climates. Many straw bale homes incorporate cob elements, and it's so much fun to mix and use that we highly recommend you give it a try!

2.2a

2.2b

2.2a-b: Adobe blocks (Inset) and earth bricks are simple to use and time tested.

Adobe and Earth Brick

Closely related to cob, adobe and earth bricks are also mixtures of sand/clay soils and natural fibers, but the mixture is put into forms and either sun baked (adobe) or compressed (earth blocks) to create rigid bricks in a variety of sizes. These bricks are often dry stacked, but sometimes laid with a clay mortar.

Adobe and earth bricks have a long and proven history and offer excellent thermal mass properties, as well as low environmental impact and cost. In some areas of North America, adobe building has been commercialized and is relatively popular and accepted by building codes.

Rammed Earth

Another soil-based building method, rammed earth utilizes a wooden formwork system into which a suitable soil is placed and then tamped or rammed to compact it, essentially creating something akin to sedimentary stone. Like the other earth based methods, rammed earth is strong, long-lasting, and has a lengthy history.

As well as providing great thermal mass and strength, low cost, and environmental impact, rammed earth lends itself to both low- and high-tech methods. Some experiments with rammed earth as a foundation system to replace concrete hold promise in northern climates.

Rammed Earth Tires/Earthships

Used car and truck tires can serve as permanent forms for rammed earth, providing a long- lasting, stable, and strong building system. A style of building dubbed "earthships" was developed in the US by Michael Reynolds. Using rammed earth car tires as massive retaining walls, earthships are typically arranged with the north side of the building backed into a hill, or buried under the earth, with the south side exposed for passive solar gain. Earthship designs also tend to incorporate systems for renewable energy, water harvesting, and waste processing that make them very self-sufficient structures. These systems are excellent models for anybody trying to lower their environmental impact, and worthy of investigation.

Rammed earth tires can also be used to create foundations for above-ground housing, like straw bale homes. The tires can be laid continuously to create a full frost wall foundation, or stacked in columns to create pier-style foundations. Often, an owner will be paid to take the tires, and the earth to fill them is free, so this is an option well worth exploring.

Earthbags

Using flood control sacks or sandbags to act as permanent forms for earthen fill, earthbag building is also known as flexible form rammed earth. The polypropylene sacks (used for sandbags and feed bags) are filled with sand or other well-draining soils for foundation building, and with clay soils for above-grade walls. Stacked in running bond (like straw bales), these earthbags can create regular vertical walls or can be stacked to create vaulted or dome-shaped buildings. Developed by Nadir Kalili (for use on the moon!), the system can be used to create inexpensive, environmentally friendly, and very beautiful buildings.

The completed earthbag structure is typically plastered inside and out, protecting the bags from ultraviolet (UV) degradation and wear and tear. As with all earthen construction, earthbag buildings provide excellent thermal mass properties, but not much in the way of insulation value. Earthbag building can be used for interior elements for straw bale homes, or to continue bale-like forms in exterior and landscaping elements.

Cordwood Masonry/Stackwall

While many builders pursuing minimal environmental impacts avoid the use of milled lumber, cordwood masonry construction makes use of "junk wood" that would otherwise be ignored. Firewood, deadfall, logging remains, and even construction scraps can be used, as can trees

harvested to thin forests producing lumber. The wood is typically cut into 24-inch lengths and laid transversely in the wall, with mortar filling the spaces on both the interior and exterior. The spaces between the logs in the middle of the wall are insulated with loose fill, often a

2.3: *Rammed-earth building.*

treated sawdust. The system can create strong, beautiful, load-bearing walls with good insulation and thermal mass properties.

It has also often been used in conjunction with straw bale walls, typically to create the lower portion of a wall that then continues with straw bale. Recent developments in the use of earth-based mortars have made the system even more environmentally friendly.

2.4: *Earthbag building.*

Light Clay-straw

In this building style, loose straw is coated in a thin clay slip and then packed into forms to create

2.5: *Cordwood (or "stackwall") house.*

a nonstructural insulation. Popular for retrofitting buildings in an environmentally friendly way, light clay-straw is also used in new wood framed structures. Inexpensive, easy, and using very low-impact materials, light clay-straw is often incorporated into straw bale structures as interior walls and as an insulative fill in areas of the wall where a straw bale does not easily fit.

Hempcrete

A mixture of finely chopped hemp stalks and hydraulic lime, hempcrete can provide an

2.6: *Below.*

2.7: *Hempcrete porch.*

2.6: *Straw/clay packed between wood studs.*

2.8: *Papercrete vault.*

insulative fill for walls framed in a variety of ways (timber framing, stud framing, etc.).

Light, fireproof, and long-lasting with an excellent R-value, hempcrete can be its own building system, or complement a straw bale structure as insulative fill in awkward cavities, as entire interior or exterior walls, or as a thick plaster. Certain mixes of hempcrete have the potential to replace insulated concrete foundations.

Papercrete and Fidobe

Similar to hempcrete, papercrete and fidobe use cement or clay as a binder around a paper fiber aggregate, creating lightweight, strong, and highly insulative material.

Cement or clay binders have also been used around sawdust aggregate. All of these methods make use of waste fibers to create an adaptable and useful building material.

Baled Waste Materials

This book focuses on the use of straw bales, but many other waste products are similarly baled and used as building materials. Non-recyclable plastics, car tires, shredded paper, and cardboard are all compactly baled for minimizing size and ease of handling. These bales, often free or inexpensive, can be used in similar ways to straw bales. (See Other Baled Stuff in Chapter 3).

Traditional Building Materials

For environmental and cost considerations, it is often worthwhile to study historical building materials and systems. Timber framing, stone masonry, wattle and daub, and thatch all offer the potential to use sustainably harvested natural materials to create beautiful, non-toxic, efficient homes.

In pursuing your ideal home plans, we encourage you to research these methods and to apply them in creative ways that are appropriate to your project, your location, and your climate. Our goal is the creation of healthy, environmentally sound, appropriate housing; we find straw bale construction to be an excellent option in this pursuit, but by no means the only option. Unique hybrids of straw bale and the materials mentioned above are often the best solution for creating the ideal building for any given circumstance.

References

Bee, Becky. *The Cob Builder's Handbook*. Groundworks, 1997. ISBN 0-9659082-0-8.

Borer, Pat and Cindy Harris. *The Whole House Book: Ecological Building Design and Materials*. New Society Publishers, 2001. ISBN 0-86571-481-9.

Chappell, Steve, ed. *Alternative Building Sourcebook: Traditional, Natural and Sustainable Building Products and Services*. Fox Maple Press, 1998.

Chappell, Steve. *A Timber Framer's Workshop: Joinery, Design and Construction of Traditional Timber Frames*. Fox Maple Press, 1998.

Chiras, Daniel. *The Natural House: A Complete Guide to Healthy, Energy-Efficient, Environmental Homes*. Chelsea Green, 2000.

Easton, David. *The Rammed Earth House*. Chelsea Green Publishers, 1997. ISBN 0-9652335-0-2.

Elizabeth, Lynne, and Cassandra Adams, eds. *Alternative Construction: Contemporary Natural Building Methods*. John Wiley and Sons, 2000.

Evans, Ianto, Linda Smiley, and Michael G. Smith. *Hand-Sculpted House: A Practical and Philosophical Guide to Building a Cob Cottage*. Chelsea Green, 2002.

Guelberth, Cedar Rose and Dan Chiras. *The Natural Plaster Book*. New Society Publishers, 2003.

Hall, Nicholas. *Thatching: A Handbook*. Intermediate Technology Publications, 1988.

Holmes, Stafford and Michael Wingate. *Building with Lime: A Practical Introduction*. Intermediate Technology Publications, 1997.

Houben, Hugo and Hubert Guillaud. *Earth Construction: A Comprehensive Guide*. Intermediate Technology Publications, 1994.

Hunter, Kaki and Donald Kiffmeyer. *Earthbag Building: The Tools, Tricks, and Techniques*. New Society Publishers, 2004. ISBN 0-86571-507-6.

Johnston, David. *Building Green in a Black and White World*. New Society Publishers, 2004. ISBN 0-886718-507-8.

Kennedy, Joseph, Michael G. Smith, and Wanek, eds. *The Art of Natural Building: Design, Construction, Resources*. New Society Publishers, 2001. ISBN 0-86571-433-9.

Laporte, Robert. *Mooseprints: A Holistic Home Building Guide*. Econest Building Company, 1993.

McHenry, Paul, Jr. *Adobe and Rammed Earth Buildings: Design and Construction*. University of Arizona Press, 1985.

McRaven, Charles. *Building with Stone*. Garden Way, 1989.

Norton, John. *Building with Earth*. Intermediate Technology Publications, 1997.

Reynolds, Michael. *Earthship, Vol. 1: How to Build Your Own House*; Vol. 2: *Systems and Components*; Vol. 3: *Evolution Beyond Economics*. Solar Survival Press, 1993.

Roulac, John. *Hemp Horizons: A Comeback of the World's Most Promising Plant.* Chelsea Green, 1997.

Roy, Robert L. *The Complete Book of Underground Housing.* Sterling, 1994.

Roy, Robert L. *Cordwood Masonry Housebuilding.* Sterling Publishing Co., 1995. ISBN 0-8069-8590-9.

Smith, Michael G. *The Cobber's Companion: How to Build Your Own Earthen Home*, 3rd ed. Cob Cottage Company, 2001.

Steen, Bill, Athena Steen, Eiko Komatsu, and Yoshio Komatsu. *Built by Hand: Vernacular Buildings around the World.* Gibbs Smith Publishers, 2003. ISBN 1-58685-237-X.

Wells, Malcolm. *The Earth-Sheltered House: An Architect's Sketchbook.* Chelsea Green Publishers, 1999. ISBN 1-890132-19-5.

Wojciechowska, Paulina. *Building with Earth: A Guide to Flexible-Form Earthbag Construction.* Chelsea Green Publishers, 2001. ISBN 1-890123-81-0.

CHAPTER 3

What are Straw Bales?

As bales are the essential building blocks for your home, it is important to know your bales. If you are going to make the right choices, you should understand how bales are made and what qualities to look for.

Speaking of Straw

Rectangular bales dotting the fields in mid-summer is a familiar sight to a lot of people. An essential rural icon, a field of bales is often a symbol for wholesome rural ideals. But are those bales straw or hay?

Straw Is Not Hay!

It is common for people to confuse straw with hay. While bales of the two are the same size and shape, they are different substances. Hay refers to any combination of field grasses that are grown to maturity, cut while still relatively green, and baled to use as livestock feed when fresh grasses are not available. High in moisture content, food energy — a full course meal for critters big and small! — and having the potential to sustain microbial activity that can cause rotting and mold, hay is not what you want in your walls. Build your house with straw. Feed the hay to your livestock!

BEN POLLEY

"I'll Grind Your Seeds to Make My Bread ...."

Straw, the dried stems of grain-bearing grasses, is harvested as a by-product of cereal grain farming. The nutritious seed head is cut — threshed — from

3.1: *The seed heads of this summer barley are what the farmer wants to harvest. Once they are removed, the stalks are baled into a great building material.*

the top of the plant once it is fully mature. With the seed head gone, the stalks are dried and baled.

The most common types of straw are wheat, oats, barely, flax, and rice. All of these are commercially farmed in most parts of the world. But any kind of straw can work, including hemp, spelt, rye, and other specialty grain and seed plants. It is possible to bale and build with almost any fibrous plant stems. As long as the majority of seed heads are removed and the stems are thoroughly dry before baling, anything growing nearby can be baled and used.

Farmers may use their straw as bedding for livestock, and gardeners use straw to mulch crops. But grain production outstrips our current minimal usage of straw; it is largely considered a waste by-product of grain production. In some places, excess straw is burned in the field, contributing seriously to air pollution.

Tiny Trees in Fast-growing Forests

Each stalk of straw resembles a long, thin, hollow tree trunk. The resemblance is more than skin-deep, for trees and straw share a similar chemical structure — cellulose and lignin — and a similar strength and durability. But because of the smaller dimensions, straw grows to maturity in just one season.

All straws vary in their physical properties, and crop quality can also vary depending on weather and soil conditions. Typically, if a type of straw has been grown and stored successfully in your climate, then it will be an appropriate type of straw to use for building, since you will essentially be storing the straw in your walls.

Get to Know Some Straw

Each little tree trunk of straw is remarkably strong. Straw is capable of quickly dulling metal cutting blades and is hard to tear apart by hand. It also resists decomposing quite well, which anyone who has mulched with it will confirm. Pick up a piece of straw — even long dry grass at the edge of your lawn will do — and you'll be amazed at its strength and resilience. Imagine thousands of these rugged tiny trees packed tightly together to create your building bales.

About Bales

The Harvesting Process

Commercial grain fields are harvested by a combine. This machine cuts the grain stalks close to the ground, then threshes the seed heads. The bare stalks — straw — are deposited on the field in straight lines to await baling.

A baling machine is pulled over the field, sweeping the lines of straw up into a chamber where a mechanical plunger compacts the loose straw into thin square flakes. (You'll hear a lot about flakes later on.) A number of these flakes are pressed together in the chamber and mechanically tied with twine into a bale. The bale is either redeposited onto the field or kicked into a trailing wagon. Different baling machines produce bales of differing quality. Even bale quality from the same machine can vary dramatically, depending on the sharpness of the cutting blades and the adjustments made for the tightness of the strings.

How to Find Bales

You can't order bales from the local construction supply yard, unlike most other building supplies — not yet, anyway! So, when it comes to finding your bales, you're on your own. However, anywhere grain is harvested, so is straw. Chances are good that there is straw within a reasonable distance of your chosen building

Other Baled Stuff

Bales of straw are not the only way to create energy-efficient buildings out of useful by-products. Very successful structures have been created using bales of boxboard, waxed cardboard, shredded paper, nonrecyclable plastics, and car tires. Straw, too, comes in other baled forms, including jumbo bales (3-by-3-by-9 feet and 4-by-4-by-12 feet) and super-compressed bales (jumbo bales squished down to regular bale size).

Straw bale building is all about using abundant resources available locally, and sometimes the above baled materials may just meet these intentions better than the straw bales we describe. In some cases, straw bales can be used in conjunction with other baled wastes. If you choose any of these materials, know that there are people who already have experience with them, and do as much research as possible. You'll find that many of the concepts and construction details covered in this book will apply to these other baled materials.

— *Chris Magwood*

The Last Straw, no. 42, focused on many of the above alternative baled materials. You can find TLS online at <www.thelaststraw.org>. ∎

3.2a: *Boxboard bales used as a load-bearing wall.*

3.2b: Shredded *paper bales being installed within a frame.*

3.2d: *Stranbloc is made from any waste fibre.*

3.2f: *Waxed cardboard bales.*

3.2c: *Plastic bales being used as a foundation.*

3.2e: *Tire bales can make good foundations.*

3.2a-f: *Straw is not the only baled "waste" that can be used to build. Buildings have been created using bales of boxboard, shredded paper, non-recycleable plastic, waste agricultural and lumber fibres (under the name Stranbloc), used car tires and waxed cardboard.*

site, even if the site is urban. Many cities are built near or *on* prime farmland, and the farmers who have maintained their land near these areas are often producing some grain crops. But how to find the right farmer with the right bales?

Go Where the Farmers Are

You can look for bales in several ways. A drive along some rural roads where active farming is taking place will show you who is growing grain, and as often as not you'll see a sign at the end of a driveway advertising straw and hay for sale. You can also approach a local feed mill, farmers' co-op, or grain elevator. They will know who is growing grain and might be able to put you in contact with an appropriate source. They may be willing to broker the sale for you, although they will add a percentage to the cost for providing the service. Farmers' markets, agricultural fairs, farm equipment sales centers, or any other places that farmers frequent can be good places to start. An advertisement in a few small town newspapers or wanted flyers can also put you in direct contact with farmers who have bales. As bale building grows in popularity, regional bale building associations are formed. These groups can put you in touch with good bale suppliers, as can bale home owners, designers, and builders. *The Last Straw*'s annual *Resource Guide* lists bale suppliers by state and province.

Old Bales, New Bales, No Bales

You can use bales that have been in storage from previous harvests, or you can preorder your bales from the current grain harvest. Remember that bales are an agricultural product and therefore are susceptible to fluctuations in weather, crop prices, and demand. There are both lean and abundant bale years. Where grain production is modest in scale, farmers will sometimes reserve their entire harvest for their own use. For this reason, it is best to source your bales as early as possible.

Round Bales Don't Work

In recent years, baling machines that create large, round bales have come into favor with many farmers. However, you can't build with round bales. You'll have to specify that you need square bales. If contacted prior to harvest, some farmers who currently bale round might use their old square baler in order to make the sale to you. It can sometimes be frustrating to see literally tons of straw at hand but in a form you can't use. Be persistent — somebody out there has square bales for you.

Plastered round bales may perhaps make for an interesting way to create structural columns, but nobody to our knowledge has tried this ... yet!

Two-string versus Three-string Bales

Much of the pioneering work in reviving straw bale construction was done in the southwestern United States. There, large three-string bales are common. In areas of small-scale grain farming, two-string bales are the norm. Both are suitable for building purposes; the kind you use will be determined by the baling standard in your local area.

The Three Bale Basics

When faced with a towering mound of hundreds or thousands of bales, it's good to know what to look for. You have three basic concerns: tightness, dryness, and size. Before making your purchase, be sure you are satisfied on all three counts.

Tightness

You want your bales tight. Bales can be tied with polypropylene string, sisal twine, or metal wire. Any of these options is fine. It is the solidity of a straw bale that allows it to be used as a building material, and that solidity — or lack thereof — is a direct result of how tightly the bale has been tied. A farmer can adjust the baling machine to vary the tightness. Really tight bales use less twine or wire to bale an entire field but are heavier and harder to handle. If you are preordering your bales, be sure to specify that you want them on the tight side. But what exactly is tight?

Methods for assessing tightness vary from the low tech to the scientific. For the low-tech method, pick up the bale by its strings and check that they don't lift from the bale by more than five to six inches. The bale should also maintain its integrity if you lift it by just one string and shake it around. If it spills out when you do this, the bales are too loose. Be sure you sample a number of bales from different places in the stack.

Some attempts have been made to more scientifically quantify tightness. The Arizona and California Straw Bale Codes specify that bales shall have a minimum calculated dry density of 7.0 pounds per cubic foot. This requires you to weigh, measure, and record the moisture content of the bales. If you are in serious doubt about the bale quality, these figures may be useful to generate. But don't forget, the farmer has likely been around bales for a long time. He or she will understand the concept of a tight bale, and their opinion can mean as much or more than your calculations.

Dryness

Starting with dry bales is of utmost importance. Like any organic material, straw will decompose if the right conditions of moisture and temperature exist, and by ensuring that the moisture content is low, you remove one of the essential factors for decomposition.

Like methods for determining tightness, methods for determining moisture content vary in complexity. For the low-tech option, open the strings on several different bales and look inside. Is the straw moist to the touch? Is it crisp? Does it smell damp? Are there any hints of black mold on the straw? Study the storage facility. Is the roof good? How about the floor and walls? Ask the farmer about the weather conditions when the straw was baled. Was it a damp summer with lots of rain? Typically, if bales pass these tests, they are fine to use.

PETER MACK

If you are buying bales from a previous year's harvest, the survival of the bales without rot or mold occurring can tell you that they are adequately dry.

If you want to be more scientific, use a moisture meter to get an accurate reading of moisture content. The farmer may own a meter or may be able to borrow one from a neighbor or from a co-op. Moisture meters are most

3.3: *The strings of a bale shouldn't lift more than 5 to 6-inches when you lift the bale. The bale should keep its shape and not bend or sag.*

GLEN HUNTER

3.4: *If you can find straw that is being stored in a well roofed barn, chances are it is nice and dry. Leave it in the barn until you actually need it.*

often used on hay bales but can give accurate readings for straw as well. Moisture content of 20 percent is considered the safe maximum for a building bale (this is the same figure for lumber). To calculate the dry density of a bale, subtract the weight of the moisture from the overall weight of the bale.

Keep in mind that farmers don't want wet bales either. Moist bales will mold in the barn and make for lousy bedding for the livestock. It is common farming practice to bale straw under good dry conditions, and to keep it dry once it has been baled.

Size

Size is the least important concern for building bales. As long as the bales are of consistent height

and width, their exact dimensions are not so important. Two-string bales, as shown in Figure 3.5, are generally 14 inches high, 30 – 40 inches long and 18 – 20 inches wide. Three-string bales are 14 – 17 inches high, 32 – 48 inches long, and 23 – 24 inches wide. It doesn't matter if your bales vary from these numbers, as long as they are consistent with each other so that your bale wall doesn't vary greatly in height or width.

Other Factors to Consider
Before You Buy

Some general concerns about bales should be addressed. Many modern combines chop the straw into short pieces as it is harvested. This chopped straw can be baled into good tight and dry bales, but they are much more difficult to cut, shape, and trim. The best bales contain high percentages of long, unbroken straw.

Baling machines affect bale quality, too. An improperly adjusted baler will tighten one string more than the other, producing lopsided, curved bales. If there are many such bales, avoid purchasing, since it will be difficult to bend and straighten each bale (however, if you're building a round house, these are the bales you want!). Each bale has a cut side and a folded side. The folded side will always be shaggier than the cut

3.5: Common bales come in either two- or three-string sizes, with roughly standard dimensions.

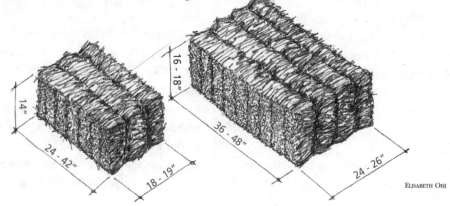

14"

24 - 42"

18 - 19"

16 - 18"

36 - 48"

24 - 26"

ELISABETH OHI

side. Examine both sides to see if they are relatively smooth and even. Smooth bales will require less trimming later on and are more desirable.

Check bales to be sure that there is not too much grain left mixed in with the straw. While some seed heads inevitably make their way into bales, large pockets of seed or a high percentage of straw with seed heads intact are grounds for declining the purchase. These seed heads attract pests and can activate microbial activity in your finished wall.

Grain crops are often treated with chemical fertilizers and sprays. While these chemicals have passed tests for use in food production, you may wish to find out which products have been used on any straw you purchase. It is possible to find straw that has been grown organically or with a minimum of chemical interference.

What Price, Fair Bale?

As an agricultural product, straw bales vary in price from season to season and from region to region. Common prices vary from Can$2 to $5 per bale. We like to offer farmers the best possible price for their bales, rather than negotiating the lowest possible price. One of the advantages of bale building is the creation of a valuable product for farmers, and we believe it is important to foster good relations with bale suppliers. The cost of your bales will be one of the lowest on your budget, even if you voluntarily offer top dollar. And offering a generous price helps guarantee that the bales will meet all your requirements.

You can also request that the farmer bale you some half-sized and smaller bales. This is a simple adjustment to make on the baling machine, and the resulting smaller bales will minimize the amount of time lost to cutting and retying bales

during the wall raising. While this may cost a bit more, it will be worth every penny later on!

Transportation costs may be included in the price of the bales or may be additional. Be sure you find out. If you live close to the source, the farmer might deliver the bales at quite a reasonable cost, or you might be able to make a few trips with a truck and trailer. If not, the farmer may suggest appropriate transportation.

Commercial carriers are also an option. Negotiate carefully with your carrier; bales require a lot of effort to move, load, and stack, and they make a big mess. Settle in advance all issues of labor and cleanup. If you have a crew on hand to load and unload a truck, it will save time and may be necessary before some transport operators will consider moving straw.

Storing Your Mound of Straw

Once you've bought your bales, you must decide where to put them. If possible, try to leave the bales in their storage barn until you actually need them. Moving and restacking bales is a lot of work, and can be minimized by having the bales arrive at your construction site very close to the time of the wall raising. If the bales arrive early, they must be stored.

Our favorite means of storing bales onsite is to have them delivered in a transport trailer. You can have the trailer delivered to your site and pay a small rental fee to have it remain there until you need the bales. This keeps your bales high and dry, and if the trailer has been parked close to the building site, you just have to swing the doors open and unload directly to the walls. A standard sized trailer can hold up to 520 well-stacked bales, which is usually enough for houses up to 2000 square feet. Special bale trailers (used by hay brokers) hold up to 720 bales, are low to the ground, and are accessible on three sides for easy unloading.

In the previous version of this book, we gave instructions for storing bales on your building site. Creating a proper bale stack, one that will stay dry and stable, is more work than we'd recommend taking on unless you have no other option. Outdoor stacks must be elevated from the ground with a moisture barrier under-

3.6: *A transport trailer is a great way to move and store bales. The trailer can be rented and left on your site until you need the straw, eliminating one round of loading and unloading.*

3.7: *From the back of a transport trailer onto an elevator and immediately into the wall: the best way to do it!*

neath. The stack should be made with a peak at the top to encourage water runoff, and well-secured, waterproof coverings must be in place. We have yet to see an outdoor stack that hasn't lost some bales to moisture, and they have definitely been responsible for some builders losing sleep on windy rainy nights.

Post and beam builders may be able to stack their bales under the completed roof of their building. Remember that bales must still be elevated and protected from water and dampness on or in the floor.

Purchase More than You Need

Plan to have extra bales on hand to compensate for broken, poorly tied, or damp bales in the stack. Extra bales can come in handy around the building site as step stools, makeshift work benches, boot scrapers, and comfortable seats during breaks.

Handling Bales

You should take some simple precautions when working with bales. Lift by their strings and wear gloves to avoid pinched or sliced fingers. Long-sleeved shirts cut down on straw scratch to your arms. Remember to use proper lifting techniques to avoid hurting your back. Depending on how and where they were harvested and stored, your bales may be quite dusty; if so, use adequate breathing masks (proper respirators, not flimsy dust masks).

In all our time building with bales, it has been very rare to come across bales that aren't suitable for building. So don't worry too much. Focus instead on good relations with the farmer, and proper transportation and storage schemes.

The color, size, shape, and smell of bales make them unlike any other building material. They're fun to play with, so go ahead and play.

CHAPTER 4

The Red Flag Questions

What about fire? What about moisture? What about insects and pests? What about mortgages and insurance? What about longevity? These are the most frequently asked questions about straw bale construction. They all have answers that should alleviate your concerns.

How Straw Bale Walls Work

Before addressing common concerns about straw bale walls, we need to explain how straw bale wall systems actually work. To be accurate we should really use the term plastered straw bale walls. The plaster — and there are many different kinds — is what seals the bales against fire, rain, wind, bugs, and big bad wolves. The plaster also gives the wall much of its rigidity and strength. Stacked bales alone can hold up a roof and keep out the weather, at least for a while, but when the walls are plastered, they take on many impressive properties.

It's a Sandwich, But Don't Eat It

When an interior and exterior skin of rigid plaster is applied to the dense insulated core of straw bales, a wall system is created that is more than the sum of its parts. A plastered bale wall creates what engineers call a stressed skin panel or sandwich panel, and it has impressive

structural capabilities. As leading straw bale engineer Bruce King says: "It is essential to understand that, once plaster is applied directly to either or both bale surfaces, with or without reinforcing mesh, the structure is now a hybrid of straw

4.1: *The unplastered bales are capable of carrying the roof loads (left side of building), but once the plaster skin is applied, the plaster does most of the work.*

31

and plaster. Effectively, any further loading — snow, people, wind, earthquakes — will go mostly, or entirely, into the plaster skins. So the assembly consists of strong, brittle, thin 'concrete walls' braced by, and somewhat elastically connected by, the straw bale core."

Pioneering bale engineer Bob Platts continues this thought: "The proven Nebraska [load-bearing] structure is not, despite appearances, a stacked block structure. At most, the straw bales take little more than the dead loads only, while the rigid skins — stucco or plaster, chicken wire reinforced — must accept all of any live loads. Any imposed in-plane loads will be taken by the relatively high modulus skins with very little further deflection; such small further strains will scarcely be resisted by the straw. In fact, the still yielding straw does finally adjust to take little of the dead loads either, after a week or two have passed. The rigid skins prevent further settling overall; the straw 'creep' manifests itself as stress relaxation; the dead loads are passed from the straw to the unyielding skins. As commonly built, the straw bale house is a stressed skin structure, of the structural sandwich type, in which the straw is simply the core which stabilizes the skins against buckling under load, takes the shear loads, and provides thermal insulation."

So as you read on, remember that all references to the performance of straw bale walls include the inherent characteristics of the entire structural sandwich, and not just a stack of bales.

Fun Facts:
Scientific answers to the most common straw bale questions

Q: Won't the big bad wolf be able to blow this house down?

A: "Both walls tested withstood the maximum static air pressure that was applied, representing a significant wind of over 134 mph (60m/s)." — ASTM E72 transverse load testing of load-bearing straw bale walls, Building Research Centre of the University of New South Wales, Australia, 1998

Q: Are these walls strong enough to hold up a roof? What about a second story?

A: "Two-string bale walls average an ultimate strength of 6156 pounds per lineal foot, exceeding ASTM E72 requirements." — ASTM E72 compression test of plastered straw bale walls, University of Colorado at Boulder, 1999

Q: Won't these walls be easy to burn?

A: "Bale walls withstood temperatures up to 1,850°F for two hours." — Fire safety tests, National Research Council of Canada

"The bale panel was tested for over two hours and withstood temperatures that reached 1942°F. The temperature rise on the unheated side averaged less than 10°F." — ASTM E-119 Fire Test, SHB AGRA, New Mexico, USA, 1993 ☞

Q: What is the insulation value of a straw bale wall?

A: The R-value varied from 30 to 40. The R-value of the straw bale walls is in the range of super efficient homes.
— Canadian Society of Agricultural Engineers, Halifax, NS, Canada

Fire

Straw bale walls have been tested for fire resistance. In these tests, straw bale walls have proved themselves far superior to standard wood framed walls.

Why Don't They Burn?

Straw bale walls are naturally fire resistant. While the dry straw that makes up a bale is easily combustible when loose, the compact nature of a bale does not trap enough air to support combustion. A good analogy can be drawn by comparing the combustibility of a single sheet of newsprint to that of an entire telephone directory. The single sheet will ignite and burn quickly, but if you drop a phone book on your fire, you'll probably put out the fire. The plaster coating effectively seals the already fire-resistant bales inside a non-combustible casing. A fire would have to burn through the plaster in order to reach the straw. When plaster is combined with the thickness of a bale wall, fire resistance is enhanced. Far from being an issue of concern, the fire testing performed around the world shows the fire-resistant nature of bale walls to be another impressive advantage of the system!

Don't Ignore the Real Fire Hazard

All of the above is true of baled, plastered straw. Unbaled, loose straw, however, is *extremely* combustible, and the large amounts of loose straw that accumulate during construction are a *serious* fire hazard. Smoking, welding, grinding, or any other spark- or flame-producing activities

Q: Won't a bale home be likely to rot or mold?

A: Straw bale walls do not exhibit any unique propensity for moisture retention. It is clear that straw bale walls can function, without incorporating an interior vapor barrier, in northern climates. — Strawbale Moisture Monitoring Report, submitted to the Canada Mortgage and Housing Corporation (CMHC) by Rob Jolly, 2000

Q: Can straw bale techniques *really* make a difference to the environment?

A: The embodied energy for the conventional frame house was 509,000 KBtus. The embodied energy for the low-impact straw bale house is 41,000 KBtus, or about one twelfth that of the frame house. — Investigation of Environmental Impacts, Straw Bale Construction, by Ann V. Edminster, University of California, Berkeley, 1995.

Q: Will a bale home be less expensive to heat?

A: Straw bale construction, along with appropriate building conservation technologies and simple passive solar design, could provide up to a 60 percent reduction in building heating loads over current practice. — US Department of Energy (DOE) straw bale assessment program, 1995 ■

should not be undertaken in the vicinity of loose straw. During construction, always be sure to have fire extinguishers and enough water available to deal with potential fires in your loose straw. Also, keep loose straw raked away from the walls to minimize the risk of any accidental fire spreading into the unplastered walls.

This is not just an idle warning. Several bale homes have burned to the ground while the straw was exposed and the site covered in loose straw, ignited most often by work site activity like soldering pipes and metal grinding.

4.2: *This single, plastered bale shows how the plaster penetrates into the bale, gripping the straw. The two "columns" of plaster carry most of the loads imposed on the finished walls.*

Loose straw (especially organic straw) makes excellent garden mulch. Rake it up, keep it under control, and don't let it catch on fire.

Spontaneous Combustion

Concerns about spontaneous combustion do not apply to straw bales. The significant microbial activity within *hay* bales can result in spontaneous combustion under extreme conditions of humidity, temperature, and storage. Straw bale walls, however, will not create or support spontaneous combustion.

Moisture

Moisture is the enemy of all builders, regardless of which materials they are using. Wood, brick, and even stone walls will deteriorate when exposed consistently to moisture. Bales, like any other building material, must be kept as dry as possible throughout the life of the building. Wet straw molds and eventually decomposes, creating an unpleasant odor, potentially harmful spores, and possible structural failures. Dryness is important.

Many excellent building practices have been established over the years to help solve key moisture problems, and it is important to apply these practices to bale buildings. There are two kinds of moisture concerns for bale walls:

- direct wetting or leakage of liquid water into the wall
- vapor penetration and air leakage into the wall

Straw builders must be aware of both these concerns in order to take adequate protective precautions.

Direct Wetting and Leakage

The most obvious source of moisture problems is the penetration of liquid into the wall cavity. This can happen in many ways, including wind-blown rain, drifting snow, splash-back from roof dripping, plumbing leaks, floods, and breaches of the wall's protective layers such as leaky roofs and window sills.

These problems are real and important considerations in any kind of building, and our chapters on bale wall design, construction, and finishing place these concerns at the forefront in every regard. Liquid breaches in the walls are preventable, and back-up protection can be included to provide a further safety margin.

Vapor Migration through Walls

Think about blowing up a balloon. You force warm, moist air from your lungs into an airtight container, creating a higher pressure than exists outside the balloon. Nature's incessant balancing act insists that the warm, moist air will do its best to leave the balloon and join the surrounding atmosphere. During the heating season, your house is essentially the same as the balloon. When you add heat to your living space, you fill your relatively airtight house with warm, moisture-laden air. Warm air naturally carries more moisture than cold, and you also add extra moisture by breathing, cooking, bathing, etc. That air will do its darndest to get out of the house and give its heat and moisture to the cold dry air outside. Moisture always drives from the warm side to the cool side.

Why Not Just Wave the Moisture Good-bye?

The warm, moist air that wants to travel through your walls does not stay warm and moist. At

Fire Testing

Straw bale architect Bob Theis composed this list of fire testing performed to date on straw bale walls as part of the movement toward a new straw bale building code in California:

1. 1993: Two small-scale ASTM E-119 fire tests at the SHB AGRA lab in Sandia, New Mexico — one test wall with plastered faces, the other bare bales — showed bales to be very fire resistant. The unplastered bale wall withstood the heat and flames of the furnace for 30 minutes before flames penetrated a joint between bales. The plastered bale wall was naturally much better, resisting the transmission of flame and heat for two hours.

2. 1996: A full-scale ASTM E-119 fire test at the University of California Richmond Field Station easily passed the criteria to qualify as a one hour wall. In the opinion of the experts present at the test, the wall would probably have passed as a two-hour assembly.

3. 2001: The Appropriate Technology Group at Vienna Technical Institute conducted an F90 test (similar to the ASTM E-119 test), which gave a plastered straw bale wall a 90-minute rating.

4. 2001: The Danish Fire Technical Institute tested a plastered straw bale wall with exposed studs on the fire side as a worst-case scenario and got these results: in a 30-minute test with a 1832°F (1000°C) fire on the exposed side, the unexposed side rose just 1.8°F (1°C). The maximum average increase permitted to pass the test is 144°F (80°C).

5. 2002: Bohdan Dorniak and members of AUSBALE tested individually plastered bales to the Australian standard simulating the heat of a bushfire front. Subject to a maximum heat intensity of 29 kilowatts per square meter, none of the nine plastered bales ignited, or even developed visible cracks. According to Mr. Dorniak, this qualifies them as noncombustible under the current Australian Bushfire Code AS 3959.

6. 2000: Flame Spread and Smoke Density tests. Katrina Hayes sponsored an ASTM E84-98 test on straw bales in 2000 at the Omega Point Laboratories. They passed the test easily; where the Uniform Building Code allows a flame spread of no more than 25, the test produced a flame spread of 10; where the code allows a smoke density of no more than 450, the bales produced a smoke density of 350. ■

some point in its journey to the outside, it will begin to cool. As it cools, the water vapor it is carrying can condense back to liquid. The point at which this condensation occurs is known as the dew point. If liquid is deposited in your walls and allowed to remain there without drying out, it will reduce the efficiency of your insulation and eventually lead to molding and rotting. In hot southern climates, the whole process can happen in reverse, especially if you use air-conditioning.

Why Aren't More Old Houses Molding and Rotting?

In earlier times, leaky windows, doors, walls, roofs, and floors kept relative humidity indoors below problem levels. Those same homes also required more energy to heat, because the heated air escaped the building through all these leaks, dissipating into the atmosphere. As better windows, doors, insulation, and building practices — especially the use of continuous plastic vapor barriers — began to make houses more airtight, the need grew to prevent moisture from migrating directly *through* the walls.

Direct Air Leaks

Moisture can also enter your walls through direct air leaks. The Canadian Home Builders' Association estimates that, over a single winter of heating, air leakage through a hole with an area of less than one square inch could allow up to eight

A Bit About Mold

Mold spores exist in the air all around us. With every breath we take we are likely inhaling at least one mold spore no matter where we live. These spores are the seeds of mold colonies and are released into the wind to settle in another area and start a new colony. Molds provide an important function when they break down plant matter, returning nutrients back to the soil just like when a pile of wet leaves are raked up and after a few days start to rot. Mold spores that settle into a moist, dark environment with a food source such as cellulose (wood, straw, cardboard) will start to grow into colonies in as little time as 24 hours.

The study on the health effects of molds came from observing animals bedded on moldy straw. Molds have two health issues: the first is allergies to the spores that we inhale, the most common symptoms being runny nose, eye irritation, cough, congestion, and an aggravation of asthma. The second is that mold colonies also release gases as they grow that can be potent mycotoxins, fungal metabolites that have been identified as toxic agents. Individuals with chronic exposure to the mycotoxins produced by *Stachybotris chartarum* fungus reported cold and flu symptoms, sore throats, diarrhea, headaches, fatigue, dermatitis, intermittent local hair loss, and generalized malaise.

The straw that is baled in a field and stacked to form walls for houses contains a high amount of mold spores that have settled out of the air and from the soil that the grains were grown in. All they need is a moisture level high enough to grow. A tarp lifted up from a pile of stored straw may reveal bales discolored with a black mold, likely *Stachybotris chartarum*, considered to be the most toxic to humans. The tarp may or may not have stopped rain getting in, but it trapped the moisture coming up from the ground. If the moisture levels in straw bales is above 20 percent then the mold spores present will start to grow. ☞

gallons of water to pass through a wall! It is critical to keep the moisture content below 20 percent in the walls.

Moisture concerns are hotly discussed among bale builders. Most of the testing done to date confirms what conventional builders already know: cracks, openings, and penetrations into the wall pose much greater risks for moisture damage than does vapor migration through walls finishes

So What About Bale Walls?

The plaster coating on bale walls is an effective barrier against damaging air leakage. If properly detailed to tie in with conventional polyethylene vapor barriers installed in the ceiling and under the floors, a bale house can be made airtight.

Throughout this book, we will address proper detailing for creating a leak free bale home without using a plastic vapor barrier over the straw wall.

Barriers

Why Build without a Vapor Barrier?

In conventional building practice, moisture is prevented from migrating into the wall cavity through the use of continuous plastic vapor barriers. This addresses the very real concern of air leakage in stud-framed homes, but it is unnecessary and a structural compromise with bale walls.

Attaching a vapor barrier to a straw wall offers many complications. The barrier can only be attached to the top and bottom of the wall,

Inspection of mold in straw bale walls has shown that in most cases the moisture entered the wall during construction with the straw not being replaced prior to plastering. It can take up to two months for a perimeter wall to dry out, which is ample time to allow molds to form. Unplastered bales can withstand some surface wetting that will dry with air exposure. If during construction the walls are exposed to moisture then they should be inspected to see if the moisture has penetrated the core of the bales. A bale should be replaced if the moisture has penetrated more than three inches into the bale and above the 20 percent moisture content. Moisture meters with long probes are usually available from local farm supply stores. When handling any bales that have become moldy, wear personal protection in the form of respirators with HEPA filter cartridges, gloves, and goggles. Strong air blowers, used in the flood and fire industry, can be rented to dry surface moisture. Moisture can also enter bale walls from floods, a leaky roof, a large crack in the plaster, poor window and door placement, or plumbing leaks as is the case with any type of wall construction. All walls exposed to moisture regardless of the type of materials, can support mold growth and should be inspected and dealt with in a timely and appropriate manner.

This book is about best building practices of straw bale construction and following the recommendations on roofs, overhangs, and foundations that will ensure a healthy, mold-free structure. People who are considering straw bale building but who have allergies to dust and the general spores found in straw bales should realize that during construction these are present and should wear personal protection. After plastering, mold spores and dust are encapsulated and will not influence health or indoor air quality (IAQ). Straw bale walls actually improve the IAQ in homes due to the slow air diffusion of the walls.

Paul Battle is a certified Bau-Biologie Environmental Inspector in Ottawa Ontario. He specializes in the detection of home health hazards and consults on ecological home construction. Contact <www.thehousedoc.ca> (613) 297-2996 ■

making it hard to maintain a taut surface unless wooden attachment points are added to the wall. A vapor barrier prevents the plaster coating from attaching itself directly to the straw. This not only makes plastering much more difficult — and will likely require more metal reinforcement for the plaster — but eliminates the substantial structural benefits of bonding the plaster to the straw. Remember, bonded together, the two materials create a stressed skin panel far stronger than the sum of their independent elements. A straw wall without a vapor barrier is less time-consuming to build and eliminates the use of a manufactured product with a high embodied energy. Finally, straw, metal stucco mesh, and plastering tools all increase the risk of introducing punctures to the vapor barrier, rendering it less effective.

To Barrier

There is no doubt that a properly installed vapor barrier is an effective tool in preventing moisture penetration through your walls. Though moisture migration has not been shown to be a problem in straw bale walls, a builder might choose — or be forced by local building officials — to spend the extra money and time and forego the structural strength and environmental bonuses of building a straw wall without a vapor barrier. In this case, you might want to use vapor-retardant paint as your barrier, rather than a layer of plastic behind the plaster. Applied to the interior plaster of your walls, the paint can achieve a high degree of protection against moisture migration while avoiding the difficulties of working with a vapor barrier over the straw. You might also decide to apply different vapor retarding strategies in different areas of your home. Bathrooms and kitchens are especially prone to high humidity and can be sealed with more vigor than other areas.

Build to Your Level of Comfort

Bale homes have been built both with and without vapor barriers. To date, only direct water leakage into the wall or rising damp from foundations have resulted in damaging deterioration of the straw. But with no complete set of data from which to work, you must decide how to build to your own level of comfort and protection. Real-life experience has indicated that both unbarriered and barriered homes operate within reasonable levels of moisture content due to vapor penetration.

Building Practices that Minimize Rainwater Penetration

Many simple, effective building techniques are used to protect bales from exposure to moisture. Generous roof overhangs and proper eave-stroughs eliminate most direct rainfall and splash-back from reaching your walls. A bale wall that is raised on a wooden curb on the foundation or floor allows any spills or floods inside the house to drain away before they soak into the walls. Plastic or tar paper placed along the top of the walls helps shed any water that may someday come through your roof. Windows and doors can be detailed to incorporate proper flashing and drip edges that shed water away from the walls.

Insects and Pests

Let's face it: we share this planet with billions of other creatures, both large and small. To say that a particular house or style of construction is pest proof is to ignore the intelligence and persistence of our "little neighbors."

What Are Pests Looking for?

To be suitable for sheltering pests, our homes must offer them openings, nests, and food. Plastered bale walls are short on all three, since their plaster coating seals the bales from foundation to roof with a difficult-to-chew barrier. Should a gap be left open in the plaster, the bales themselves are too densely packed to make comfortable housing for mice and other rodents. All those comfy spaces in your neighbor's frame walls, lightly packed with batt insulation, make a much more inviting home.

There is little food for any living creature in a straw wall; even termites tend to eschew straw. An inordinate amount of seed head in the straw *does* provide a good source of food, which is why you should check your bales for excess seed content before purchasing them. Care should be taken — as with any style of construction — to keep pests out during the building process.

While we have heard of very few pest problems in bale walls, that doesn't mean pests won't live in your roof, floor, and basement!

Mortgages, Insurance, and Resale

Perhaps the most difficult part of building with straw (or any other alternative materials or ideas) is presenting your project to the various institutions that often must be involved. Lenders and insurers are, by their very nature, conservative and averse to risks. Any construction method that is perceived as new or experimental can seem to them like a risk they'd rather avoid. It often takes time and no small amount of educational effort on your behalf to negotiate for mortgages and insurance for your project. All the evidence exists to convince them that your

proposed straw bale house will be a safe prospect for them, but you will have to be the one to present it to them.

It's Not Impossible to Get $$

Obtaining a construction mortgage, even for a conventional structure, can often be difficult, especially if you are planning to build for yourself. Banks are wary of construction projects because an awful lot of their money goes into the project before it becomes a home with any appreciable resale value. During construction, their money is in a risky spot, and they must have confidence in you, your abilities, and your overall plan. They must also have confidence in your financial situation. So you enter this scenario with several potential problems to overcome, never mind your plans for straw bale walls.

Don't panic! Many bale builders have obtained financing from regular sources. There are many things you can do to help your situation. First, it will work in your favor to bring the lender a good set of building plans that are professionally drawn and appear thorough in all their considerations. So will a thorough and realistic budget and timeline. Ensure your budget contains guaranteed quotes for materials and services you'll require. If you are a first-time builder, you may need to hire professional consultants to show the bank that there is good help available to you should problems arise. If you are hiring a general contractor to build your home, he or she will have to fill out paperwork for the bank too. Hiring someone with a good local reputation will certainly help.

The US Department of Energy has published positive findings about straw bale construction, and other government agencies have also done preliminary studies on straw bale with positive results. The CMHC (Canada Mortgage and Housing Corporation), which helps set many of the standards used by lending institutions in Canada, is quite supportive of straw bale construction, and their data can be used when negotiating for a loan. Government facts, figures, and opinions can be powerful tools when you're dealing with lenders.

Many bale builders have had to approach numerous lending institutions to find the right combination of personality and corporate culture before they secured funding. Don't let a rejection put you off. If you truly are a good risk, eventually somebody will lend you the money. It takes thoughtful preparation and patience to explain straw bale construction to a lender.

Obtaining a building mortgage is one thing; living by its strict guidelines is another. Building mortgages come with strict pay-out schedules, and money is only advanced to you when you have completed each phase to the lender's satisfaction. They will also determine percentages of the overall budget that can be used for certain expenses. For example, they will determine how much of the overall amount you can spend on windows. So your initial budgeting may need to be adjusted to work with the lender's guidelines. The lender will also hold back the final portion of the loan until they are satisfied that the project is complete. Building with a conventional construction mortgage is often stressful and occasionally requires that you have other means of financing when delays or unforeseen expenses arise.

As the number of bale homes continues to increase, it becomes more likely that a financial institution in your area has already lent to a bale home builder. Some research into existing bale homes in your area can lead you in directions where the doors have already been successfully opened to straw bale buildings.

Research Lending Options

There are many excellent references that describe methods and means for obtaining financing. Read widely before you plunge in — and remember, numerous options are still available to you should you receive an initial negative response from a banker. People have financed bale homes in all kinds of creative ways. Some have applied for numerous credit cards and run them to their maximums to build the house, and then consolidated their credit card debt with a single financial institution at good rates, using the completed house as collateral! Lines of credit can be put to use, as can retirement savings plans. Be sure to fully research any and all programs and incentives that might be offered by government agencies in your area.

Insurance

Insurance companies are concerned with facts and figures that indicate levels of risk. The existing research for straw bale homes scores positively with most insurers, especially the excellent fire ratings. Many insurance companies already have these test results on file; others are willing to consider them if you submit them with your application.

Building code approval is usually the only structural requirement of insurers, so with a permit and fire test ratings, insurance is usually attainable. Some bale homes have even been insured at rates lower than similarly sized conventional homes.

However, it may take the same kind of determination as with lenders to find the right insurer. Your role as educator, confident planner and builder, and well-researched client cannot be underestimated.

Some builders want to have their project insured during construction. In this case, the fire hazards of loose and unplastered straw may cause rates to be higher than with more conventional projects.

Resale Values

In current real estate markets, chances are good that a straw bale home will receive a lower resale value estimate than its frame-walled equivalent. However, low appraisals do not necessarily mean lower resale prices. Home buyers looking for a strong, unique, and super-insulated house may decide that the attractions of a straw bale house are worth more to them than its appraisal indicates. As a side benefit, lower official appraisals often mean lower property taxes.

Since straw bale building is relatively recent, very few homes have traded hands on the real estate market. However, those that have typically sell for the owner's asking price and within a short time frame. Sometimes it's an advantage to be selling something unique!

Longevity

The current resurgence of interest in bale construction is due in part to the rediscovery of bale homes in Nebraska dating from the early 1900s, in which the walls have remained strong and relatively unchanged from the day they were built.

The conditions that make for a long and healthy life cycle are the same for any style of construction. Do not expect a bale home to have a shorter life cycle than a wood-framed home. Kept dry, warm, and well maintained, bale homes have easily lasted for 100 years and continue to be strong and healthy. After all, the molecular structure of straw is remarkably similar to that of wood — remember, each bale is thousands of tiny trees bundled together!

Eternally Answering Questions

Straw bale construction excites a lot of curiosity, and with curiosity comes questions. Be prepared to answer red flag questions frequently, since everybody from your mother to the grocery clerk is going to ask them. Consider your patient answers — and your tolerant smile for the inevitable Three Little Pigs joke — an important educational service on behalf of straw bale enthusiasts everywhere!

References

The following list of testing documents will help you provide the information required of you by lenders and insurers:

1) Lerner, Kelly and Pamela Wadsworth Goode, eds. *The Building Official's Guide to Straw-bale Construction*, Version 2.1. California Straw Building Association (CASBA), 2000. P.O. Box 1293, Angels Camp, CA, 95222-1293, USA.<www.strawbuilding.org>

This book consolidates an impressive array of tests in one source, and frames these tests with a good introduction and resource section. You can order your copy of this book directly from CASBA <www.strawbuilding.org> or from your usual natural building book distributor. The book includes:

ASTM E72 Compression Test of Plastered Straw Bale Walls, by Matt Fitzgerald Grandsaert, 1999, University of Colorado at Boulder, sponsored by StrawCrafters and the California Straw Building Association.

ASTM E72 80 Compressive, Transverse and Racking Tests of Load-Bearing Walls, conducted under the direction of John Carrick BE, the New South Wales Environmental Protection Agency and John Glassford at the Building Research Centre of the University of New South Wales, Australia, 1998.

Straw Bale Bending and Cement Plaster/Straw Bale Bond Testing, by Jonathan Boynton, 1999, California Polytechnical State University, San Luis Obispo.

In-Plane Lateral Loading of a Stuccoed Straw Bale Wall, by Nathan White and Clint Iwanicha, 1997, California Polytechnic State University, San Luis Obispo.

Straw Bale Vault Test, designed by David Mar, structural engineer, and Skillful Means Architecture and Construction. Conducted by Bill Rothacher and Doug Stark of Consolidated Engineering Laboratories (CEL), 1998, Berkeley, California.

Compressive and Lateral Loading of Straw Bale Walls, by Ghailene Bou-Ali, 1993, University of Arizona.

Thermal and Mechanical Properties of Straw Bales as They Relate to a Straw House, conducted by the Canadian Society of Agricultural Engineering, 1993, Halifax, Nova Scotia, Canada.

Straw Bale Construction Moisture Research, by Joanna Karl, Lis Perlman and Bill Kownacki, 1995, Portland Community College, Oregon.

ASTM E-119 Small Scale Fire Test, by SHB AGRA, 1993, New Mexico.

ASTM E84-98 Surface Burning Characteristics (Flame Spread and Smoke Development) test. (These tests are available for download at DCAT <www.dcat.net> along with DCAT'S explanatory cover sheet).

Thermal Performance of Straw Bale Walls (a summary and discussion of several different thermal performance tests), by Nehemiah Stone and Tav Cummins, 1999, California Energy Commission.

2) King, Bruce, ed. *EBNet Conference CD-ROM*. Ecological Building Network, 2001. 209 Caledonia St., Sausalito, CA, 94965, USA. <www.ecobuildnetwork.org>

These proceedings from the 2001 EBNet Conference include many papers presented on both straw bale and other natural building methods:

Straw Bale Shear Wall Lateral Load Test, by Jason Nichols and Stan Raap, 2000, California Polytechnic State University, San Luis Obispo, Architectural Engineering Dept.

For the Land of Camels: A Straw Bale Test Wall for Seventeen Foot High Ceiling Structures in the Kingdom of Saudi Arabia, by Chris Stafford, Christopher Stafford Architects, Inc., Port Townsend, Washington.

A Pilot Study Examining the Strength, Compressibility and Serviceability of Rendered Straw Bale Walls for Two-storey Load Bearing Construction, by Michael Faine and Dr. John Zhang, 2000, University of Western Sydney, Australia.

Preliminary Report on the Out-of-plane Testing of an 8-by-8-foot Straw Bale/PISE Wall Panel, by David Arkin and Kevin Donahue, 2001, Mill Valley, California.

Straw Bale Construction: A Review of Testing and Lessons Learned to Date, by Bruce King, 2001.

A Status Report on the Greening of Building Codes and Standards, by David Eisenberg, 2001.

Alternative Building Materials and Systems — Understanding Technical Risk and Uncertainty, by John Straube, 2001.

The Ecological Building Network is currently engaged in the most comprehensive research and testing of bale walls ever undertaken. They report their progress and post their results regularly on their web site,
<www.ecobuildnetwork.org>

3) CMHC Testing Reports

The Canada Mortgage and Housing Corporation (CMHC) is another valuable source of testing data and documentation. CMHC is a government agency involved in social housing, mortgage insurance, research, and advocacy on housing issues. To this end, they have provided funding for straw bale housing research that has been important and influential.

A sampling of key CMHC tests includes:

Developing and Proof-Testing the "Prestressed Nebraska" Method for Improved Production of Bale Fibre Housing, by Fibrehouse Limited with Scanada Consultants Limited, 1995.

Strawbale Moisture Monitoring Report, by Rob Jolly, 2000.

Moisture Properties of Plaster and Stucco for Strawbale Buildings, by John Straube, 1999, University of Waterloo.

Pilot Study of Moisture Control in Stuccoed Straw Bale Walls, by Bob Platts, 1997.

Many other tests are also available from CMHC. You can browse all of CMHC's material at <www.cmhc-schl.gc.ca/> and order documents online, or by calling 1-800-668-2642 (or outside Canada, 613 748-2003), faxing 613-748-2016 or mailing to CMHC, Suite 1000, 700 Montreal Road, Ottawa, ON K1A 0P7.

4) Straw Bale Building: An Information Package for Building Officials in Ontario, 2004.

This booklet is available from the Ontario Straw Bale Building Coalition, and contains structural, fire and moisture control data. Order from: <info@strawbalebuilding.ca>. Ontario Straw Bale Building Coalition, c/o 2025 Ventnor Road, RR#3, Spencerville, ON, Canada, K0E 1X0. <www.strawbalebuilding.ca>

5) University of Manitoba

Design Dead Load of a Straw Bale Wall, by E. Arbour, 2000.

Design Approach for Load-Bearing Strawbale Walls, K.J. Dick and M.G. Britton, 2002.

Resistance to Shear in Stuccoed Straw Bale Walls, by Lisa Stepnuk, 2002. All three papers available from Department of Biosystems Engineering,

University of Manitoba, Winnipeg, Manitoba, R3T 5V6, Canada, 204-474-6033, <www.umanitoba.ca/faculties/afs/biosystems_engineering/overview.html>

6) Other Test Documents

The following tests have been performed at university labs or by interested individuals. Many of these people will, understandably, ask for a fee for their document(s):

A Comparison of the Load-Bearing Capacity and Behaviour of Earth- and Cement-Rendered Straw Bale Walls, by M.A. Faine and John Zhang, University of Western Australia, <j.zhang@uws.edu.au>

House of Straw: Straw Bale Building Comes of Age, by the U.S. Dept. of Energy, 1995. Available online only at <www.eren.doe.gove/EE/strawhouse/>. This report studies thermal performance and construction cost issues, with positive results.

Straw Bale Exterior Pinning Report, by Sustainability International, 1998. Contact Bob Bolles to purchase copies <bob@strawbalehouse.com>. Engineering results on a rebar-exterior-pinning system which gained approval from the Tucson/Pima County building department.

Moisture Control in Straw Bale Homes: Report to Ontario Building Code Commission, John Straube, 1999. Building Engineering Group, Civil Engineering Department, University of Waterloo, Waterloo, ON., Canada, N2L 3G1. An important look at how straw bale walls handle moisture

Community-Built Housing Solution: A Model Strawbale Home Design, by David Riley and Sergio Palleroni, 1999.

Strength Testing of Stucco and Plaster Veneer Straw Bale Walls, by D. Riley, G. MacRae, and J.C. Ramirez, 1998. Contact Prof. David Riley, Dept. of Architectural Engineering, Penn State, 104 Engineering Unit A, University Park, PA 16802, USA, <driley@engr.psu.edu>.

Moisture in Straw Bale Housing - Nova Scotia, by S.H.E. Consultants, 1998. Contact S.H.E. Consultants, RR#3, Comp. 308, Wolfville, NS, Canada. Blower door tests on several bale homes, and a "refining" of the term "breathable walls."

Investigation of Environmental Impacts: Straw Bale Construction, by Ann V. Edminster, 1995. Contact Ann Edminster, 115 Angelita Ave, Pacifica, CA 94044, <avedminster@earthlink.net>

Evaluation of a Straw Bale Composite Wall, by Edwin R. Schmeckpepper and Joe Allen, 1999. Contact Joe Allen, PE, Allen Engineering, 917-10th Street, Clarkson, WA 99403. Tests performed on an unusual light-gauge steel/straw bale wall system.

7) Code Testing Video

Straw Bale Code Testing, Black Range Films 1996. This video documents the Arizona compression and lateral loading tests (three-string bales), the 1993 Nova Scotia moisture testing, and the NM lateral load and E-119 fire tests (two-string bales) with very positive results. Includes interviews with code officials. Available from Natural Building Resources, <www.StrawBaleCentral.com>.

This list was compiled by Chris Magwood, with extensive help from Mark Piepkorn, Lars Keller, André de Bouter, and many of the testers themselves. A version of this list appeared in The Last Straw, *issue #40.*

CHAPTER 5

The Hotly Debated, Often-Distorted Question of Cost

So what does one of those straw bale houses cost?" Such a common question, such a difficult answer. The issue of cost is complex, and while bale building can be done less expensively than conventional framing, so much is up to you.

Much that is written, and even more that is rumored, about straw bale building hails it as the perfect option for people wanting to build on the cheap. Before we get into the specifics of designing and building your straw bale house, we'd like to address the hotly debated, often-distorted question of cost.

All About Money

There is No Such Thing as Cheap

Building a house is an expensive proposition. This is true whether you are using straw bales or any other materials. From the cost of the property on which you build, to permit and start-up costs, right through to the hinges, knobs, and handrails of the finished house, the list of expenses is long and weighty. There is no way to avoid expense, especially when you are building for longevity, efficiency, and to meet codes.

The Less Expensive House

Since truly cheap housing methods — lean-tos, shacks, or tents — are not what is commonly deemed "suitable" in much of North America, we prefer to use the term "less expensive" housing when talking about straw bale building. Many people have heard of the $10-per-square-foot straw bale house. Be assured, a $10-per-square-foot house is very simple, roughly finished, not necessarily efficient, and definitely not erected where a building code is enforced. Building a home to modern building code standards can never be considered cheap.

Money — or lack thereof! — is always a central concern when you design and build your house. Building your house is going to absorb whatever budget you allocate. Rather than focusing on how cheap straw bale building can be, it makes more sense to focus on creating a building that can be completed within your means. This can often mean keeping the size down and planning to expand in the future. At every juncture in this book, we will be assessing costs and trying to point out ways to save money.

How Can Bales Save Money?

Straw bale buildings can certainly hold a cost advantage over conventional styles. By replacing both wall-framing lumber and insulation — plus vapor barriers, nails, glues, etc. — with a single, inexpensive material, the cost of building super-insulated walls can be lowered. The interior and exterior plaster cladding, depending on the choice of ingredients and method of its application, can be comparable with other cladding systems such as drywall, vinyl or wood siding, or brick.

You might also save money on framing labor. Because bales are more user-friendly than other wall systems, many people are encouraged to put up their own walls, which can cut down on costs. But if you are hiring people to build straw walls for you, you won't necessarily save money on labor. The cost of hiring labor for frame homes and bale homes is very similar.

The Buck Stops at the Top of Your Wall — Underneath It, Too!

With the exception of the exterior walls, the rest of the construction costs for a straw bale house can be identical to any other building style. Most contractors estimate the cost of the wall system at about 10 to 15 percent of the total budget. As a building material, your straw bales are going to directly affect only that percentage of the total cost. To truly save money, a straw bale builder must turn his or her attention to all the other aspects of the building and lower costs at each stage. Fortunately, straw bale construction lends itself to the use of plenty of alternatives that can reduce the overall cost of a project.

Comparing Apples to Oranges

When comparing the costs of a straw bale home to those of a conventional home, it is important to make a fair comparison. The 2-by-6-inch frame-walled, airtight house is the current building standard and benchmark for comparison. If you use straw bales to build a house of identical square footage, the costs are likely to be similar to that of a frame-walled building or perhaps a little lower. However, such a direct comparison is misleading. To equal the thermal performance of a straw bale wall, conventional builders would need to opt for a double 2-by-6-inch stud wall, or use furring strips and a layer or two of Styrofoam insulation to raise the R-value. This kind of frame wall construction definitely tips the cost scales in favor of the straw bale wall.

Building super-insulated frame walls also requires the use of more manufactured materials, upping the levels of embodied energy in the house and raising the environmental costs even farther beyond those of a straw bale wall. The idea is not just to spend less money, but to maximize the efficiency and energy savings of the finished home. With a straw bale wall, you can raise thermal efficiency while maintaining or undercutting standard costs in both dollars and environmental impact.

— *Chris Magwood*

How to Really Save Money

The choices you make concerning labor, materials, and finishing will determine whether or not you are able to build within a certain budget.

Labor costs will have a big impact on your construction budget. Doing it all yourself will eliminate labor costs. Doing some work yourself and hiring for some will raise costs proportionally. Having your home entirely built for you by others will increase costs even further. Remember that if you build the house yourself, you will have to make a serious commitment of time. While you may not be paying for labor, you may be losing your own earning potential. It is quite possible to mix and match your talents and interests with those of local professionals and find a good balance between your budget, time, and level of expertise. Finding the right blend of personal sweat equity and hired help is crucial as you try to establish an accurate budget.

Materials choices will similarly cause wide variations in cost. Right from the early stages of your design work, the choices you make — especially about foundation, roof, windows, and mechanical systems — will have major cost implications. Research your choices carefully, and be sure to weigh initial costs against long-term costs; sometimes extra money spent up-front in the building process can save lots of money in the long run.

The chapters on budgeting and going shopping will help to clarify some issues around choosing materials.

Interior finishing also makes up a significant portion of a typical house budget. Bathrooms and kitchens are the most expensive spaces in the home. Take into account what kinds of flooring, doors, windows, kitchen cabinets, appliances, curtains, rugs, bathroom fixtures, etc., you want.

The same basic building shell can be finished in wildly different ways, resulting in astronomically different budgets.

What You Spend Now versus What You'll Spend Later

Even if you're looking for the lowest possible costs, take care to weigh the advantages of bottom-dollar prices with other factors. Used, single-pane windows may be dirt cheap, but you will pay for that choice with higher heating costs for the rest of the building's life, and many building codes do not allow single pane windows. Cheap

JOY ALLAN

toilets are another common "money saver"; they won't last as long and they use more water.

Salvaged materials can be free, or at least significantly less expensive than new. But, they can also require large amounts of time to clean, prepare, and fit. This is fine if you have lots of time, but otherwise could offset the cost advantage. If you are willing to put in a bit of extra legwork, you may produce excellent and inexpensive options for many building materials, but

5.1: *Friends and families, from kids to grandparents, are usually glad to be part of a bale raising. This can help save on labor costs and be a lot of fun, too.*

rate their usefulness, condition, and long-term performance carefully.

Over Budget Is the Norm

The building that is completed without going over budget is rare. Never plan to spend everything up to your last available penny at the budgeting stage. There are always problems, delays, or unforeseen costs, and they can add up significantly. Be sure to leave yourself plenty of breathing room. It is better to plan more modestly and finish your project than to plan grand and fall short of completion.

The Real Savings Are Long-term

Your straw bale house will inevitably save you significant amounts of money when it comes to heating and cooling costs. Long after you've finished the house, those savings will keep multiplying for you. So even if you don't build the cheapest house in the world, you likely will be building the cheapest house in which to continue living in the long term.

The Final Word

Well, there really isn't a final word on cost. Each house is unique — even when created from the exact same set of plans — and only you can make all the ongoing, complicated decisions about cost. The price tag is up to you. We put affordability high on our list of priorities when planning and building, and we hope you'll find some good advice in this book to help you keep your costs as low as possible.

References

Roy, Rob. *Mortgage Free! Radical Strategies for Home Ownership*. Chelsea Green Publishers, 1998. ISBN 0-930031-98-9.

Chapter 6

Getting Focused

Most owner-built homes start with a dream and a basic desire to shelter oneself affordably, creatively, and adequately. But as soon as you decide to realize those dreams, actually getting started can be daunting. You've entered the thinking stage, and now it's time to get focused.

Whether you intend to build every part of your house by yourself or hire a contractor to build it all for you, it is important to get focused and answer some basic questions very early in the process.

Work Smart

Putting Thinking ahead of Building

When most people envision building their home, they picture themselves with a hammer in hand, hoisting a bale, or in some other way being actively engaged in the physical building process. For those who have never built before, acquiring manual skills and technical building knowledge appears to be the most daunting part of such a project. In this book, we work with the assumption that the major difficulty faced by potential builders is visualizing and articulating what they want from a building and learning what will be required to achieve their goals. The thinking tools are the most important

tools you will acquire. In comparison, actual construction — whether done by you or by hired labor — is a matter of basic achievable mechanics.

Wrong Turns, Bad Decisions, and Mistaken Assumptions

Every builder inevitably has a list of "I shouldas" at the end of a project. It identifies points where knowledge and understanding came after the physical process of building was finished, or at least well underway. It's impossible to predict and understand every variable a house building project will throw your way, and the only way to keep the "I shouldas" from overwhelming your project is to allow yourself plenty of thinking time in advance. Even builders with decades of experience will take away something new from each project; it is this acquired knowledge that often allows them to usually do things faster, better, and more economically than novices.

The Three Big Questions

Why Build at All?

The potential answers to this question are as many and varied as the people asking. List your answers and keep coming back to them as you progress through the thinking and design stages of your project. If your reasons for building are not being adequately addressed by the designing and planning you are doing, it's time to reassess. Don't allow the project to fuel itself — keep track of why you are doing what you are doing. For example, if one of your primary reasons for building is to lower your current shelter costs, then be sure you are thinking toward a detailed budget. If, during the thinking process, you realize you won't be able to build within budget, you may need to reconsider. You may want to scale back your ambitions, rethink your financing, alter your time frame, or perhaps postpone your project for the time being until your preconditions for building have been met.

It is all too easy to let momentum take over in a building project, and that momentum can launch you in directions far from your original intentions. Only by writing down your intentions and focusing on them clearly can you ensure that you are running the project and not having the project running you!

What Do I Really Want?

Your set of answers to the question What do I really want from the house I build? will provide a foundation for the thinking and planning you do. Make sure your answers to questions one and two are compatible. If not, your wishes and desires will outstrip your intentions. Plan to spend quite a while answering this question.

Don't assume that any point is too small or too obvious to include on your list. In fact, you can divide the list into large and small concerns. On the large side, take note of your preferred locations, surroundings, and exterior appearance you want your home to have. On the small side, keep a list of specific design details that are important to you. It will be a long time before some of the smaller details become a real concern, but get to know them early.

Ask yourself what rooms you envision for your house. Write down the names of those rooms and list the attributes you associate with each one. Do not limit yourself to what you already know and have experienced. This is a time to consider your ideals. Does your kitchen serve a central role, functioning as a place for food preparation, art work, and long, intimate teatimes? Is your bedroom only a place where you sleep, or do you enjoy certain activities — reading, writing, or watching television — in that room? Do you want a dining room? Is your bathroom merely functional, or is it your personal getaway? Which rooms can be multipurpose? All these considerations are important. Include contradictions if they arise; they will be solved later.

If you find that a traditional room does not appear on your list, don't force it to be there. Perhaps the typical living room function will be served by your kitchen, or by a den or library. Invent new room names if necessary.

Room uses, furniture items, ambiance, noise levels, views, storage capacity, and counter space — whatever presents itself as important to you should be included. Be exhaustive, and allow yourself time to change and modify the lists.

Mapping Your Movements

Take the time to study and think about traffic circulation in your home — if you have kids, it may be more along the lines of air traffic control!

What works in your current home? What needs improvement? You can begin this process by studying different kinds of movement. Movement in and out of the house is important; movement within key public rooms — especially kitchens — is also important. Examine traffic patterns between rooms, noting which patterns are most common. Make lists and notes about circulation. Do you often entertain crowds? If so, what happens to human movement under these conditions? Does movement change with the seasons?

Be sure to note all your current gripes! If you know what's wrong, keep track of the negatives. Solutions will be forthcoming.

Keep Your Eyes Wide Open

Don't limit your examination to your current home, but think about other residences you've lived in or places you've visited. Every time you are in a building, be conscious of its layout, the features of its rooms, and its traffic patterns. Take notes wherever you go, either mental or written. Building a home gives you the opportunity to blend the best and avoid the worst of everything you've ever known or experienced, so keep your eyes wide open.

This Is Not a Chore!

Don't look at this stage of your design process as a chore. We call it the Design Game because it can be a lot of fun. You have access to a rich architectural and cultural history. Enjoy it! Revel in it! When you finally stop seeing new things and being excited by possibilities, you're probably at the end of the process.

Don't Forget Your Family

Your family will be sharing the house with you, so involve them in the process. You'll be amazed

JULIE BOWEN

at how attentive to detail kids can be if they are told what to look for! Think back to when you were young. Whose house did you like to visit? Why? What did you like and dislike about your own childhood homes? Think about your future needs. Will children be arriving? Will parents, siblings, or friends be moving in? Will your home be accessible to people with physical challenges? If you have children, you'll have to think about their future needs, too. Inevitably, conflicts between various needs will arise. Let them come to the fore, and soon enough you'll be able to start making compromises. Planning for everybody who

6.1: *You can use hand-drawn "bubble" lists for initial room arrangements. You might want to assign each room some proportion, based on the size of your list of characteristics.*

will share the house is vital if it's going to work well for all concerned.

Once you know what rooms you want and how they will be used, start arranging them in ways that accommodate your movement patterns. One way to achieve this is to write the names of your rooms on individual pieces of paper, including key features and arrows that indicate the kind of traffic flow you expect that room to handle.

Start arranging these pieces of paper in different ways until they start to make sense to you. When you find an arrangement that seems suitable, make a drawing of it. Then start over again. There are many possible arrangements that might work, so don't stop at one. At each stage in the Design Game, give yourself lots of time. You can even make your design puzzle the center of an evening with friends and family. Invite everybody to create their own house out of your individual elements — their designs will bring fresh perspectives to your own puzzling.

It's Not a Matter of Life and Death!

It is easy to become so wrapped up in the Design Game that you feel you must have everything perfect. Don't sweat it. Every house is full of compromises — even warm-spirited, inviting, and comfortable homes have their share of little problem areas and "shouldas." Some people — those who don't have building code concerns! — just start laying things out on the ground, and design as they build. That, too, can work. By the time you work your way through the Design Game, you'll have learned an awful lot about what you want your house to be like. This awareness — even when it's an awareness of flaws — is invaluable. It is your first important thinking tool.

Where to Build — City, Suburbs, Town, or Country?

If you do not currently own property on which to build, you are facing a task about which entire books have been written. Chances are, you'll already have decided to live within a certain region due to family ties, employment, love of the landscape, or some other personal reason. When buying property, it is helpful to define a boundary for yourself and concentrate your search within it.

City Sites

City builders must consider issues of lot size and availability, local zoning and building restrictions, neighborhood quality, availability of services, proximity to employment and schools, and transportation networks. Don't forget to research the city's development plan to see whether or not your prospective neighborhood is slated for major zoning changes. Talk to people who live in the area and find out what they have to say.

If the lot you are considering has been empty for a long time, find out how it has been used in the past. Be suspicious of former industrial sites or sites that have been used for gas stations or other polluting businesses. Paying for a soil analysis is a good idea if you harbor any suspicions or concerns. Don't forget to consider noise and light pollution. Excessive shading of your site by other buildings, proximity to high-wattage street lights, signage or factory lighting, and car headlights can become constant irritants for urban dwellers.

To date, straw bale homes have been idealized in rural settings. Straw bale construction, however, works well as urban housing. The remarkable sound-proofing nature of thick bale walls can significantly lower the amount of ambient noise in your home, making it a more relaxing environment. By virtually eliminating noise transfer, straw bale dividing walls can remove a major disadvantage of multi-unit structures. Furthermore, bale construction allows for design adaptations to surrounding home styles without requiring higher expenditures for conventional materials.

While the ideals of clean, environmental living that are identified with straw bale homes might seem incongruous in urban settings, urban living offers us many opportunities to lower our personal environmental impact. Using bicycles and public transportation make environmental contributions as valuable as building with bales.

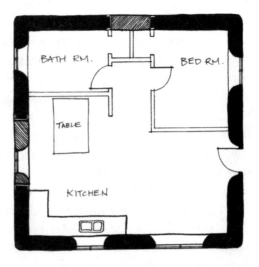

6.2a

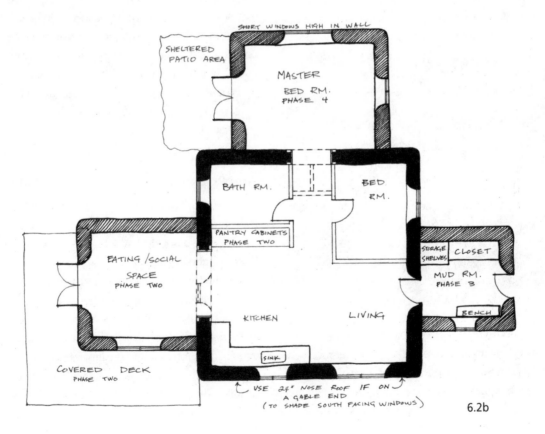

6.2b

6.2a - b: *This type of hand-drawn floor plan shows all the main features of the space. Plans for additions to be constructed later should be thought through at this point, allowing a small initial structure to grow smartly into something more spacious.*

Suburban Sites

If an urban site does not appeal to you, you may want to build in the suburbs. Suburban sites offer builders more opportunity to take advantage of passive solar gain than do many urban sites. Exterior appearance is often highly regulated in suburban neighborhoods. Fortunately, straw bale designs can easily be made to blend in with dominant architectural styles, allowing builders to retain maximum efficiency without resorting to conventional building practices.

In general, suburban sites represent the most environmentally unfriendly option for building. Due to the lack of local markets, infrequent public transportation, and general "isolation" of many suburban communities, residents are often forced to use automobiles when they go out, creating environmental impacts that can negate any advantages offered by building with bales.

6.3: This large straw bale structure is in the midst of one of Canada's most densely populated area.

Town Sites

Small towns can offer a balanced compromise between urban and rural choices. Prices for town lots can be very reasonable and edge-of-town lots can be quiet and very rural in feeling. There are likely to be fewer appearance restrictions in smaller towns. Environmentally, town living can cut down on automobile use.

Country Sites

Rural living and straw bale homes seem well suited to one another. Rural sites have many advantages. Under proper conditions a builder can harvest both straw and lumber from his or her own property. Code restrictions can be less imposing — or possibly nonexistent — in rural areas. Be careful not to jump into rural life without adequate forethought, especially if you are a long-time urban dweller. While rural life can be quiet, beautiful, and inspiring, it also requires adaptations in lifestyle. From an environmental perspective, rural homes are often the most energy-intensive dwellings. Automobiles must be used frequently, fuel sources need to be transported long distances, and road construction and maintenance consume vast amounts of energy. If you are committed to lowering your environmental impact, think carefully about how you plan on living after you've built your straw bale home in the country.

About Property

Find Property That Agrees with You

Allow yourself some room for intuition when choosing property. If a particular site feels good and meets your price and location needs, go with that choice. Similarly, if a site meets all your requirements but simply doesn't turn your crank, then let it go and keep looking elsewhere. If possible, visit your potential site several times and over a few seasons; seasonal changes can radically transform the land of your dreams. Anticipate the view when the trees are with and without leaves. Examine the ground for signs of spring flooding and water movement.

Look for the Microclimate

An ideal building site for energy efficiency and added comfort would have trees (especially evergreens) to protect the site from prevailing winter winds and to trap the sun's heat. Southerly and easterly exposures benefit from clearings and a few deciduous trees, which will allow the sun to help heat the home and immediate surroundings. Perfect microclimates are few and far between but definitely worth looking for.

You Can Grow Your Site

Remember that sites are not unchangeable nor unchanging. Sites that do not currently offer ideal microclimates or appear naturally beautiful can be grown into functional, lush, attractive sites over time. That lot with the two gorgeous mature oak trees may be nice now, but how will it look when those trees inevitably come down as they die? Try to look ahead. You can always transform your site to meet your needs, and if the lot you're interested in is clear, beginning with a clean slate is not always a bad thing.

Wherever You Build, Think about More Than Your House

Regardless of your choice of location, don't forget to plan for more than just your house. Assess the property for its natural characteristics, including trees, vistas, bushes, hills, and other features. Harmonize friendly outdoor spaces with your plans. Think about storage buildings and workshops, and leave room for such outbuildings even if you don't need them now. Situate the house to make gardening possible, remembering that a good microclimate can bring part of the yard to the south of a house one growing zone warmer, lengthening the growing season and possibly creating a mini fruit belt.

Property Hunting Schemes

Searching for property can be a long frustrating process. Real-estate agencies are a good place to start, but be sure to let agents know all your requirements early on. Listings for vacant lands are considered the doldrums at many real-estate offices. Be sure to ask for complete listings in your preferred area; otherwise, you may only be shown newer listings or those an agent is keen to push. Expect to see a lot of what you don't want. You can also place ads in local newspapers, specifying your needs and price range. Quite often, the prospect of a keen buyer can motivate property owners into selling lots that are not currently on the market. Tax foreclosures, property dealers, and rezoned lands are all worth researching, too.

Don't Design Too Early

Without a piece of property on which to build, don't spend too much time creating a finished design for your home. The land should — and will — be responsible for shaping your design.

References

Books

Alexander, Christopher, *A Pattern Language: Towns, Buildings, Construction.* Oxford University Press, 1977. ISBN: 0195019199

Allen, Edward. *How Buildings Work: The Natural Order of Architecture.* Oxford University Press, 1995. ISBN 0-19-509100-0.

Brooks, Hugh. *Illustrated Encyclopedic Dictionary of Building and Construction Terms.* Prentice-Hall, 1976. ISBN 0-13-451013-5.

Brown, Azby. *Small Spaces: Stylish Ideas for Making More of Less.* Kodansha International, 1993. ISBN 4-7700-1495-3.

Crowther, Richard L. *Ecological Architecture.* Butterworth Architecture, 1992. ISBN 0-7506-9171-9.

Holloway, Dennis and Maureen McIntyre. *The Owner-Builder Experience: How to Design and Build Your Own Home.* Rodale Press, 1986. ISBN 0-87857-643-6.

Preston, Edward. *How to Buy Land Cheap*, 4th ed. Loompanics Unlimited, 1991. ISBN 1-55950-064-6.

Rybczynski, Witold. *The Most Beautiful House in the World.* Penguin Books, 1989. ISBN 0-14-010566-2.

Taylor, John S. *A Shelter Sketchbook: Timeless Building Solutions.* Chelsea Green Publishers, 1997. ISBN 1-890132-02-0.

Woods, Charles G. *A Natural System of House Design: An Architect's Way.* McGraw-Hill, 1996. ISBN 0-07-071736-2.

CHAPTER 7

Design Considerations

After playing the Design Game, you'll have come to certain conclusions about the house you want. Before you move on to a scaled drawing or design, there are some technical aspects to be addressed. It's time for you to become aware of some key design considerations.

The results from your Design Game are an important beginning. You will have gained some clear understanding about your future home and learned about the kinds of decisions and compromises that must be made along the way. Depending on your level of experience and the range of your personal concerns, you may or may not have addressed certain technical issues in your version of the Design Game. These elements must be addressed before the Game is over and the working design is created.

Some New Pieces for the Design Game

Passive Solar Design

Early cave dwellers knew about it, wild and domestic animals know about it, and some cultures still practice it, but passive solar design has been neglected in modern home design. Incorporating passive solar elements into your house is easy to do, and the rewards are significant. Given the importance of the sun in all aspects of how we function in our built environments, it is really quite remarkable that paying attention to the sun's interaction with our buildings isn't part of mainstream building practice. It seems odd that such an important topic is rarely addressed, and when it *is* addressed, it's as though it's a specialty concern. It should be fundamental: if you're undertaking a building project, please don't ignore the sun!

Ever watched a cat or dog stretch out on the floor in a pool of warm sunlight? Passive solar design can maximize your home's exposure to those warm rays and give them a chance to heat your home in the colder months. At the same time, proper passive solar design ensures those same rays are kept out when you are trying to keep your home cool in the summer. By simply taking account of the sun's position in the sky, you can lower the cost of winter heating and summer cooling dramatically, while improving occupant comfort.

Passive solar design is premised on the changing position of the sun from morning to night (east to west), and from winter equinox to summer equinox (low on the horizon to high). At each time of day and in each season, we want our buildings to coordinate their performance with the sun's position.

There is no one-size-fits-all strategy for appropriate passive solar design. Much will depend on your geographical location (your latitude), your

7.1: *This is a good example of effective passive solar design. South-facing windows on both floors are shaded in summer and open to the sun in the winter. The "eyebrow roof" is slanted at a good angle for mounting solar panels.*

MARK GODFREY

climate, the specifics of your building site, and your daylighting needs inside the building. There are three basic elements to consider in passive solar design:

- building orientation and shape
- window placement and shading
- occupant needs and movements

Building Orientation and Shape

The classic passive solar strategy calls for a building that is oriented so its longest side faces south (reverse for the southern hemisphere), creating a building along an east-west axis. This allows you to maximize your south-facing windows for passive heat gain in the winter. It is a good strategy,

and when the site and occupant needs allow for such a shape, it is simple and effective.

However, a lot of building sites do not allow for this long and skinny approach. But that doesn't mean you have to give up on passive solar design. There are many building shapes, some simple, some complex, that allow for good use of the sun. Even on sites where southern exposure is limited or the building is constricted by lot size, there are ways to maximize passive solar aspects.

When siting a house to face south, simply locate the sun around noon. That's the direction you want! A compass will point you in a direction that is not quite true solar south, since magnetic north and true north are not aligned perfectly. If any bias is to be made away from true south, it is best to shift a bit to the east to maximize your morning exposure and minimize late afternoon overheating.

Window Placement and Shading

There is more to passive solar design than just aiming a bunch of windows to the south. Too often the attempt is made to simply capitalize on passive heat gain during the winter, without considering the different needs that accompany each season. Those who employ the "massive south glazing" strategy, covering the south face of the building with windows, often come to regret this approach when the house overheats in the summer and cools down very quickly at night in the winter.

You must first consider that fact that the sun's rays have very different qualities at different times of the day. In the morning, the sun is low to the horizon, giving it a long penetration into the building. Typically, it is good to encourage your access to this morning sun, even in the summer, because your house will have cooled

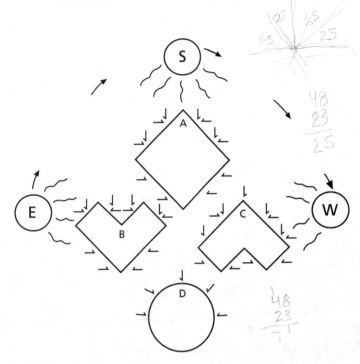

over night, and early morning sun will start to warm it quickly, with little chance of overheating because the rays are still quite weak.

As the day progresses, the sun moves higher into the southern sky. In the winter, you want to encourage this mid-morning to mid-afternoon sunshine to enter the building, but in the summer you want to exclude it. The key to benefiting from both heat gain in the winter and heat deflection in the summer is to have a good shading strategy. Summer shading can save you as much, if not more, energy than winter heat gain, and all too often this is not taken into account.

There are many ways to adequately shade your south-facing windows to allow for winter sun and cut out summer sun. Properly calculated roof overhangs are one effective method. All you need to know are the maximum and minimum sun angles for your latitude (you'll find charts in many of the resources listed at the end of the chapter, or you can go and look outside!), and the maximum and minimum heights of your windows. From this, you can set the overhangs and windows such that the shadow cast by the overhang just covers the lower sill at midsummer and allows full exposure to the top of the window in winter. Two-story buildings will require additional shading over the first story windows because the roof overhang will not shade them.

Buildings incorporating photovoltaic panels or thermal solar panels can mount these over south windows to provide the same kind of shading as a roof overhang. Retractable awnings over south windows will allow you to customize the amount of sunlight accessing your windows.

Trellises are another good strategy. The trellis will be covered in thick leafy greenery in the summer, cutting out the sun to the windows, but those leaves will have died off by late fall,

letting the sun come in. Deciduous trees planted (or already existing) a proper distance from the house can have the same effect (but don't forget the height of the canopy will change as the tree grows!).

A common error in passive solar design is too much glazing and/or inadequate shading on the west. As the sun begins to sink in the afternoon, the low rays become more difficult to exclude, and even in the winter, after a full day's worth of heat gain, the afternoon sun can raise the indoor temperature uncomfortably. Roof overhangs that create a porch space to the west can solve this problem, as can smaller windows. Shrubs and bushes planted close to the building can also work well.

Window sizing is a very important consideration. It must be remembered that, even in a house with good passive solar design and the highest quality of glazing, the windows are still

7.2: Good passive solar qualities can be achieved with a wide range of building designs. A shows a square building set for optimum solar exposure. B and C show typical L-shaped homes arranged for good passive solar qualities, and the round house, D, also gets exceptional solar gain.

net losers of heat in the winter and net gainers of heat in the summer because they are the least insulative element in your building shell. The further north you build, the more important this consideration, as winter hours of sunlight are short and summer hours long. A balance must therefore be struck between adequate light and excessive heat loss or gain.

The most energy-efficient building would have no windows at all, just nice thick bale walls and lots of roof insulation! However, most of us don't want to live in a dark cave, even if it's super-efficient. But the lesson here is: the bigger the windows, the lower the overall efficiency of the building. It doesn't take huge windows to allow in enough winter sunlight to warm the air effectively. Choose window sizes to suit your day-lighting needs and to create a space you will find comfortable in terms of views and ventilation. Remember that most building codes include minimum window sizes for specific rooms in a home.

Larger windows are most desirable on the east and south, smaller ones on the west and particularly the north, since they can only be net losers where they never see the sun. And we can't overemphasize the importance of using high quality windows.

Passive Solar: Theory and Practice

The passive solar design of my house is one of its most effective and important elements. On a sunny winter day, even if the outdoor temperature is –20 degrees Celsius, there is no need to heat our straw bale home! However, a lot of what I was told and read about passive solar was misleading for northern climate applications. The further north you go — we're at 44 degrees north — the fewer hours of sunlight you get in the winter. Plus, winter sun is very often obscured by clouds. This means that when you really want its benefits, the number of hours of passive solar gain is much lower than the number of hours of thermal loss, since heat escapes through windows at night and on cloudy days.

Counting on passive solar gain to significantly warm concrete floors or any other thermal mass can be a mistake in northern climes, unless extreme design strategies are undertaken — windows extending to the floor and no rugs or furniture blocking access to sunlight. The thickness of bale walls means that much of the direct sunlight will fall on your window sill, not on the floor. By incorporating some thermal mass — thick plaster, tile, or stone — into your wide window sills, you will gain some warming effects, but your floor and any interior walls will not see enough sun to raise their temperature appreciably.

When it is shining, the winter sun will do an excellent job of heating the air — not the mass — of your home, and it doesn't require massive south facing windows to do so. Sizing your windows too large will put you in a negative gain situation. Standard-sized windows are quite adequate, as long as enough of them see the sun.

Shading your south windows against direct sunlight in the summertime will do a remarkable job of keeping your home cool. This is an equally important part of the passive solar equation, and one that is too often overlooked. However, the standard practice of using the high- and low equinox points of the sun's angle will block the sun's heat in early spring, when you may still need it, and start letting it back in during the late fall, when you may not want it. While the static shading on our house works well, adjustable awnings would allow us to pick and choose when we wish the sun to do its remarkable job of replacing our woodstove.

— *Chris Magwood* ∎

Occupant Needs and Movements

The final consideration for good passive solar design is effective daylighting inside the building, allowing natural light to replace electric light as much as possible.

Everybody will have different daylighting needs. For early risers, place your bedroom on the east side of the building where the sun can greet you as soon as it rises. Late risers will want to do the opposite, placing bedrooms far from the morning sun, on the west or north side. Consider your movements through the house during the day. What are your main daytime activities? Make sure the rooms for these activities have maximum southern exposure. What activities do you only do at night? Rooms for these should be on the north, since electric light will be used anyway. When do you take your leisure time? When do you read or watch television? When do you socialize? Where and when do your kids do their homework? You'll want to trace the timing of these activities in your life and assign them placement in your design to suit the available light.

This strategy will accomplish two things: create a healthier atmosphere (our bodies prefer natural light to artificial) and save on energy. The energy savings are particularly important for those considering off-grid living.

Your own version of a passive solar design will be uniquely dependent on your specific situation. For now, add this new aspect to your current efforts in the Design Game.

Building Size

Home sizes in North America have increased dramatically in the past two decades. Regardless of how energy efficient or green the design of a building may be, there is a basic, foolproof guarantee: the bigger the home, the more energy required to build it, heat it, and cool it. There is a direct correlation between a building's size and its cost and environmental impact. We urge you to save yourself money and the planet some strain by creating a thoughtfully designed building with the smallest possible dimensions. Bigger is not better.

As much as we would like to see a return to sanely scaled buildings, it is important to check your local building codes to see if there is a minimum square footage requirement in your jurisdiction. Often these minimums can be

shockingly high, especially for homes intended for only one or two residents.

Bungalow or Multi-story?

You may already have decided whether you are building your home on one or two levels. (Three stories plus a basement is the maximum allowable by many residential building codes.) If you haven't decided, now is a good time to consider your options. Size alone may dictate whether your building is one or two stories. Tiny houses don't need an extra level, while

7.3: *This 1,000 - square-foot bungalow leaves a small footprint on the planet, was affordable and easy to put up. It's also more than enough space for a family to live comfortably.*

7.4a

7.4b

7.4c:

very large buildings usually do. However, with a moderately sized building — 1000–2500 square feet — you have the option of going either way.

It may seem that the added complexity of an extra level would be more costly to construct, but a reduction in footprint size can often cancel out such cost factors. A 2000-square-foot building constructed on one level will require a large foundation/floor area and a large roof (often the most expensive elements). However, if you build two 1000-square-foot stories, you half the size of the building's footprint and the costs that go with them. You will end up adding expenses for stairs, second-floor joists, and flooring materials for the two-story option.

When making this decision, take into account your mechanical systems (which are most efficient when kept centralized), your building experience (two stories is more complex), your passive solar strategy (shading considerations), and your choice of materials.

The biggest factors in making this decision are your level of experience, confidence, and intended involvement in the construction. There is no doubt that multi-story construction offers many more logistical and practical barriers to owner-builders, ranging from the need for scaffolding to the construction of staircases to fear of heights. Bale homes, in particular, offer challenges on multi-stories. Scaffolding will need to be rented and erected. Bales must be lifted into place, as must plaster and plasterers, causing work

7.4a - c: Your own design goals and the nature of your site will both inform your decisions during the design game. As these three very different examples of bale homes demonstrate, there no real limitations imposed on your design by the use of bale walls.

times to rise significantly as the building gets taller. Experienced crews may not be affected as much by taller walls.

Rounds, Curves, and Creativity

One of the great attractions of bale building is the potential for creating spaces that are unique. The combination of bales and plaster offers endless possibilities for form and texture. At some point in your Design Game, don't forget to include some aspects that will make your home uniquely yours.

Bales can be laid sideways underneath windows to create wide bench seats; buttresses can grow into the interior or outside the building, the orientation of the bales can be changed over and/or around windows and doors to add weight lines; shelves, ledges, and niches, can be formed in or on the walls. It is possible to add these elements at the spur of the moment onsite during construction, but it is worth having some fun right at the design stage, so these elements become part of an overall vision of the space.

Modern construction avoids rounded and curved elements because wooden framing, plywood, drywall and other manufactured materials do not lend themselves easily to such details. Bale walls are quite adaptable to curves, allowing for design possibilities foreign to most modern home plans. Curved and rounded walls lend a remarkable feeling to a space and are worth considering. Keep in mind that your round or curved bale wall will still have to blend with your foundation and roof, both of which are likely to use straight materials (see sidebar on round roofs in Chapter 9).

Learning to Juggle

You will discover as you begin this part of the design process that there is nothing simple or easy about it. It can be, in turns, fun, challenging, and frustrating. The number of ideas, considerations, and technical requirements you have to juggle will only keep growing as you delve deeper into the design of your home. Don't worry if you drop an item or two as you juggle. Work at a pace that is comfortable to you and progress at a rate that matches your understanding. Expect to ride an emotional roller coaster, with high highs and low lows. In the end, remember that you are building a house, not attempting to reach a state of perfection. There is plenty of room for learning — and for mistakes — as you move forward. The more you think about the design of your house now, the easier the building or hiring process will be later.

References

Aho, Arnold J. *Materials, Energies and Environmental Design*. Garland STP Press, 1981. ISBN 0- 8240-7178-6.

Beckstrom, Bob. *Home Plans for Solar Living 1*. Home Planners, Inc., 1989. ISBN 0-918894-67-0.

Broome, Jon and Brian Richardson. *The Self-Build Book: How to Enjoy Designing and Building Your Own Home*. Green Earth Books, 1995. ISBN 1-900322-00-5.

Canada Mortgage and Housing Corporation. *Tap the Sun: Passive Solar Techniques and Home Designs*. Canada Mortgage and Housing Corporation,1998. ISBN 0-660-17267-4.

Ching, Francis D. K. *Building Construction Illustrated*. Van Nostrand Reinhold, 1991. ISBN 0-442-23498-8.

Clark, Sam. *Independent Builder: Designing and Building a House Your Own Way*. Chelsea Green Publishers, 1996. SBN 0-930031-85-7.

Cole, John N. and Charles Wing. *From the Ground Up*. Atlantic Monthly Press, 1976. ISBN 0-316-15112-2.

DiDonno, Lupe and Phyllis Sperling. *How to Design and Build Your Own House*. Alfred A. Knopf, 1987. ISBN 0-394-75200-7.

Jones, Robert T., ed. *Authentic Small Houses of the Twenties: Illustrations and Floor Plans of 254 Characteristic Homes*. Dover Publications, 1987. ISBN 0-486-25406-2.

Kachadorian, James. *The Passive Solar House: Using Solar Design to Heat and Cool Your Home*. Chelsea Green Publishers, 1998. ISBN 0-930031-97-0.

Pearson, David. *New Natural House Book: Creating a Healthy, Harmonious and Ecologically Sound Home*. Simon and Schuster, 1998. ISBN 0-684-84733-7.

Shurcliff, William A. *Super-Solar Houses: Saunders' Low-Cost, 100% Solar Designs*. Brick House Publishing Co., 1983. ISBN 0-931790-47-6.

Todd, Nancy Jack and John Todd. *From Eco-cities to Living Machines: Principles of Ecological Design*. North Atlantic Books, 1994.

Wylde, Margaret, Adrian Baron-Robbins, and Sam Clark. *Building for a Lifetime: The Design and Construction of Fully Accessible Homes*. The Taunton Press, Inc., 1994. ISBN 1-56158-036-8.

CHAPTER 8

The Many Styles of Bale Building

There are many kinds of straw bale wall systems, and once you've decided to build with bales, you'll be faced with the key decision of how exactly the bale walls will be constructed. The variation you choose will have important implications for your entire building project, and this choice must be made before any detailed planning can be completed.

There are three categories of bale wall systems: load-bearing (or Nebraska-style), post and beam infill, and hybrids that combine the two.

Load-bearing or Nebraska-style Walls

The first builders of straw bale homes used bales because of a lack of available lumber, stone, or suitable sod. These Nebraska pioneers saw the tight, thick, and durable bales of field hay they were harvesting — yes, they used hay! — as a solution to their housing needs. They stacked them up, built a roof, plastered, and moved in. As with other styles of pioneer buildings, Nebraska-style bale homes featured simplicity, ease of construction, and the use of local materials. These same features are the main attraction in modern load-bearing straw bale homes.

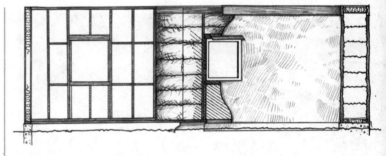

Bales as Structural Elements

As is implied by the term "load-bearing," a building of this style uses bale walls as structural components. The weight of the roof structure bears directly on the top of the wall, which in turn transfers the loads to the foundation. No supporting framework is used to create the wall structure, just bales and plaster. And therein lies the appeal

8.1: *In this side-by-side comparison, you can see the difference between frame wall construction and bale wall construction. On the left, the frame wall has regularly spaced studs and blocking, and these cavities are filled with insulation. On the right, the bale wall has framing only around the window and at the top and bottom plate.*

of Nebraska-style construction. Expense, complexity, and lumber consumption can be reduced, and the skilled work of framing or creating

8.2a

HANK CARR

8.2b

CLEMENT & DENISE PILON

8.2a - b:
*Load-bearing
structures
can be small,
simple
bungalows
or very large,
two-story
structures.*

any sort of skeleton structure is replaced by the relatively easy task of stacking bales and plastering. The walls can be built quickly and affordably with a minimum of materials, resulting in a cost saving and a less dramatic environmental impact.

Can Bales *Really* Support a Building?

For many people, it is a considerable leap of faith to believe in the strength of a straw bale wall that is unsupported by lumber or any other structural framework. However, as both experience and scientific testing show, load-bearing walls exhibit a strength equal or superior to standard frame walls. But how can this be when bales are a compressible material? Shouldn't the walls sag or give?

There is a double-edged answer to this question. Yes, straw bales can support the roof of a building. But, no, they don't actually hold up the roof, even in a load-bearing building. Confused? So were many bale builders, until some engineers started to analyze the performance of the walls to determine how they really function.

Creating a "Stressed Skin Panel"

A straw bale wall is an interesting combination of two strong, but brittle, plaster skins bonded to the dense, but elastic, bales. The thin plaster skins alone are remarkably strong in compression, strong enough to hold up the roof of a large building. But standing on their own, they'd be too prone to buckling to function in a structural manner. However, since the plaster skins are well anchored to the straw bales, they are prevented from twisting or buckling, and structural loads pass through the plaster skins in their strongest direction.

This understanding of load-bearing wall behavior often helps to reassure skeptics (other types of stressed skin panels are commonly engineered for construction purposes), and also helps to inform load-bearing building practices. Since we understand that the plaster skins are responsible for much of the structural strength of a load-bearing wall, and that the bond between the plaster and the straw is essential to that strength, we can apply these principles to our designs for load-bearing walls.

Precompression of Load-bearing Walls

Load-bearing straw bale walls are unique in the realm of construction materials for their need to be precompressed. The precompression serves three important functions: getting rid of the "squish" in the walls, leveling the top of the wall, and providing a structural tie from foundation to roof plate.

Getting Rid of "Squish"

Straw bales are not rigid blocks, and though they can hold up a roof, they will compress under that load over time. The tighter the bale, the less "squishiness" in the wall, but even very tight bales will settle. Once the plaster is applied (and has cured), this settling stops because the plaster skins are not compressible. But we don't want to apply plaster to a wall that will be getting shorter as the plaster is trying to cure!

The Nebraskan pioneers addressed this issue by building the roof structure on top of unplastered walls and allowing time for the walls to settle under the weight of the roof. Once the settling stopped (this could take four to six weeks), they plastered the compressed bales, creating the structural skin of the stressed skin panel that results in such remarkably strong and rigid buildings.

In most modern construction scenarios, it is not practical to leave a building to settle over such a long period of time. Modern straw builders use a variety of mechanical systems to pre-compress their load-bearing walls and then prepare the walls for immediate plastering, since roof loads will no longer cause the bales to settle.

There are many techniques for pre-compressing, most of which are low-tech and easy to employ. They all share the common concept of tying some form of continuous structural roof plate to the foundation at regular intervals around the building. These ties are then subjected to a mechanical force that draws the roof plate down toward the foundation. This mechanical force is a substitute for the weight of the roof — and for additional weights and forces to which the roof is subject. As a testament to the compressive strength of bales, even large mechanical forces usually produce only one to four inches of immediate compression in a wall with seven courses of bales. Properly tensioned, the walls are remarkably strong and resistant to flex in all directions, even before plastering.

Leveling the Wall

Because bales are not perfectly square blocks, and because there will be variations in density between bales, the top course of a bale wall will not necessarily be level. Mechanical precompression systems all use ties that are spaced at regular intervals around the building, and differing amounts of force can be applied to each point to achieve a level top plate.

Attaching Roof to Foundation

Neither plaster skins nor stacked bales provide a whole lot of resistance to lifting forces, to which your roof may be subject. Whatever form of mechanical tie is used to precompress the wall is left in place to provide this resistance to uplift, and this function should be taken into account when materials and methods for precompression are being chosen.

Precompression Techniques

Ideal tensioning devices must be relatively inexpensive, strong, durable, and easy to work with, allowing you a simple way to add and remove tension with a minimum of hassle. A wide variety of methods have been tried over the years. The most common and successful variations use a system of wire or cable ties. Looped through the foundation and over a rigid roof plate assembly on top of the bale wall, a come-along Grippler, a patented wire tensioning system, or other such tensioning device can be applied to the two ends of the wire where they meet. This shortens the loop and forces the top plate to come down.

Typically, these loops are created with galvanized wire, stainless steel cable, or metal or plastic binding. Each option requires its own specific attachments or fasteners, and each will also require special tools for applying tension. They all seem to work equally well, so choosing is a matter of availability, cost, and your own level of comfort.

These loops can be affixed to the foundation in a variety of ways, depending on the style of the foundation. There should be a tie approximately every four feet around the building. Ties at each corner should be equidistant from each other — approximately two feet from the outside corners. You'll want to avoid running ties across door and window openings. If you aren't certain where your openings will be, you can overcompensate and provide an excess of attachment points for the ties, and use only those that end up being appropriate.

Another precompression method uses threaded steel bars which are embedded in the foundation and run through the middle of the bales to protrude through the top plate. Compression is applied by tightening a nut against the top plate. Most builders have abandoned this practice because it is costly, overly complex, and because it is buried in the wall, it is difficult to access should a rod break or the threads strip (a common occurrence).

If you should devise your own method for precompressing walls, be sure to record the materials and strategies you used, and share your results with others. If your system works, it could be a big help to future bale builders. If it doesn't work or needs improvement, it could help others avoid similar mistakes. Bale building is too young to have all the answers, so every new contribution is useful.

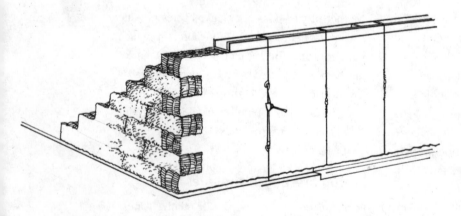

8.3: A 9-gauge galvanized wire straps the building from foundation to roof plate at 4 foot centres. A come-along and a pair of fence stretchers or a Grippler add the tension. Plastic or metal banding is another suitable option.

Obstacles to Load-bearing Designs

Skepticism — both personal and institutional — is by far the biggest hurdle facing a builder who chooses a load-bearing design. Building a home is a large investment and one that we hope is long-term; you definitely do not want to have doubts about the strength of your walls. If testing data and the experiences of others do not inspire a healthy trust in you, a load-bearing design may not be a suitable option for you. If you can see its numerous benefits and can make the perceptual leap, you must still convince your spouse, family, and building inspector, lender, and insurer that the idea is a good one. The best way to convince yourself and others is to go and see a load-bearing straw building. Its solidity, permanence, and strength will be obvious.

Even if you are convinced that a load-bearing design is for you, you still have to deal with the construction community. Many builders are concerned about obtaining building permits for load-bearing straw bale designs. Most building inspectors are unfamiliar with the concept and may be resistant to it. However, permits have been issued for load-bearing straw homes in most American states and Canadian provinces. Most jurisdictions that already include straw bale construction in their building codes make provisions for load-bearing straw walls, and these existing codes can be used to support claims of methodology, strength, and soundness of construction when you meet with your building inspector.

The most commonly cited disadvantage of load-bearing walls is the fact that they are built before the roof, which can leave the walls vulnerable to wet weather. This susceptibility to wet weather will be directly related to climate, building size, and the experience of the building crew.

Obviously, if you are living in an area that has a predictable rainy season (or a good probability of major rainstorms) you will want to time your bale raising so it doesn't occur during that season, or consider post and beam options. Otherwise, in most climates, it's not too difficult to find two or three days without rain in which to safely raise your walls.

The true joy of load-bearing construction is the speed at which the walls can be erected.

If the window and door frames are already constructed and in place and the roof plate pre-built and ready to be installed, it often takes only a day or two to raise all the bales and install the roof plate. It is only while the tops of the bales are directly exposed to rain that real moisture damage is likely; bales can get quite wet from the sides and still dry out, but, if they are soaked into the core, they will not. Once the roof plate is in place, it helps prevent water from soaking the top course of bales, and a roll of plastic or a tarp should be used if rain is expected.

CHRIS MAGWOOD

We have successfully built large (over 2,000 square feet) one- and two-story load-bearing buildings in a climate with unpredictable and often heavy rains, so it's not impossible or even particularly difficult, but it does require some forethought (have tarps or other coverings at hand) and planning (quitting work early enough to leave time for tarping).

Designing for Load-bearing Walls

Load-bearing buildings create some challenges for builders. A load-bearing bale wall in the

8.4: For most two-story, load-bearing buildings, the first floor bales are stacked, compressed, and plastered, and then the second story is built onto the floor platform.

process of being built can seem like an entirely unfeasible proposition. Often wavy and unstable, it's easy to be convinced that there is no way this is the basis for a strong, long-lasting building! But there are some design and construction tricks that help to make the process manageable, and you will find these in the chapters on straw bale construction plans and wall raising.

At the early design stage, there are a few considerations to keep in mind if you're going to build load-bearing. Early ideas about load-bearing building cautioned against wide window or door openings and limited the length and height of load-bearing walls. Most of these limitations are false: there is very little in modern home construction that cannot be done with load-bearing walls. Wide window and door openings (four-foot or wider) will require additional lintels or a stronger top plate, and long or tall walls may require temporary bracing, but these are not obstacles to load-bearing designs.

Two-story buildings present some interesting challenges, mostly because of the additional time that can be required for construction, leaving walls exposed to weather longer. There are two basic ways to create two-story load-bearing buildings. They can be platform style, in which the first-floor walls are built and plastered, followed by the floor system and then the second-floor walls. They can also be balloon style, in which the walls are built to full height in one step, and the floor is either hung from a box-beam built into the wall or supported by posts and partition walls on the inside of the building.

Which Way to Orient My Bales?

Most bale buildings tend to have the bales laid flat (no strings showing on the face of the wall). This standard was established early on, when the very first tests were performed on bare unplastered bales. In these tests, bales laid flat offered less resistance to compression than bales laid on-edge (with strings showing on both sides of the wall), but did not experience the same kind of ultimate failure that on-edge bales demonstrated.

This early bias has never really gone away, even though we now understand that the bales themselves will never be subjected to the kinds of loads imposed in these tests because the plaster skins will be handling this structural role. Bales on-edge are used in post and beam settings, but it is still considered experimental to use them on-edge for load-bearing structures, despite the fact that some of the historical bale buildings in Nebraska were built with bales on-edge.

Thermal testing of bales in both orientations has shown that there is no significant difference in the R-value. Flat bales have a slightly lower per-inch R-value, but more inches; on-edge bales have the inverse.

Advantages to bales laid flat:

- a wider wall can be more stable
- easier to notch around framework
- more depth for carving window openings and niches
- testing data supports this orientation
- easier to plaster if mesh is not being used

Disadvantages to bales laid flat:

- loss of floor space due to greater width
- need more bales for same wall height
- use of more lumber for framing
- more compression and settling
- need to trim the folded side prior to plastering ☞

You Don't Have to Be Conventional!

Load-bearing bale walls are unique creatures. You can certainly create walls that are perfectly level, square, and plumb, but don't forget that this isn't an absolute necessity. Conventional walls need to be perfectly square and level or else all the prefab finishes applied to them (drywall, plywood, brick, etc.) won't work. But your plastered bale walls are their own beasts, and a wavy top plate that would give a conventional framer a heart attack can be intentionally beautiful in a bale wall!

Most of the strategies you'll use to create sound load-bearing plans do not translate into higher costs or undue construction complexity. A well-planned, well-built, load-bearing building is cost-effective and relatively easy to construct. However, if you find yourself resisting a load-bearing design, perhaps post and beam will better suit your needs.

Post and Beam Infill Systems

In any form of post and beam construction, structural loads are handled by a series of upright members (posts) that support suitable horizontal beams. With this type of structural system, some kind of insulative infill is used to close in the walls. Straw bales and plaster make an attractive option as an infill wall system.

Post and beam construction has a long history, and many builders, architects, and building inspectors are familiar and comfortable with its application. Most commonly, large-dimension lumber is used to construct the load-bearing structural framework, but concrete, steel, or

Advantages to bales on-edge:

- less floor space used
- need fewer bales for same wall heigh
- two-string bales create 16-inch-wide walls, well-suited to efficient use of standard building materials
- less compression and settling
- little or no trimming required

Disadvantages to bales on-edge:

- no testing data (yet) to support load-bearing applications
- more difficult to notch around framework
- can be more difficult to plaster if mesh is not being used

Each builder must decide which way to orient the bales for a particular building, based on which of the points above are most important. You can't really make a wrong choice; they work well in either orientation!

— *Chris Magwood* ∎

combinations of these materials can also be used. By infilling with bales, all the excellent insulation capabilities of straw buildings are retained. Bales still offer an unbeatable price; walls can still be put up quickly and easily; and the character of the plastered bales will remain the dominant feature of the home.

There are two major reasons typically cited by those who choose post and beam systems for bale buildings. The first is the familiarity of the materials and engineering, which can make bale building more approachable and understandable for designers, building officials, and builders used to conventional materials. The second is the ability to complete the framework and the roof prior to installing the bales, reducing some of the weather-related concerns that can arise when working with bales.

There are many ways to make a post and beam frame, and many ways again in which to blend the bale walls into the frame. Each offers advantages and disadvantages, and very different results can arise depending on the combination you choose.

Post and Beam Variations

Timber frame

The classic timber frame, with its large-dimension lumber and carefully crafted joinery, is very beautiful. Timber-framed buildings have an elegance and solidity that is impossible to duplicate, and its recollections of the craftsmanship of the past have brought the style a recent resurgence in popularity.

If you are building for the first time or have never tried timber framing, you must recognize that it requires a good deal of skill and practice. It is entirely possible to learn these skills, but do not expect to erect your building quickly as a first-timer. If you decide to hire out, there are many experienced timber framers with a variety of styles. They can do beautiful work in a reasonable length of time, but timber-framing can be expensive.

Timber-framing occupies an unusual place in many building codes. Recognizing its historical validity, many building officials will allow its use without requiring an engineer's approval, especially when an experienced framer is responsible for the design and/or construction.

Advantages: beautiful, strong, long-lasting, satisfying to build

Disadvantages: costly, large timbers often not sustainably harvested, steep learning curve for beginners, complications integrating bales.

Mechanically connected post and beam

Mechanically connected post and beam techniques and materials can substitute for the notched joinery used in timber-framing. A variety of mechanical fasteners can be bought or fabricated to attach posts and beams together. Commercial brackets and fasteners are generally accepted by building officials; homemade versions may require special approval. Carefully assess your choice of connectors if you are exploring this option; often they are expensive, and it is not difficult to end up spending as much money on mechanical fasteners as you might do on hiring a timber-framer.

Post and beam systems often eschew the large-dimension lumber used in timber-framing in favor of site-made or commercially available laminates. To create an onsite laminate, a number of pieces of standard dimension lumber are joined together using a certain nailing or bolting pattern. These laminate posts and beams may be suitable for your project and accepted by your building official, and often cost less than a comparable solid timber.

Commercially available laminates are also an option. They are made from glued strands of wood and are designed to equal the load-bearing capacity of large-dimension lumber. Their cost is often reasonable, especially if you must otherwise import solid timber from a great distance. Some environmentalists praise commercial laminates because they are made from waste wood and therefore save large trees; others are less positive because of the nature of the glues used to create the laminates. If the chemical composition of the glues concerns you, be sure to do some research before inviting them into your home. Commercial laminates are often available complete with appropriate fasteners and joinery from lumber supply yards.

Manufactured joists are also an option for creating beams. These joists use oriented strand board (OSB) — a product similar to plywood — sandwiched between lengths of small dimension lumber to create strong I-beams. They can be ordered to meet your length and strength requirements, and use fewer glues overall than do full-sized laminates. They are also much lighter to carry and lift into place.

Advantages: building code friendly, relatively simple to construct, can choose more sustainable lumber options

Disadvantages: can be costly, complications integrating bales, can use a lot of lumber

Modified Post and Beam

Modified post and beam designs can blend the lumber-saving elements of load-bearing designs with the structural advantages of post and beam. This style uses a structural top plate, similar to that used for a load-bearing structure, as a continuous beam and transforms the window and door bucks used in load-bearing buildings into structural posts. Since a regular post and beam design would use similarly strong window and door bucks, lumber savings can be significant. The posts are rigid box beams constructed of small dimension lumber — usually 2-by-4s — and plywood or OSB, which means that only small reforested trees need to be harvested. The 2-by-4 and plywood supports can be stuffed with straw

to provide nearly identical insulation values to the rest of the wall. Simple to construct and relatively miserly in lumber usage, this option allows for a post and beam framework that can be completely buried in the straw wall without any need to notch or cut bales. You save time and space. Until such designs become common, however, it may take an architect's or engineer's stamp for a modified post and beam design to get permit approval.

8.5: *A traditional timber frame (in this case using recycled timbers) can be erected as a stand-alone structure, then wrapped or in filled with straw bales.*

8.6a

Advantages: simple, low lumber usage, easy integration with bales

Disadvantages: needs special engineering

Standard Stick Framing

It is relatively easy to use a conventionally framed stud wall system with straw bales. In this system, the bales would be stacked between the studs. Two-string bales can fit quite well into a standard 16-inch stud spacing if stood on their ends. Some additional framing will be required to compensate for the extra width of the bales, but this is easily accomplished at the design stage.

Advantages: simple, code accepted

Disadvantages: high lumber use, difficulty integrating bales

Truss Systems

Full truss systems, wood or steel, are comprised of all-in-one wall and roof trusses, which are spaced at regular intervals. Bales can be placed between

8.6b

8.6a - c: *These thin posts are used to frame door and window openings and corners, creating a lightweight frame that is then infilled with bales. When the posts are as wide as the bales, no notching and cutting is required.*

8.6c

the trusses. Strapping is added between the trusses to help stabilize them, and plaster eventually gives the whole structure further stability.

Buildings of this sort can be erected very quickly, and because the trusses will be manufactured to the specifications of an in-house engineer, code approval should be relatively easy to obtain. The truss engineer will need to be aware of bale thickness and the odd spacing bales will require, but these dimensions shouldn't prove to be a problem. A truss system could be designed to allow bales to be used continuously from walls to ceiling, since truss spacing would be tailor-made for bales, anyway.

The cost of executing a truss design varies greatly, depending on the simplicity of the design. A relatively straightforward square or rectangular design will use identical trusses for the entire structure; a complicated design will require a series of varying-sized trusses that will up the cost significantly.

Advantages: simple, pre-engineered, easy bale integration, low cost

Disadvantages: high lumber use, can't build your own trusses

Concrete

Concrete columns and concrete top plates can be used together or in combination with other materials. Stacked concrete blocks or poured concrete columns can support roof loads. Blocks are easily dry stacked, and the hollow cores can be filled with cement and rebar when the column is at full height. This option requires no form work and little experience. Poured columns require either homemade or prefabricated forms to contain the wet concrete. The simplest and cheapest forming system is the Sonno-Tube, but since it creates a round column, you'll have to figure out how to blend the finished column with the bales. In either case, it is important to use adequate rebar to support the column. Check your building code or ask an experienced professional for guidance.

While concrete columns may cost less than certain lumber options and may be easier to build if you are unfamiliar with woodwork, they do have two drawbacks. First, columns built to the inside of the straw walls remain visible in the house after the walls are erected. Forms that incorporate interesting patterns, pigment in the concrete mix, or a simple surface paint job could help solve the esthetic problem of exposed concrete. Second, columns that are buried in straw walls create a thermal bridge, allowing heat to transfer outside much more quickly and lessening the overall insulation value of the wall. Styrofoam or other rigid insulation can be used to reduce this effect.

A concrete top plate — for post and beam or load-bearing designs — can be formed on top of straw walls to replace the typical unit made of wood. Formed with lumber that remains in place to allow for the attachment of roof framing and stucco netting, this option could be cheaper and faster to construct than a wooden unit. A concrete top plate creates a good seal against the bales and produces a level upper surface. The pour will bond with the top layer of straw and fill in any uneven surfaces along your top row of bales. For load-bearing designs, wires or cables can easily be looped over the entire unit or routed through tubing embedded in the concrete.

Concrete beams are also an option. A concrete beam will add significantly to the dead loads your framework and/or straw walls will have to carry and reduces the allowable span between posts or the width of the openings in a load-bearing wall. Check with your building inspector before you commit to this option. At the finishing stage, concrete is easier to plaster over than wood. As with concrete posts, concrete beams create a thermal bridge at the top of your walls unless Styrofoam or another rigid insulation is used inside the wooden forms.

For both concrete top plates and beams, adequate rebar should be used to ensure that the concrete is well reinforced against the loads they will carry. Lightweight concrete is available and could be used to lessen dead loads on the walls.

Advantages: long lasting, moisture resistant
Disadvantages: high environmental impact, poor thermal performance

Metal Frames

Prefabricated metal buildings have been very successfully integrated with straw bale walls. Prefab metal building kits are widely available and the prices are extremely competitive, and usually the kits come pre-engineered for building code acceptance.

Site-built steel frames are also feasible. Metal columns and I-beams are widely used in industry and have been building code rated, giving you accurate load figures with which to work and specialized information from which to draw should you choose to build with metal. Metal components can be combined with wood and concrete in various ways — an advantage if, for example, you have found some inexpensive steel joists that could ride on wooden or concrete posts. It is quite possible to find used or surplus components at a reasonable cost that can be incorporated into your design. As with

concrete, you must account for the minimal insulation value of metal and plan around the esthetic effects of exposed steel in your home.

A site-built metal frame will require that you have welding skills and specialized metal-working tools, or you will need to hire appropriate labor. Kit buildings often just need assembly with nuts and bolts.

Advantages: simple, cost effective, long lasting, pre-engineered
Disadvantages: kits limited to basic rectangles, poor thermal performance, possible condensation issues in bale walls

The Bale/Frame Connection

If you choose to build with a frame of some kind, you will immediately face a second choice: How will the frame interact with the bale walls?

There are three ways for frames and bale walls to interact. Chapter 13 offers specific detailing advice for each of these possibilities, but at this stage you need to consider the design implications of each in order to choose appropriately for the kind of building you want.

Framework outside the bale walls

Advantages: freeform bale walls unrestricted by roofing complications allow for creative designs under a simple roof structure; no complicated interface of bale walls with posts and beams
Disadvantages: separate foundation footings required for posts and bale walls

Framework buried in the bale walls

Advantages: straightforward interfacing of frame and bale walls, shared foundation for frame and bales

Disadvantages: thermal bridging concerns, steel and concrete must be separated from straw, hollows in straw wall will require stuffing and meshing

Framework inside the bale walls

Advantages: aesthetics of exposed timbers in the home

Disadvantages: loss of floor space, foundation can be complicated, plastering more difficult

It is also possible to combine these strategies in different parts of the building to achieve different design results. All of these options can certainly work, but make sure you are making the choices in material and frame placement that best suit your needs and abilities.

Hybrid Systems

Straw bale builders are not limited to an either-or choice between load-bearing and post and beam. Many successful hybrids have been constructed that take advantage of the best aspects of both; many others await creative invention. Rammed earth pillars, stone, lumber, concrete, and earth berms support walls — all can work well in conjunction with straw.

The most important consideration in any hybrid design is the calculation of the finished height of the load-bearing straw walls. Exact finished height is dependent on bale size (it is easier to cut lumber to meet even courses of bales than it is to cut bales to meet post heights!) and the amount of pre-compression applied. It isn't difficult to make a very close guess as to the finished height of a load-bearing wall, but reaching an exact height will take careful precompression and calculation of bale heights, as well as the thickness of curb rails and top plates.

Hybrids created from a central frame with load-bearing walls use a simple structure of lumber, rammed earth, stone, brick, block, or concrete with perimeter walls of precompressed straw bales. The central frame is erected first, followed by construction of the bale walls. Since the roof framing will extend down from the central frame to the bale walls, compression of the walls will only change the roof pitch minimally, and bales need not be the same height as the solid material. The bales that are used to infill the space between the roof plate and the angled roof framing are not load-bearing, since the roof framing is bearing the full loads.

Jack posts are adjustable steel posts. They can be used in load-bearing designs to provide support where load-bearing walls of a material other than straw will be employed. The threaded end of a jack post can be adjusted to meet the height of the compressed straw wall.

Earth berm homes — sometimes called earthships — are dug into hillsides. While straw bales wouldn't be appropriate to use against the earth berm due to moisture concerns, they could be used to build walls that are not buried, in either a load-bearing or post and beam design.

Mortared bale structures use straw bales just like concrete blocks. If you have plenty of experience with mortar and blocks, you may find this option suits your talents. Bales are set down on a thin bed of mortar, and more mortar is poured between the abutting ends. This technique can create a strong structure and does not require a framework or any pre-compression. It does require a lot of time and mortar. It also creates thermal breaks between each bale, causing the insulation rating of the entire wall to suffer because the spaces between the bales offer only the minimal R-value of concrete. Building with mortared bales eliminates one of the main advantages of straw walls — walls do not go up quickly and simply.

How to Choose: Load bearing, Post and Beam, or Hybrid?

The factors that weigh into the load-bearing versus post and beam debate are so many and varied that there is no hard-and-fast rule about which way to go (despite what the hard-core advocates of both styles would have you believe!). The following are some issues to consider.

Building Code Compliance

Many people assume that it will be easier to get a building permit for a post and beam home with bale infill. However, most prescriptive building codes require post and beam structures to be individually designed and approved by an engineer, the same as load-bearing buildings. The existing bale building codes (where they exist) recognize load-bearing and post and beam styles, and the engineering data to design both is well established, so there shouldn't be major code barriers to either option.

Load-bearing buildings, however, will often be subject to more questions and concerns, especially in a jurisdiction that has never approved one. This shouldn't prevent you from building in load-bearing style, but it may mean some extra effort to convince officials of the feasibility. Chapter 13 has many suggestions for approaching building departments, regardless of which style you're planning on adopting.

8.7: The load-bearing walls of this building are plastered, then the central post and beam structure is built to the finished height of the walls.

Cost

Cost is one of the most obvious differences between the two styles. Because the bale walls will use a similar quantity of time and materials to construct in either case, the additional materials and time that go into creating a frame weigh heavily on the budget. Add in the complexity that often occurs when installing bales into a frame system, and costs can go up again, especially if you are hiring people to raise the bales walls.

The simplest and/or prefabricated frames may not tip the scales too heavily. Modified post and beam, prefab steel and truss systems can all be very reasonable in cost, but they will have higher materials costs than a load-bearing building.

Environmental Impact

Once again, the addition of extra materials necessary in a post and beam option means that your building is consuming more resources than its load-bearing equivalent. If you plan your frame around reclaimed or sustainably harvested timbers, recycled steel, or other low-impact materials, then there is not necessarily an environmental price tag attached to a post and beam frame.

Every framing system will have its own range of environmental impacts. Less is always more in environmental terms, and recycled is better than virgin.

Building Size and Complexity

Both styles of bale building can be successfully employed on most residential projects, but really large buildings or those with multiple floors or levels are sometimes easier to complete under protection of a roof in a post and beam context. Larger load-bearing structures are best tackled in sections, building and plastering the walls and raising the roof in manageable stages.

For buildings with curved walls and/or lots of jogs and changes in wall direction, load-bearing walls will be easier to construct, as framing materials are much more cumbersome to employ in such designs. However, it is possible to form these creative walls under a straight and square roof in a post and beam context.

Nobody has tested the strength of load-bearing walls over 12 feet high, but regardless of whether or not they are strong enough (which they very likely are!), it does get difficult to build load-bearing over this height. Keeping the walls plumb, installing top plates, and pre-compressing all become cumbersome at these heights, and infill might be a better solution.

Larger and more complex buildings always use more materials and take more time than smaller, simpler ones. If size or complexity is starting to inform your decision toward either style, it might be wise to reconsider the parameters of the design, rather than the building method!

Knowledge and Experience

Your own knowledge and experience (or that of people you hire) will be an important factor in this decision. If you have framing experience, or are planning on hiring a conventional contractor to build your bale home, then it might make sense to choose an infill technique. There is definitely a learning curve to building with bales, and load-bearing designs put a premium on the bale work.

However, building bale walls isn't rocket science, and for those with little or no experience, it's probably easier to figure out bale stacking than it is to figure out post and beam framing.

Esthetics

Straw homes can be made to suit a wide variety of esthetic preferences. Plastered straw will be the dominant visual theme inside and out, and in the end, the esthetics of your building will have more to do with how you trim, sculpt, and finish your bales than with whether you choose a load-bearing, post and beam, or hybrid design.

No Wrong Choices

When it comes right down to it, your bale walls are going to work to your advantage, regardless of whether they are load-bearing or infill. There is no wrong choice, only choices that are more or less appropriate for your site, budget, construction experience, local codes, and concern for the environment.

Bales in Other Parts of Your Building

Straw bales have been used successfully as ceiling and floor insulation. For roof or ceiling insulation, framing must be beefed up to handle the extra weight of the bales. The large dimensions of bales often precludes the use of standard spacing for framing members. The installation of the bales can be a tricky and heavy procedure and can expose the bales to rainfall before the roof sheathing is installed. Unplastered bales will also be exposed to the air on the top side — as in any roof or ceiling installation — creating a home for pests and, possibly, creating a fire hazard. Borax and other chemical treatments have been used to lower these risks, as have thin slip coats of plaster. If you plaster the open side of the bales, you add considerably more weight to the bales and create complications in the application process. However, with creative thinking and a clever use of resources — especially manufactured wooden I-beams — you may devise a suitable way to use bale insulation in your ceiling.

Bales have been used as floor insulation in concrete slab floors. For slab floors, bales are placed a few inches apart in rows. Concrete is poured between the bales, creating a honeycomb of bales and concrete that is eventually covered with the top few inches of the slab. There are valid concerns about the amount of concrete this slab floor (or any slab floor) uses and about the performance of bales in the moist environment of a concrete slab on-grade. We do not recommend the use of bales in any below-grade applications.

Bales as a frame floor insulation may make the most sense, especially where TJIs™ (wooden I-beams created with pressboard and narrow lumber) or open web joists (narrow lumber joined with steel spacers) can be sized and spaced to accommodate the bales with the least amount

8.9a

8.9b

BRETT KENCAIRN

Prefabricated Bale Walls

In the spring of 2000, we went on a cross-country tour to promote the first edition of this book; and to support our talk, Pete and I built a large section of portable straw bale wall. This wall traveled thousands of miles and was subjected to all kinds of abuse, and yet at the end of it all showed very little cracking or damage. This got us thinking about prefabricating plastered bale wall panels. These prefab panels are built *and plastered* in the controlled conditions of a warehouse or factory. They are then shipped to the building site on a boom truck, which lifts the panels into place on the foundation. The walls are then immediately ready to receive a roof.

Our initial experiments with this method were very encouraging, resulting in a very beautiful and simple-to-install demonstration room at the Toronto Home Show.

Further work on the panelized system has led to drastic reductions in time and material use. The biggest savings is in plastering. Rather than fighting site conditions and gravity, using a three-coat system and lots of labor, the prefab panels are plastered while lying flat on the factory floor. In this way, the full thickness can be poured in one coat (just like making a sidewalk!), which is then easily screeded using the temporary sides of the frame to create a consistent finish. Plaster curing takes place out of the sun and wind in controlled conditions. When prefabricated, bale walls cost much less than commercial stud frame walls, even with shipping and crane time figured in. ☞

of trimming, cutting, and use of oversized lumber.

While many builders have met the challenges of using bales in ceilings and floors, the availability of other lightweight recycled insulation materials such as cellulose fiber and spun rock wool, means you must carefully weigh the advantages and disadvantages of using bales. Be sure the costs, materials, and risks involved do not exceed those of other materials.

8.8: *Bales go into a roof with framing that is spaced perfectly to fit.*

A prefab bale wall factory requires only some basic woodworking tools and a roof overhead. The same concept can be applied by owner-builders, who could create tilt-up wall panels onsite.

Prefab straw bale ... as strange as it sounds, it could be an idea whose time is about to come!

— *Chris Magwood* ■

8.9c

8.9d

8.9e

8.9a - e: *Prefabricated bale wall panels are assembled in frames with permanent top and bottom plates and temporary sides. Plastered lying flat, they are then moved with a crane or forklift, shipped and assembled on site.*

References

The Timber Framer's Guild of North America, P.O. Box 1046, Keene, NH 03431, USA; phone: 603-357-1706. A non-profit organization devoted to the advancement of timber framing.

Books

Benson, Todd. *The Timber Frame Home: Design, Construction, Finishing*. The Taunton Press, Inc., 1993. ISBN 0-942391-60-8.

Borer, Pat and Cindy Harris. *Out of the Woods: Ecological Designs for Timber Frame Housing*. New Society Publishers, 2004. ISBN 1-89804-912-2.

Chappell, Steve. *A Timber Framer's Workshop: Joinery, Design and Construction of Traditional Timber Frames*. Fox Maple Press, 1998.

Mitchell, James. *The Craft of Modular Post and Beam: Building Log and Timber Homes Affordably*. Hartley & Marks Publishers, 1997. ISBN 0-88179-131-8.

Roy, Rob. *Timber Framing for the Rest of Us: The Guide to Contemporary Post and Beam Construction*. New Society Publishers, 2004. ISBN 0-86571-508-4.

CHAPTER 9

Structural Design Options: Foundations, Roofs and Partition Walls

Having visualized the space you'd like to create, it's now time to start making some practical decisions regarding the structure of your building. Important among these decisions are the foundation and roof, which will have a major impact on all aspects of your building. It's time to blend the practical with the personal.

The decisions you make about your home during the Design Game reflect your individual tastes. But to realize your design dreams, you must be able to translate them into a physical structure that can meet the demands you put on it. Foundations and roofs are important parts of that physical structure and must be considered before you progress and finalize the actual plans for your building.

A variety of foundation and roofing systems can meet stringent building code requirements. Experimental options also exist but may be more difficult to get approved. Before you finally decide about your foundation or roof, be sure to research the methods that are used in your area, and talk to other builders and homeowners about what's appropriate for your region. In many cases, roof and foundation designs will need to be approved by a structural engineer, even if the wall system of the structure does not.

Foundation Options

Get to Know Your Frost

There is a big difference between foundations in areas with significant frosts and those without. The deeper the frost penetration, the more substantial the foundation must be.

When the ground freezes, water retained in the ground also freezes. The expansion of frozen water will exert a force of 150 tons per square inch as it increases in volume by nine percent! This is enough to lift or heave your building, causing damaging strain to many structural elements. You need to build a foundation that will prevent frost from penetrating the soil directly under your building. You will have to design with a specific regard for the soil conditions at your site and for the frost penetration depth in your region — in our part of Ontario, for instance, it's four feet.

Site Soil Conditions

It is important to first assess the site's soil conditions because these will dictate what kinds of foundations are possible:

- *Sandy soils* can drain water and are easy to excavate. They can be unstable when trying to create trenches.
- *Clay soils* tend to hold water and therefore be prone to expansion when frozen and instablility when thawing.
- *Rocky soils* have varying sizes of large stone, surrounded by either sand or clay. Depending on the size of the stones and the surrounding soil, drainage can be good or poor, and trenches may or may not be stable.
- *Solid rock* can be found at the surface, or just below, on some sites. Solid rock is very stable and not prone to frost heaving, but can require drilling or blasting for foundation work.

By digging some test holes, you will gain important information about suitable foundation options. Don't trust just a single hole; dig several and dig deeply, so that you know what conditions exist to the full depth of frost penetration. Only once you know the soil conditions can you properly design your foundation; otherwise you could spend too much money trying to make a particular foundation work in unsuitable conditions. If you don't have the ability to dig test holes, information can be gleaned from local excavators and builders, who will have worked with the soils in surrounding areas. Existing vegetation can also give you important clues as to what lies beneath the surface.

Some engineers may require soil testing to determine its bearing capacity. They will be able to recommend appropriate labs to do this kind of analysis.

Foundation Styles

Foundations come in three basic styles: perimeter wall foundations — including full basements — pier foundations, and grade foundations. Each style can be matched to your design requirements, and versions of all three should be allowed by your local building code.

Perimeter Wall Foundations

Perimeter wall foundations extend the vertical walls of your house down to a wide, secure footing below the frost line. They are sometimes used to create a below-grade basement space or crawl space in a building.

Concrete Stem Walls

In their most conventional form, the foundation perimeter walls are made from poured concrete or concrete block. Concrete stem walls will sit on a wide poured concrete footing and run continuously to a determined height above the finished grade level. *There is no need for a concrete stem wall to be any wider than normal to suit a straw bale wall!*

There are a few options for concrete stem wall foundations:

- Concrete stem wall creating a useable basement space. This version typically uses a wooden floor joist system resting on top of the stem wall, and the bale walls are built on this floor platform.
- Concrete stem wall creating a crawl space. This version also uses a wooden floor joist system resting on top of the stem wall, but the space created under the floor platform is not conditioned livable space. There

will likely be minimum and maximum heights for this crawl space specified by your building code, as well as ventilation requirements.

- Concrete stem wall with a slab floor contained inside. This version involves building a slab floor of some description on the existing grade within the confines of the stem wall. This slab can be concrete or earthen, or stone, brick, tile, or other surface of choice on an insulated sand or gravel bed.

Other Perimeter Wall Options

While concrete may be the most conventional material for creating perimeter wall foundations, there are many other suitable options. All have been used successfully in different climates and conditions, but will likely require an engineer's approval, since they are not typically described in most building codes.

- Rubble trench foundations. A rubble trench foundation creates a solid footing for a building on frost free ground on a deep, wide trench filled with mixed, compacted stone. The stone, once compacted, can easily transfer building loads to the undisturbed soil below. Because the stone will not trap or hold water, the foundation is not prone to frost heave damage. A concrete perimeter beam can be poured on top of the rubble trench to provide a flat, stable surface for building the bale walls. A slab floor of some description can be created inside this perimeter beam, or a wooden floor deck can be built on top of it.

- Rammed earth tire foundations. Much progress has been made in recent years in the use of rammed earth car tires as a perimeter wall foundation. This type of foundation is used for a style of home called earthships, which use the tires — packed tightly full of earth and built-up in numerous courses — to create conditioned indoor space below grade, making this style of foundation suitable for creating either basements, crawl spaces, or stem walls. A perimeter beam of concrete or

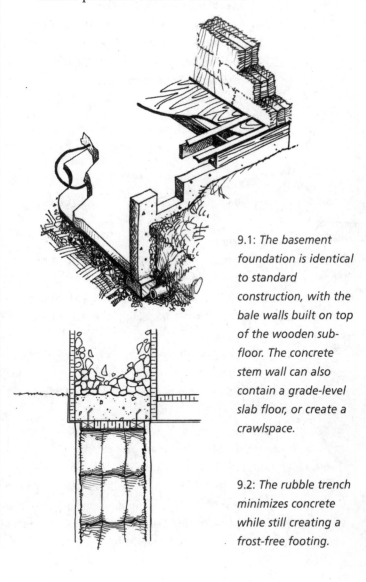

9.1: *The basement foundation is identical to standard construction, with the bale walls built on top of the wooden subfloor. The concrete stem wall can also contain a grade-level slab floor, or create a crawlspace.*

9.2: *The rubble trench minimizes concrete while still creating a frost-free footing.*

treated wood on top of the tire wall creates a platform for the bales or for a wooden floor deck.

- Sandbag foundations. Poly sandbags (familiar to many as grain bags or feed bags) can create a wide, stable footing and perimeter wall. Laid up in continuous courses, the sandbags can be filled either with sand (for a well-draining foundation) or with moist earth, which is then tamped (or rammed). Being porous, sandbag foundations are appropriate for providing a stem wall containing a slab floor, or for creating a wooden floor platform over a crawl space, but not for constructing basements.

- Mortared stone. If your site has plenty of accessible stone, you might consider using it to create your perimeter wall. Many early builders used stone and mortar, and their homes are still standing today. You can also use local stone in conjunction with cement. Use the sides of your dig as a form, and add stone to site-mixed or pre-mixed concrete as you pour. The stone can displace a fair bit of concrete without sacrificing strength.

- Dry-stacked stone. Many historical buildings used flat, dry-stacked stone to create a perimeter wall. It's very similar to the rubble trench foundation, except the stone is deliberately chosen and stacked to create a stable platform for the wall above.

- Rammed earth. Where soil conditions are suitable, a stabilized rammed earth

What To Do About Cement?

Cement: It's Everywhere

Nothing summarizes modern construction better than the image of the concrete truck. Its slowly turning barrel-on-wheels is likely to make at least one appearance on the site of every new building in the Western world, and a high percentage globally. As the key ingredient in concrete, our reliance on portland cement is staggering; there is not a city on the planet that would be left standing if the cement was taken out, and many of our "eco-friendly" bale homes would likewise disappear.

Why Try to Reduce Cement Usage? In many ways, concrete seems like an ideal building material. It is strong, reliable, slow to deteriorate, works above and below ground, and has the useful property of being created as a liquid that quickly sets into a solid, so it can be formed into any shape that is required.

Concrete may seem to be fairly benign on the jobsite — just add water and stir — but the cement content comes with a very high environmental price tag. The creation of cement involves large-scale quarrying and burning of limestone, a very energy-intensive, polluting process. In 1998, worldwide cement production reached 1.52 billion tons (with China, Japan, and the USA leading in production). For every ton of cement produced, 8.5 million Btus of energy must be expended, and one ton of CO_2 will be emitted. Worldwide production of cement is estimated to be responsible for 7 to 10 percent of the world's CO_2 emissions, second only to electricity generation. We ignore this significant contribution to atmospheric pollution and greenhouse effect at our own peril. ☞

Right: The Cook home sits on the edge of one of Canada's fastest growing urban areas, yet retains a country charm that combines the heritage designs of the area with a modern presence.
Cook residence, Kanata, Ontario

Below: Settling a home into its landscape so it looks like it belongs is one of the great challenges to designers. Form and color must work together seamlessly, as with Pat Marcotte and Sherry Smith's owner-built home.
Marcotte/Smith residence, Bancroft, Ontario

PAT MARCOTTE / SHERRY SMITH

CATHERINE WANEK

Below right: Natural light loves the slightly irregular surfaces of natural materials.
Dilschneider residence, Ferndale, Ontario.

LAURA TAYLOR

Right: Round log timbers act as floor joists for the second floor of this two story, load-bearing bale home, and were harvested from the property where the home was built, lowering the building costs and blending well with the plastered walls.
Greg Magwood residence, Eldorado Ontario

Right: Found objects often find new life in bale walls, in this case as a "truth window" into the bale wall of Jan Cohen's owner-built home.
Jan Cohen residence, Steamboat Springs, Colorado.

JAN COHEN

Bottom: A thickly plastered window sill makes a light-filled home for plants.
Greg Magwood residence, Eldorado, Ontario

LAURA TAYLOR

Right: Wood, stone and plastered straw complement each other as natural materials.

Below: Straw bale walls can blend perfectly with timber framing techniques, as evidenced by this home in Routt County, Colorado. The main house is a bale-wrapped timber frame, while the garage in the forefront is conventional frame construction. Both photos Routt County, Colorado home designed by Robert Hawkins, Architect

DAVID PATTERSON PHOTOGRAPHY

*Right: A home settles subtley into
its surroundings without being
shy of colour or form.*
Warburton residence,
Hockley Valley, Ontario

*Below: Uneven wall edges catch and
bounce interior light in a soothing way.*
Joy Allan, Bert Weir residence,
Parry Sound, Ontario.

JOY ALLAN

MELINDA ZYTARUK

Right: New straw bale buildings can recreate architecture of the past. This home echoes the churches and school houses of the early settlers. Wise/Jansman residence, Centreville, Ontario

Below: The soft shapes of plastered bales can inspire playfulness with other building materials. Bringing the bale wall half-wall into the room provides division of space without stark delineation. Designed by Robert Hawkins, Architect

Bottom right: Wood and creatively stained plaster help Jan Cohen's home blend well with its snowy surroundings. Cohen residence, Steamboat Springs, Colorado

foundation might be possible. You will likely need to do a fair bit of research and experimentation before attempting this foundation, but the process could be fascinating and rewarding.

Pier Foundations

Pier foundations utilize a grid of columns to transfer building loads down into footings that rest on frost-free soil. The columns are used to support a wooden floor deck system that rests above the finished grade. This type of foundation is definitely the least intensive to build in terms of materials, labor, and site impact, but is not used to create conditioned space under the floor. Special considerations must be made for running water lines into a building on a pier foundation, as there is no frost protection in the soil under it.

Post and beam designs may call for an individual pier to be constructed on its own footing for each supporting post because of the high point loads imposed on the framing columns. Where posts are placed outside the shell of the house — as for porch supports or to create wide roof overhangs — each post will definitely require its own pier. A shallow, insulated slab on-grade can be poured around such piers, or you could use them to support a raised, wood-framed floor system.

There are four basic types of pier foundation:

- Poured concrete columns. Tubular concrete forms used to pour piers come in a variety of common sizes and are typically left in place around the finished column below

Reducing Cement Use By Design. Most typical foundations use quite a bit of concrete. Slabs, frost walls, and basements are construction norms, and all three rely on massive quantities of concrete. The first step in reducing cement use is considering foundation styles that call for little or no concrete. Rubble trenches, sandbags, rammed earth tires, pier-and-beam, natural stone, gabion basket, helical piers, and pin foundations, among others, exist as minimal or zero concrete usage foundations.

Careful research into local soil conditions, available materials and expertise, and structural requirements are all necessary before making a foundation decision, but if minimizing concrete use is maintained as a priority, a large impact can be made. There is almost always a less concrete-intensive way than the current norms.

Unfortunately, many bale buildings employ the worst possible concrete use strategy: footings the full width of the bales extending all the way down to the frost line. With such massive use of concrete, it is questionable whether the performance of the building will ever make up for the energy expended in providing all that concrete.

Lowering Concrete Use in Slab Foundations. Slab foundations are popular for bale homes but use a lot of concrete. The attributes of concrete that make it a good medium for slab floors (especially heated ones) can be obtained with more benign materials. If concrete use is limited to a grade beam under the bales, the floor portion can be created with adobe (earth), soil cement (earth with five to ten percent cement content), sand beds (with brick, tile, or stone over top), or even sustainably harvested woods. Many of these materials will provide good thermal and wear characteristics with a lot less environmental impact. ☞

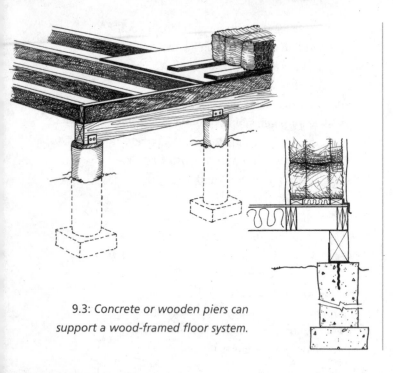

9.3: *Concrete or wooden piers can support a wood-framed floor system.*

grade. Some tube forms can be purchased with an attached boot that forms the footing, as well as the column, in a single pour.

- Concrete block columns. Concrete blocks can be mortared together or dry-stacked on the footing to create columns. The hollow cores of the blocks are then filled with concrete to create a stable column. Blocks of many sizes and shapes are available.

- Wooden columns. Heavy wooden columns can be used as a foundation, but special consideration must be made to protect the wood against rot below grade. Choosing a rot-resistant species is important. Pressure-treated wood can be used, as can creosote and other preservatives. Charring the surface of the wooden column is a

Lowering Cement Content in Concrete

Cement Stabilized Earth. In some situations, rammed earth that has been stabilized with small amounts of cement can provide adequate structural qualities to replace the use of concrete. In places where rammed earth construction enjoys code recognition, this option may be easily implemented. Where rammed earth is still considered on the fringe, it may be difficult to get approvals.

Fly Ash. Where concrete is called for, it is possible to reduce the actual cement content for the same volume of concrete. One such option has been receiving a lot of attention recently — the addition of coal fly ash to concrete mixtures. As a by-product of coal burning (mostly at power plants), fly ash can replace a fairly high percentage of cement and provide a concrete that is at least as strong and stable. This has the double benefit of reducing cement use and providing a market for a waste product that is often sent to landfills in vast quantities. Fly ash may be obtained from your local concrete dispatcher and batched with your order. Rice husk ash is being used similarly as a replacement binder in concrete, although availability is not as common as fly ash.

Waste Fillers. There are many products, both commercially available and experimental, in which waste materials are added into concrete mixtures to reduce the required volume. These include mineralized wood chips, recycled foam particles, and hemp hurds. These additives not only reduce the overall concrete content, they have the added benefit of providing the concrete with a much-improved insulation value, and can eliminate the need for below-grade foam insulation.

Autoclave Aerated Concrete. Aerated concretes use a minute portion of aluminum paste in the concrete mixture to create a chemical reaction that results in hydrogen bubbles foaming the concrete mixture. This typically reduces ☞

less conventional but very effective deterrent to rot. Regardless of the treatment, wood below grade will eventually rot and require replacement.

- Rammed earth tire columns. Car tires rammed with earth can be used to create columns to support building loads. Tires of an appropriate diameter can be chosen, and may not require a separate footing due to their width. The tires will need to be protected against UV rays above grade.

There are two less common pier foundations, both of which use very minimal materials and have very slight site impact.

- Helical pier foundations. Helical piers are basically giant screws that are wound into the ground (capable of being used in soils or solid rock) to provide a stable, frost-protected base for homes. The helical piers will need to be installed by qualified professionals.

- Pin foundations. Similar to helical piers, except that tripods of long, slender metal pins are driven deep into the ground to provide support for a perimeter beam.

Shallow, Frost Protected Slab-on-Grade Foundations

A slab on-grade foundation is a monolithic a concrete pad that is designed to float on the grade surface of your site. Excavation is minimal: only the topsoil — the part that supports organic matter — needs to be removed. The thick concrete pad acts as a base and supports the walls and floors of the building.

the volume of concrete by 66 percent, and creates a product that has good thermal characteristics (R-1.25 per inch). Autoclave aerated concrete can be made with a very high fly ash content and a cement-lime mixture to further reduce cement use. Unfortunately, these aerated concretes are cured under pressure at high temperatures, adding back some of the energy use they eliminate. Aerated concrete can come in block form or as precast structural panels. In both cases, the need for additional insulation products is reduced or eliminated.

Other Benefits of Reduced Concrete Use. Concrete is a relatively expensive material, and it often requires significant formwork and manual labor to install and finish. Choosing low-concrete foundation options can reduce the cost of a building, without necessarily raising the amount of labor involved. Concrete is not a very forgiving material, and inexperienced builders often find the formwork and finishing surprisingly difficult, and mistakes are not easily corrected. Many of the available options lend themselves to use by owner-builders.

Making the Effort Will Make a Difference. With each ton of cement creating a ton of CO_2, it is not hard to calculate the impact that reducing cement use in your building can have on the environment. That's a one-ton reduction in CO_2 for every 23 bags of cement you don't use! And, these figures don't take into account the pollution created in shipping, storing, and moving the cement to your site!

— Chris Magwood
A version of this article appeared in issue 38 of The Last Straw, *2002.*

■

Slab foundations are unique. No attempt is made to secure the foundation to soil below the frost line. In climates where frost is a concern, slab foundations use an insulation blanket around the perimeter of the foundation to prevent frost penetrating the soil beneath the slab. The insulation blanket extends from the foundation just below grade level and remains in the ground when the soil is backfilled. For perimeter insulation, the rule of thumb is that six inches of insulation is required for every foot of frost penetration being protected against. The insulation must be specifically designed for below-grade applications.

Foundation Combinations

You are not restricted to a single style of foundation for your house. Styles can be combined to match your needs and site conditions. In fact, it is possible to have the best aspects of two or more styles working together. Take time to consider how different foundations will meet and attach to one another and how they can provide a suitable platform for the bale walls that will span their intersection.

Foundation Considerations

Bale Specifics

Make sure you design a foundation that lifts the bales far enough above grade level to prevent snow and rain from making continuous contact with the base of the wall. In northern climates, a minimum of 8 to 12 inches above grade should be used. Building codes often specify a certain above grade height for any plastered wall finish, so be sure to check for regulations in your area.

Additions

Very few houses remain unchanged over their life span. Additions are common, and if you do some early planning, you can make the job much easier for yourself — or for those who own the house after you. Consider which orientations are most suitable for expansion, taking into account site restrictions, room uses, entrance points, light conditions, roof shape, and specific plans you may have for the future — a greenhouse, office, triplets, etc.

You can provide for future foundations as you build if you fit rebar and/or anchor bolts into the foundation or leave suitable attachment points in concrete for additional framing. If plans for an addition are fairly certain, it may be worth the extra time and money to build the foundation now. That way, you won't have to spend twice for digging equipment and material delivery. Plus, you may be more likely to go ahead and build that addition if the groundwork has already been laid!

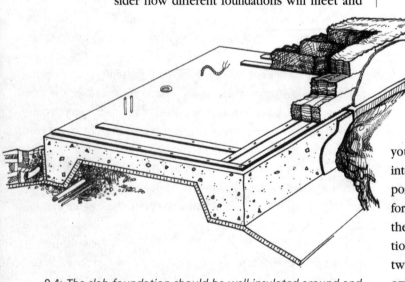

9.4: *The slab foundation should be well insulated around and below, and have all service lines, conduit and heating tubing placed prior to pouring.*

Temporary Foundations

For temporary and nonresidential structures, you may choose to use a simpler foundation. Railroad ties or other large-dimension lumber can be laid on a gravel bed. You can use deck supports like piers to build a structure above grade or set wooden pallets on-grade over a gravel bed. Your comfort level and the function of your building will determine which system you use, but these foundations will definitely not meet building code requirements for residential structures.

Choose Carefully

Many structural elements can be changed once your building is erected, but a foundation is permanent, so be sure to choose the style that is right for your project. Your foundation is not the place to cut corners on cost or quality; a good one is worth the investment.

Roofing Options

Roof *framing* deals with the structural materials of your roofing system, and roof *sheathing* deals with the waterproofing membrane that covers the framing. A variety of options exist for both, and most can be used in combination.

Roof Designs

Your roof design must integrate performance with appearance. Roofs play a very important structural role that can't be compromised. At the same time, their size and shape affect the overall appearance of your house. Their capacity to create shade, duct rainwater, deflect winds, and blend with their environs are also important. Don't forget passive solar requirements when you design your roof. You are not restricted to a single roof style. You can combine them, tip them, play with the pitch, and add dormers to

achieve the combination of function and appearance you wish. Remember, though, that every complication — intersection, angle change, or interruption — will result in higher costs, a lengthier construction time, and potential leakage points.

The best way to assess different roof designs is to pay careful attention to the vast array you

9.5a: *This house utilizes a small concrete block basement in one corner for all the mechanical equipment, and a pier and beam foundation for the rest of the structure.*

9.5b: *A rubble trench foundation follows the curvy path of the bale walls, while piers will support a rectangular frame and roof.*

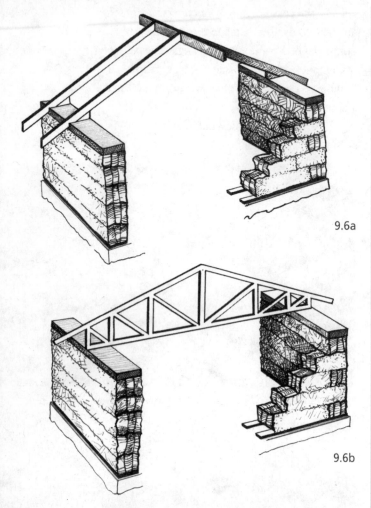

9.6a

9.6b

9.6a - b: A site-framed roof uses heavy rafters on a ridge beam, while a truss roof uses an internally braced design to provide support using smaller lumber.

that meet your design requirements. It's a good idea to take a look at these span charts early in your design process, since they can help you decide on overall roof dimensions. You don't want to plan a roof that is prohibitively difficult or expensive to frame.

There are several ways to go about framing a wooden roof system:

- Site framing with dimensional lumber. Using the span charts in your building code, you can cut the rafters, joists, and collar ties required by the design of your roof and use the appropriate connections and fasteners to assemble the roof.

- Manufactured roof truss systems. Manufactured trusses are engineered to use small-dimension lumber — 2-by-4 and 2-by-6-inch — to meet the load requirements specified for your region. They are engineered to fit your plans, are factory built and assembled, and delivered to your site. Their cost is often equal to, or lower than, the cost of the heavier lumber you'll need if you frame the roof yourself. The truss company employs an engineer to design the trusses, so prices include the cost of having an engineer stamp your roof plan. If you are paying a carpenter for framing, manufactured trusses are likely to be a cheaper option. For complicated roofs, a combination of manufactured trusses and site framing may be optimal. Building inspectors often prefer manufactured trusses over site-framed roofs, especially if the builder is a first-timer. Environmentally, the small-dimension lumber used for manufactured trusses can be more sustainably harvested than

see around you. Look for shapes that you find attractive, and that would create the kind of indoor space you want. Take photos as a way for you to remember the roof shapes you like best and for your design professional to see the shapes rather than just have you describe them

Wooden Roof Framing

Most roof framing uses lumber. Wooden roof frames are strong, lightweight, and easy to construct. Your local building code will contain span charts specifying the lumber dimensions

the heavier lumber used for traditional framing.

- Wooden I-beams. Manufactured wooden I-beams can be used to site-frame a roof with spans that would have made regular-dimensional lumber prohibitively large and costly to the environment. The wooden I-beams use a glued, oriented strand board (OSB) to create a deep, thin beam with small-dimension lumber on top and bottom as stabilizers. Lighter and less prone to warping and cracking than dimensional lumber, they can prove easier to work with. The costs are comparable to the dimensional lumber they replace.

- Timber framing. A timber-framed roof uses very large-dimensional lumber with traditional notched joinery to create a strong and beautiful roof frame. Although usually part of an entire timber-frame shell, it is quite possible to have a timber-framed roof only. Sheathed and insulated on the outside of the timbers, the exposed woodwork is left visible inside the building.

- Mandala framing. Mandala roofs (also called the reciprocal-frame roof structure), use large-dimensional round or squared timbers arranged in a circular pattern, and designed such that each member rests on its neighbor in a self-supporting system to create roofs that are typically used to cover round buildings, but can also be adapted for square or multi-sided structures.

Steel Roof Framing

- Steel framing. The use of steel framing is becoming more popular in conventional home building. It is stable, long-lasting, and available to meet a wide variety of roof styles. Steel framing is usually done by experienced installers. Most framing steel uses a high recycled content, but this is not necessarily the case, so it's good to inquire before purchasing.

- Steel conical roofs. Designed primarily for agricultural use (topping grain bins), these conical steel roofs are unique in that they are a structural sheathing, meaning that they are self-supporting without any additional framing requirements. Prefabricated panels bolt together to provide a round roof that is very simple to construct and remarkably inexpensive.

FRIEDEMANN MALHKE

Exterior Appearance and Interior Space

It is inadequate to choose a roof design merely for the sake of appearance. How you intend to use the space under the roof must play an important role in your decision-making process. Cathedral ceilings, lofts, second-story living space, or attics will all need to be figured into your roof design.

9.7: *This mandala framing system creates a self-supporting structure with no central support.*

Porches

Your roof design can easily accommodate plans for a porch. Design your roof to overhang the building and create a sheltered area outside the building's shell. Wrap a porch around one or more sides of your building, or create a simple awning over an entrance way. Porches provide good weather protection on the north side of your building; a screened porch can be a comfortable outside living space in areas where mosquitoes and other insects are troublesome. You can even plan for an addition to be built at a later date under the existing roof.

Overhangs and Bale Walls

It is an important practice to provide bale walls with a wider-than-average roof overhang. If you extend the roof further, less rain can fall directly on the walls and snow cannot pile up against them. When planning, consider the direction of prevailing winds that will drive the rain and the availability of sun that will help with drying. There is no magic number for overhangs, but you should plan for a minimum of 24 inches. Wider overhangs can become a defining characteristic of your home and, used well, can add a unique visual appeal.

Bale Specifics

While roof framing for a straw bale building is very similar to that for a standard home, there is a key difference. Load-bearing and modified post and beam designs use a wide top plate, and the roof framing must accommodate this width. If the entire weight of the roof is allowed to bear only on the outside edge of the top plate, the force may tend to make the wall buckle — not to the point of wall failure but enough to cause cracks in the plaster. Custom-framed roofs can use wedges of lumber to equalize the downward force over the entire width of the top plate, and manufactured trusses can be designed to provide a bearing point in the center of the top plate. Roof design for post and beam buildings must take into account the location of the beams in relation to the straw bale walls. Depending on the placement of the framework, the beams may be outside, inside, or directly over the walls. Each variant will differently affect the placement of the roof framing.

Roof Sheathing

The framework of your roof will support some form of waterproof membrane to keep rain and snow from finding its way into your house.

Metal Roofing

Sheets of galvanized or painted steel or aluminum have a good track record as a sheathing option. They come in a wide variety of styles and colors, are relatively fast and easy to install, are very durable, and rank among the longest lasting of the sheathing options. Snow tends to slide off, rather than accumulate on, metal roofs, making them a good choice if you are concerned about snow loads. The gauge, rib style, and color of the metal sheets will affect the price. Be sure to look at a wide selection before you buy.

Metal roofs are often identified with barns and rural architecture, and may be frowned upon in urban settings. They can blend with urban architecture, however. Metal roofing has been styled to look like shingles, slate, or ceramic tiles.

Anybody who has been inside a barn during a rainstorm may wonder about noise. You needn't worry. Inside your home, the roof will be separated from your living space by a substantial layer of insulation that will dampen the sound of rain to a barely audible patter. Outside, though, or under a porch roof, the sound will be loud.

Metal roofing requires plenty of resources and energy to produce — aluminum more than galvanized steel — but lasts a long time (50 to 80 years) and is recyclable when it is removed.

Cedar Shakes

Where supplies of cedar are abundant, this style of roofing is attractive and long-lasting. Cedar shakes can be purchased ready made, or can be made by hand or machine onsite. The process is time-consuming, but the visual and environmental rewards make it a system worth considering. Cedar shakes do create a fire hazard, so check with your local building officials before going ahead

with this system, especially in a densely populated area.

Asphalt Shingles

Unfortunately, the dominance of petroleum companies in our society has led to the proliferation of asphalt shingle roofing. Relatively low in cost, shingles also have a relatively short life span, and when replaced can only be hauled to a landfill site. This wasteful practice is an environmental disaster, as is the energy-intensive process required to create the shingles. The shingle industry offers many color and texture choices, and qualified installation companies abound.

Asphalt shingles should not be used where rainwater is going to be collected, since the

Grain Bin Roofs over Straw Walls

My frequent driving throughout Alberta and Saskatchewan provided me plenty of opportunity to see two of the most common icons of the Prairies: straw bales and grain bins. As an ecodesigner and house builder, I began to study the conical grain bin roof as a potential roof for a straw bale yurt.

Thus was the beginning of a design adventure. And soon opportunities presented themselves, leading to the construction of seven houses that use the conical grain bin roof. They range from 1 to 3 floors, and from 500 to 1,600 square feet in size. With a round roof and a three-foot overhang, they have an Asian flavor to them.

Why consider a grain bin roof for a house? They are long-lasting, easy to assemble, and readily available throughout the Prairies and other parts of the country. A key advantage is rapid roof assembly. The roof sheets usually go up in one day to create quick protection for the rest of construction, including bale work. Several different sizes are available.

The grain bin roof system is free spanning and needs support only on the outside perimeter over the straw walls. Walls can be post and beam style or load-bearing (a circular load-bearing straw bale wall has added structural strength over a straight wall). So rather than concerning ourselves with a post in the middle of the building, the top center of the roof can become a four-foot diameter skylight.

In addition the roof is truss-free, so we can skip that construction step. More importantly we can use the vaulted interior space created by this modular conical roof system. The roofs are sloped at 30 degrees, resulting in a wonderful large teepee-like interior. We have finished the ceilings with plywood or canvas on half-round wood poles. The interior volume of this roof means we can build four-foot high straw walls for the second level of a house and still have a spacious second floor. ☞

impregnated stones wear off and petrochemicals can be transferred to your water.

Ceramic Tile

Tile roofs are often associated with Spanish and Latin-American architectural styles. Originally made from local clays, modern tiles are mass-produced, fired, and weatherproofed. More expensive than some options, tiles still use natural materials in their manufacture, look good with the plaster finishes common to bale homes, and provide excellent protection. Installation is slower than with some sheathing, and cutting for angles is likewise slow work. High winds have been known to damage tile roofs, so if you live in an area prone to severe wind conditions, check with your building official or other roofers before using tile.

Slate Roofs

Slate is a sedimentary stone, quarried in thin, strong tiles that can be nailed to the roof as shingles. The stone is heavy and the work slow. Slate roofs were once very popular, especially in areas that were close to a quarry. Ranging in color from black to green or red, a slate roof can be stunning when completed. Its natural colors and texture blend well with plaster finishes. Very durable, a slate roof will last indefinitely with some regular attention and timely replacement of loose or broken slate.

PAUL BELANGER

9.8a

PAUL BELANGER

9.8b

9.8a - b: The conical grain bin lid roof can be used on post and beam or load bearing bale buildings, octagonal or round.

These conical roofs offer incredible wind resistance. A 350 km/h hurricane would not affect such a structure.

The octagon was first used as the design shape, and fit well under the round roof. The wall system has 14-inch-thick posts and beams with infill straw bales. Last year we built our first round straw bale wall to fit under the conical roof. For this we created a simple post wall with 34 2-by-8s equally spaced to create a 1000-square-foot cottage using a 42-foot grain bin roof system painted green.

Off the shelf, the grain bin roof is not rated for Canadian residential snow loads. Therefore we have designed and engineered 12-inch-deep rafters that attach to the underside of the ribs of the roof sheets.

In addition to the strength improvement these rafters create the depth needed for R-50 cellulose insulation. Installing these rafters actually takes more time than the roof sheets themselves. With this level of insulation, the roof is very quiet. You cannot hear rain or hail through it. Sound studio quality acoustics are achieved if the interior ceiling is finished with canvas.

Challenges and disadvantages. Off-the-shelf roof sheets are galvanized, a long-lasting finish which is visually all right in a rural site. But when a colored roof is desired, the galvanized finish is costly to paint over. ☞

Thatch Roofs

Thatch is made from bundles of grasses or reeds that are carefully arranged in thick layers and attached to the roof frame to provide protection against water. Thatch has been in use for centuries and, despite its antiquity, is still a reasonable roofing method. Appropriate natural materials are available in most regions of the world.

Although any style of roofing requires special skills, good thatching is particularly dependent on knowledgeable hands. You may find it difficult, if not impossible, to find a good thatcher in North America. A thatch roof is a perfect match for straw bale walls and is long-lasting (40 to 50 years) when regularly maintained.

Living Roofs

A living roof is an intriguing option. A waterproof membrane is laid down over wooden roof sheathing to prevent leakage, and a layer of drainage medium and then soil — which is appropriately planted — is laid over the membrane. A living roof

9.9: Bundles of reed are spread and fastened to the wooden roof strapping.

MICHEL POST

Another issue we had to face early on was permit problems. The roof system required complete engineering to get a building permit. Separate engineering per roof building is costly. Consequently we designed a generic roof sheet/rafter combination with a standard 50-pound snow load (suitable for most places in Canada). We then spread out this engineering cost over six buildings. After four years of R&D (and fooling around) we now sell the roof system along with the post and beam package with the engineering included.

A construction disadvantage is the fact that the roof assembly requires skills that, typically, framers or carpenters cannot offer. This means that a different trade needs to be hired to build the roof. You could do it yourself if you are the adventurous type and good at following instructions.

The smaller roofs are cost effective especially when combined with designs that reduce the wall height to create a second level. The largest grain bin roof available — the 48-footer — is more costly per square foot than the smaller roofs, but is still cheaper than high-end conventional roof systems.

Future frontiers. We have decided to turn some of the grain bin roof sheets into solar collectors and have begun testing this on one building in sunny Alberta. We simply added another layer of tin to the underside of the south quadrant of the roof to create a one-inch air space. With some ductwork and a fan we have a large amount of free hot air that is then circulated through a concrete floor. Another version of this produces hot water instead.

Overall, the grain bin roof system, in combination with simple post and beam design, has created lower-cost straw bale housing than any other method of construction I know.

— *Paul Belanger, ecological designer,*
Living Design Systems <www.sunandstraw.com>

■

9.10: *The living roof on this bale building is offering up a crop of poppies, and could be used to grow any type of garden.*

can be very heavy and requires substantial roof framing to handle the load; you will need to do some research and design carefully if you use this option. While it makes a strong environmental statement and creates an unusual visual effect, a living roof may necessitate the use of significantly more structural and sheathing materials than conventional roofs.

Roll Roofing

A very inexpensive but unattractive and short-term way to sheath a roof, roll roofing is an asphalt impregnated paper that is stapled to the roof in wide swaths. It is quick to install but not nearly as durable as other options. Like asphalt shingles, roll roofing is made from petrochemicals and is not recyclable when its short life is over. Best used when you cannot afford other options, roll roofing can be overlaid with other sheathing materials at a later date.

Professional Roof Design

If you know what style of roof you want, it may be best to let an architect, engineer, or truss company complete your roof plans. Actual structural design of a roof can be quite a technical workout, even with building code span charts and reference books to help you. And, the more you stray from simple roof designs, the more reluctant your building inspector is likely to be to accept a homemade framing plan.

Leave Your Roof Open to the Future

If you think your house may grow someday, make sure your roof isn't a hindrance. As with foundation designs, it is good to think about future additions when you plan your roof. It's easy to

Cover Those Bales

CMHC moisture testing of bale walls in Alberta found that contact with rainwater, especially on northern exposures where the sun provides little or no drying potential, was a much greater concern than moisture migrating through the walls from inside the building.

In conventional home design, protecting walls from moisture has been a matter of applying moisture-resistant siding materials or using latex or oil paints. In bale home design, protecting the walls starts with proper roof design. Generous overhangs (24-inches minimum) are the start of protective design, but hip roofs, eyebrow roofs, porches, and other strategies should be employed in a site-specific manner. When using gable roofs, consider framing out the entire depth of the gable, otherwise the peaked portions do not offer much protection to the wall below.

Not only will creating a properly designed roof help to protect your walls, it will help keep snow and rain from your foundation, too, resulting in a building less prone all around to moisture problems.

The CMHC report on moisture in bale walls in Alberta was authored by Rob Jolly. It can be viewed on the CMHC website <www.cmhc-schl.gc.ca/publications>. ∎

expand in the direction of an open gable end but not so easy to expand in the direction of a sloped roof. Try to think ahead. If you have to tear up an existing roof, it will complicate your addition projects greatly!

Interior Partition Options

Most people assume that 2-by-4 studs and drywall will form the interior partitions of their building. There are other options, and you can mix and match them to create different partitions in different rooms. Most of these options are not suitable for load-bearing partition walls.

Stud Walls

Wooden 2-by-4-inch studs clad with drywall are most commonly used for partition walls. Quick and efficient, they are made using standard framing principles. Steel studs can be used at a comparable cost, and sheathing for stud walls doesn't have to be drywall. Straw panels, paneling, wood — weathered barn board is attractive and recycled — and other claddings exist.

Straw Bales

The common complaint about interior bale walls is that they take up too much space. While it's true you might not want to make every partition from bales, the esthetic possibilities of using bales (often on-edge, or cut in half) will often more than compensate for the loss of floor space, especially in common living areas. In places where you want an effective sound barrier, bales are also a good option.

Strawboard Panels

A recent addition to the construction palette, strawboard panels are made from straw that is heated and pressed into panels that are faced in kraft paper, similar to drywall. They are thick enough that they can act as stand-alone partition walls, or used to sheath ceilings or existing stud walls. Heavier versions are available for use as exterior walls.

Cob

Cob is a clay-straw mixture that is sometimes used to build entire homes. It can be hand formed or poured into wooden forms to create interior partitions that are thinner than bales and that blend well with exterior bale walls. Cob is easily sculpted to create bench seats and other interior elements. Cob work can be slow, but it is simple and very inexpensive.

Woven Twigs

Studs of any sort — including saplings — can have long, thin sticks or saplings woven between them. The partition wall can be left with the sticks exposed or can be plastered over with gypsum, cob, or any other plaster.

Bricks, Stone, and Concrete Block

Bricks, stone, or block can make attractive partitions

9.11a

9.11b

9.11a - b: *A portable lumber mill can be put to effective use as a bale cutter, creating custom sized bales for building partition walls or fitting between roof or floor framing.*

9.12: *This pressed-straw panel is a good option for both partition walls and ceiling sheathing. It offers good thermal and sound-dampening properties, and is made from one of our favorite resources!*

PETER MACK

and function especially well if they can be used as heat sinks behind woodstoves or in the path of direct sunlight. If the partition is not load-bearing, you can be creative with your brick and block laying and incorporate patterns, protrusions, built-in shelving, and other arrangements.

Other Mortared Materials

Mortared bottles, cans, cordwood, or other common recycled materials can make interesting walls at minimal cost, with beautiful esthetic possibilities. They can be fun, too!

Screen Dividers

Removable, changeable, and rearrangeable room dividers may be all that's necessary to mark out space and provide a bit of privacy. From home-

9.13a

CHRIS MAGWOOD

Building a Roof on the Ground

Here's a strategy worth considering when planning your roof: Build it on the ground! Much of the labor that goes into building a roof is tied up with lifting people and materials up to the roof. And the dangers of roofing have to do with the height above the ground.

It's entirely feasible to build your roof on the ground, or even on your foundation, and then lift it into place with a crane. We did just that when faced with a very steeply pitched roof at the top of a 34-foot-high tower. So we created the roof on a top plate on the ground, framed and strapped the roof, and attached the metal sheathing, all at a reasonable working height. The only thing we didn't do was place the ridge cap at the peak. Even the soffit and fascia finishing were done on the ground.

The crane arrived and the operator put his straps through the open ridge cap and looped them around the ceiling joists. He then lifted the entire roof up to the top of the tower where we guided it into place on the posts and fastened it. ☞

made versions to expensive, traditional Japanese varieties, screen dividers can be beautiful and effective. Even if they are not a permanent solution, they can allow you to experiment with different room layouts before you commit to more solid walls.

Mix and Match

No option has to exist on its own. A straw bale base can be topped with woven twigs; bricks can be placed below studs; or you can create other variations. Wall materials can be divided in non-horizontal fashion as well. Be creative!

9.14: *Mortared log ends and bottles make an effective and attractive partition.*

It was so easy! And the crane rental was for about one hour, or around $100! This has made us think about all kinds of other possible applications for this kind of thinking, including building the roof for a load-bearing house on the foundation, lifting it aside with a crane, and then setting it down on the walls immediately after they are raised. Presto, completely protected walls!

— *Chris Magwood* ■

9.13a-c: *This progression of photos shows a roof framed and sheathed on the ground, then lifted by crane to its position on top of the walls. The economics (and ergonomics!) of this choice make it worth considering.*

9.13b

9.13c

References

Atcheson, Daniel. *Roofing: Construction and Estimating.* Craftsman Book Company, 1995. ISBN 1-57218-007-2.

Herbert, R. D., III. *Roofing: Design Criteria, Options, Selection.* R. S. Means Company, Inc., 1989. ISBN 0-87629-104-3.

Jenkins, Joseph. *The Slate Roof Bible.* Jenkins Publishing, 2003. ISBN 09644258-15.

Portland Cement Association. *Concrete Solutions: 1998 Catalog Supplement.* P.O. Box 726, Skokie IL 60076-0726 USA.

Ramsey, Dan. *Builder's Guide to Foundations and Floor Framing.* McGraw-Hill, Inc., 1995. ISBN 0-07-051814-9.

"Roofs and Foundations." *The Last Straw,* no. 38, Summer, 2002.

Scharff, Robert. Roofing Handbook. McGraw-Hill, 1996. ISBN 0-07-057123-6.

Steen, Athena and Bill Steen. *Earthen Floors.* The Canelo Project, HCI Box 324, Elgin AZ 85611 USA. <Absteen@dakotacom.net>

West, Robert. *Thatch: A Complete Guide to the Ancient Craft of Thatching.* The Main Street Press, 1988. ISBN 1-55562-044-2.

CHAPTER 10

More Design Options: Mechanical Systems

With the physical characteristics of your home well established, it's time to consider the mechanical systems that will provide you with water, heat, light, electrical power, and waste disposal. Your choices of mechanical systems will have a major impact on the cost and long-term performance of your house.

Too many owners and builders do not consider their mechanical systems until too late in the design process, figuring that they can just be added into any design. But the best and most efficient homes are designed with their mechanical systems fully in mind, so they are well integrated into the building.

Heating and Cooling Options

We use a lot of energy to moderate the indoor temperature of our living and working spaces. Too often, our heating and cooling systems are inefficient, unimaginative, and poorly integrated into the structures they serve. The forced air furnace has become the "inexpensive" standard in the home construction industry, but there are many fine options that better serve our needs and don't threaten dwindling fossil fuel supplies.

"A Candle Oughta Keep That Place Warm ..."

Many people erroneously assume that the high insulation value of a straw bale wall eliminates the need to carefully consider heating and cooling systems. In some climates this will hold true, but wherever extremes in temperature are the norm, some form of heating and/or cooling will be required. Straw bale walls can significantly decrease the amount of energy you require to make your living space comfortable, as can well-insulated floor and roof systems and quality windows and doors.

Passive Solar Design

Reducing your reliance on mechanical heating and cooling systems begins with passive solar design. We've already talked about taking advantage of the natural heating capabilities of the sun (see Chapter 7), but we'll stress the point again. Orient your building's main bank of windows in the direction of the sun, and let its rays bathe your home during the cold months of the year. During the warm months you'll appreciate the shade won by that carefully plotted eaves overhang. Remember, the eaves don't shade early morning or late afternoon sun, so large west (and to a lesser extent, east) windows may cause overheating. Straw bale homes have far less heat loss and better inherent thermal mass than passive solar homes of yore, so don't overdo it on the windows. This type of design is easy to create and one of the best energy investments you'll ever make.

Heating Air versus Heating Mass

Heating systems can be categorized into two types. One type, a forced air system, directly heats the air in your building. Modern forced air furnaces — oil, propane, or natural gas — burn their fuel to heat air, and a fan pushes the heated air around the building through ducts. Air, being of minimal mass, heats quickly. But it loses heat just as quickly — through open doors, drafts, cold windows, and cooler walls and floors. Heated air also rises, concentrating near the ceiling far from where our bodies can feel it. So, while forced air systems are the current standard in the home building industry and are relatively inexpensive to buy and install despite their comparative complexity, they are also the most inefficient and uneconomical systems available. The ductwork used for forced air systems also has inherent health issues, due to dust, mold spores, and other contaminants that can blow into your living space.

The second type of heating system — a radiant heat system — imparts heat to some kind of dense mass that, in turn, warms air and other objects indirectly. This is the way we receive our heat from the huge hot mass of the sun, and the sun is a good heating system to replicate! Your home can be designed to contain a suitable mass in the form of a stone, brick, tile, cob, adobe, rammed earth, or concrete floor. Suitable mass can also be designed into partition walls of these materials. More efficient than a forced air system, a radiant heat system requires lower input temperatures, retains its heat for longer, and produces a steady, ambient warmth. Usually, once you've experienced the comfort of a well-designed mass heating system, you won't consider anything else!

Different Ways to Store Radiant Heat
Radiant Floors

Radiant floor heating is becoming increasingly popular. Silent and hidden from sight, this system uses the entire floor area of your home as a heating device. Though they take time to bring up to temperature, radiant floors are not prone to large temperature fluctuations once they are fully operative. Though many systems use standard thermostats to control the input of heat, many people with slab floors find the reaction time too slow and use timers that work better and cost less than thermostats.

Because of its large mass and surface area, a radiant floor can be maintained at a lower overall temperature than would be comfortable with another system. These floors distribute heat evenly and put it at your feet, where it is most appreciated. The price of radiant heating is dropping as more people choose this system; it's now quite competitive with forced air systems. Most radiant floors use piped water as the heating medium, but air systems are also a possibility.

Radiators

Many older homes use metal radiators, through which hot water is circulated. These are making a comeback today, with many interesting designs and applications. Because their surface area is limited compared to the area they must heat, radiators operate at higher temperatures than slab floors. Metal radiators distribute heat less evenly and take up valuable space. Still, if you have access to a supply of used or new radiators, they may be worth considering.

Walls

Radiant heating can be run through walls of appropriate mass. Some bale builders (particularly in Europe) pin their heating tubes to the bale walls and then use a thicker application of plaster to increase the thermal mass. Interior partition walls of masonry, earth, or other heavy materials can make excellent radiant heat sinks.

Sources of Heat

Hand in hand with deciding what heating system to use, you must also choose a fuel source to provide that heat.

Solar heat

While passive solar gain can heat your house on sunny winter days, you will need an active solar heating system if you want to derive all, or most, of your home heating from the sun. Active systems collect the sun's heat using collectors, transfer it to another medium — water or air — and direct it to its intended destination in the home. Solar collectors can be purchased ready to install or can be built at home. Commercial vacuum-tube solar collectors — used for heating water only — are highly efficient, but also expensive. Commercial or homemade flat plate

collectors — for heating air or water — are less pricey and effective.

In general, active solar systems utilize a fan or a pump to circulate the heated medium from

CHRIS MAGWOOD

10.1a

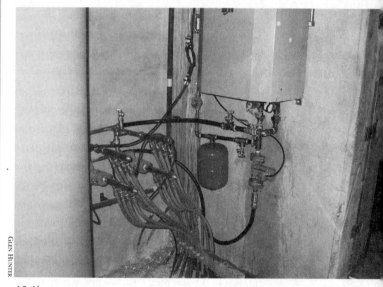
GLEN HUNTER

10.1b

10.1a - b: *The continuous tubing of a radiant floor heating system is laid out and tied in place before it is buried in or under the floor. The tubing comes together at the manifold, where the pumps, controls, heaters and storage tanks are located.*

the hot panel to a storage medium, and from there it is sent to any of the radiators mentioned above. The amount of storage capacity compared to the amount of sunshine expected will determine the percentage of the heating capacity of the building that will be provided by the sun. Solar energy can be used in conjunction with other fuels to meet your heating needs, eliminating some of the capacity requirements of a solar-only system, while minimizing the use of other fuels.

Solar energy is free, non-polluting, and usually abundant. Some homes in northern climates meet all heating needs by a combination of active and passive solar. The design and construction of such a home requires study, careful planning, and creative building. The rewards for using only solar are remarkable: you will be heating for free and treading very lightly on the planet.

Planning issues for solar heat. Solar heating systems don't have to be complicated, just well planned. Solar collectors need direct, unblocked southern exposure to be effective, so if you are designing with active solar heat in mind, you must plan to have your collectors (and there may be many of them) properly aligned. Collectors can be designed to act as the shades for the passive solar component of your house, combining the requirements and efficiencies of both systems.

The more integrated your solar heating system is into your house, the more efficient it will be. Keep storage mediums — hot water tanks, stone boxes, and entrance points to radiant floors — close to the panels. The cheapest systems use convection loops that take advantage of the natural upward flow of heated air or water, without using pumps or fans. These can increase efficiency

but also add cost and complexity. Keep in mind that the house itself is often an active participant in the collection and distribution of solar heat.

At this point in its development, active solar heating is wide open to innovation and creativity. If you want to put your mind to it, great results may follow your discoveries!

Ground Source Heat Pumps

Ground source heat pumps are like buried solar collectors that tap the huge reserves of solar energy stored in the earth itself. Capitalizing on the constant temperature of the earth below the frost line and using a process similar to that used by your refrigerator, these systems use long buried pipes to circulate liquid through the ground — or through a deep well or pond. The predictable temperature at which this liquid will enter the system allows for a compressor to convert a liquid refrigerant into a gas at this temperature, creating usable heat (think about the radiator on the back of your refrigerator). This heat can then be distributed in the house via a radiant floor or forced air system, while the liquid is recycled back through the ground loop to regain its lost temperature.

Ground source heat pumps extract from a free heat source, but their installation requires professional assistance, and the costs of digging trenches, buying and burying pipe, and obtaining the heat pump are all quite high. They require heavy-duty circulating pumps and a fair bit of electricity. But a well-designed system can be an excellent investment.

Planning issues for ground source heat pumps. Most ground source heat pump units are compact, but they can be quite noisy. It's worth considering a small shed near the house to isolate this equipment, or at least a well-sound proofed room. They can be hooked up to radiant or forced air distribution; we recommend a radiant option. Site considerations are key when thinking about ground source heating. You will need a site that offers enough space to lay the required amount of underground piping. Bedrock, high water tables, small lots, and buried services in urban areas can all present obstacles. Deep wells or bodies of water can also be used if trenching is not possible.

Fossil Fuel Appliances

Oil, propane, and natural gas are the most common fuels used in radiant or forced air heating systems. Our culture has a century-long tradition of subsidizing fossil fuel production and distribution. While supplies last, many people will continue to rely on these sources of energy. Modern combustion technology has led to cleaner burning appliances, so be sure to research efficiency and cleanliness ratings before buying a furnace. Do think of the future, though, and be sure that your heating system is adaptable, so you can switch over if supplies of fossil fuels should dwindle or escalate in price.

Planning issues for fossil fuels. Standardized building practices have been developed for the installation of all types of fossil fuel heating systems. Most building codes outline common options, and many reference materials are available from the conventional housing market. A well-designed bale home should have significantly reduced heating requirements, so be sure you size your heating system accordingly. For instance, a domestic hot water tank can often provide enough heat input for a radiant floor or wall heating system in a bale home, rather than an expensive boiler.

Biodiesel

Many oil-fired heating devices can burn a fuel known as biodiesel with little or no modification to the equipment. Interest in biodiesel (made from virgin or recycled vegetable oils) has blossomed in the past five years, with most of the focus placed on using this eco-friendly fuel in diesel vehicles. However, it offers the same advantages of cleaner combustion, fewer emissions, and a renewable resource to those using oil-fired heaters. Check with manufacturers of equipment and biodiesel fuel before switching over. Biodiesel can be made at home from used restaurant cooking oil, enabling home-owners to create their own fuel source from a local waste product!

Wood-burning Devices

Much of the world's population still uses wood as a primary heat source. Four basic wood heaters are used in modern homes.

Masonry Heaters

When you need good heating ideas, turning to the Scandinavians and the Russians is not a bad idea. Masonry heaters have been used in northern European homes for centuries to provide dependable radiant heat. Masonry heaters temper the boom-or-bust heat available from the more common, metal airtight woodstoves. The masonry heater's firebox does not exit directly into a metal chimney but into a convoluted masonry chimney that ducts exhaust gases through a labyrinth before releasing them to the outside. Masonry heaters can burn at remarkably high temperatures, and initial exhaust gases — the ones that escape unburned in most wood-fueled devices — are fully combusted, generating intense heat and nearly completely using the potential energy of the wood. The heater's thick masonry walls absorb the heat of combustion and radiate it into the house slowly and gently. Often combined with a baking oven, masonry heaters can be finished beautifully in brick, stone, stucco, tile, or ceramic and can be a visual treat.

Masonry heaters are an exciting heating option. They are virtually creosote and pollution-free when fueled with dry wood. Short hot fires are what they require, so softwoods are a viable fuel, and the wood you use need not be cut in thick, heavy lumps. You'll burn less wood overall in a masonry heater than in a regular woodstove.

The sheer size of a masonry heater requires that it become an integral part of your house design. Your foundation must be able to accommodate the heater's great weight, and enough floor space must be allocated for its external dimensions.

A high level of skill is required to build an efficient masonry heater. Many come in the form of precast kits. Professionals can provide you with an outstanding heating device, though it will come at a steep initial cost. If you want to undertake the task yourself, you should study design and construction techniques very carefully.

Woodstoves

Woodstoves produce an uneven heat — extremely hot when they're burning and cold when the fire is out. In a well-insulated straw bale house, this boom-or-bust heat can be managed and used to maintain a comfortable living space. Plan to position your woodstove centrally, so heat can travel throughout your house. Heat from a woodstove rises quickly, so if you want your bedroom to be cool, don't put it above the woodstove! Bathrooms, on the other hand, make good upstairs neighbors for a woodstove.

Most older woodstoves — even those billed as airtight — are relatively inefficient and allow much of the potential energy in a piece of wood to go up the chimney as smoke. Smoke deposits creosote inside the chimney and is the cause of dangerous chimney fires. Woodstove design is improving; many newer units burn cleaner and more efficiently than ever before, though their greater efficiency also brings higher costs. Nowadays, many building codes require that you install expensive insulated chimneys if you intend to heat with a woodstove.

Outdoor Furnaces

Located outside the shell of the house, prefabricated outdoor furnaces burn wood to heat water that is piped into the house for heating and domestic use. Many of these systems burn very efficiently and safely and can burn softwoods or fuel sources other than wood, such as corn husks or sawdust. Although some users will make claims about outdoor furnaces burning even wet wood, it's best to resist this temptation; creating steam saps efficiency no matter how large the firebox. Outdoor furnaces are relatively expensive but eliminate the need for an indoor chimney system. You won't need to create space inside your building to accommodate a heating unit or worry about the smells or oxygen consumption associated with an indoor

10.2: *A masonry heater is a very efficient way of burning wood, and becomes a centre piece for the home. Even, long-lasting heat and clean burning are the two big advantages over regular woodstoves.*

PETER MACK

stove. Though you won't have to haul wood into the house, you will have to go outside periodically to stoke your furnace.

Fireplaces

Set into an exterior wall, traditional fireplaces — even those with heat recovery equipment in the chimney — have a largely esthetic value and should not be relied upon as a central heating source unless the climate is quite moderate.

Planning issues for wood burning devices. Indoor wood heaters require central placement in your house and a chimney pipe with as few bends as possible. Plan for a fresh air vent that can provide a direct and dedicated oxygen source for a wood-fueled heater. Be sure you plan to make it easy to move and store wood inside. The less time you have to spend moving your wood, the happier you'll be!

Trees are a valuable and dwindling resource. Large-scale and indiscriminate burning of hardwoods is not sustainable, especially if wood is cut elsewhere and transported to your home. Still, if you have access to a suitable woodlot and manage its resources well, burning wood can be a relatively inexpensive heating option once you've made the initial investment for equipment.

Don't Squander Your Heat!

No matter how you heat your home, you can always find ways to prevent heat waste. Create sheltered entries so doors don't open directly outside. Mud rooms, boot rooms, and closed porches are more than just practical; they save on energy costs, too. Inside the house, match heat distribution to activity. An office, where you sit for long periods, will likely require more heat than a kitchen, where you are moving about or creating

heat with the oven. Finally, be moderate with your temperature settings, and treat your heat like the valuable resource it is.

Heat Recovery Ventilators

Modern airtight construction can lead to air-quality and moisture problems in the home, especially if indoor combustion is used to provide heat. Many jurisdictions now mandate the use of heat recovery vents (HRVs) that exchange stale, moist indoor air for fresher, drier outside air, with a minimum of heat loss. These units can be expensive, and installation and balancing usually require a trained professional.

PETER MACK

While we agree that there are some true benefits to having a source of fresh air in the home, we think it is unfortunate that these systems are required by code in many jurisdictions. The HRV is a sort of Band-Aid fix for the off-gassing chemicals that pollute the air in many new homes and for the excessive moisture buildup that can occur in homes sealed with vapor barriers. By choosing healthy building materials, finishes and

10.3: A stone and brick shroud around a woodstove can even out the spikes in temperature caused by the combustion cycles of an airtight stove.

furniture, you can reduce or eliminate the poisons in the air your breathe. And by undertaking to create a building in which the materials are

10.4: *This heat recovery ventilator (HRV) draws in fresh outside air and reclaiming some heat from the outgoing exhaust air. Such devices are required by code in some jurisdictions. Find out if you will require one, and plan for the cost and the ductwork in your budget and design.*

capable of absorbing moisture from the indoor air and releasing it when the air is drier (unpainted or unvarnished wood and unpainted plaster are two effective choices), you can drastically reduce moisture buildup. Your health will benefit as much as the planet does from these choices.

There are many effective strategies for keeping indoor air fresh that don't involve a complete HRV installation, but if you do need to install one, be sure to plan early for the routing of the required ductwork.

Cooling

The principles that apply to heating also apply to cooling. It is not as effective or efficient to cool air as it is to cool a mass. Radiant floor systems can help keep your house comfortably cool in the summertime. Hot indoor air will be moderated by the floor, which, even when fully heated, does not exceed 73 degrees Fahrenheit (23 degrees Celsius). Ground source heat pumps also act as cooling devices in the summer, since ground temperatures are likely to be consistently cooler than air temperatures.

Don't stop with flooring when you think about cooling. Shade your south-facing windows from the summer sun; it is the most effective step you can take to keep your house cool. Plan for adequate ventilation by taking into account the usual direction of summer breezes, and allow for cross ventilation from one side of the house to the other. One of the best ways to beat the heat is to plan for an enclosed porch area on the north side of your house. Constantly shaded, this space can provide cool outdoor living quarters that are naturally air-conditioned!

Water and Sewage Options
Water Sources

Water collection methods vary by region. If you are new to your area, ask neighbors and local officials about standard practices, and keep in mind that the standard option is not necessarily the only option.

Municipal Service

If it's available, a municipal water supply offers you easy access to water. Guidelines and costs will be outlined by the municipality.

Drilled Well

A drilled well is a narrow shaft that has been drilled by machine to access underground water supplies. Wells can range in depth from 15 feet to 200 feet or more; the depth of the drilling determines their cost. The deeper the well, the stronger the pump you will need to lift water to your home. Ask around to find a well driller who knows the geology of your area.

Dug Well

An older version of the drilled well, this well is dug by hand and/or back hoe to access a water supply close to the surface. Well tiles — usually made of precast concrete — are inserted into the hole to prevent cave-ins. Dug wells are usually shallower than a drilled well. Insist on properly grouted joints between tiles, or you will be drinking cloudy rainwater and pumps may prematurely give up the ghost.

Lake, River, or Stream Collection

Water can be drawn from a natural body of water. Fast-moving water is likely to be of better quality, but it is rarely possible anymore to find safe drinking water from a surface source. Treatment of some kind will likely be necessary.

Rain Water Reservoirs

Rainwater can be collected and stored in above grade or below grade holding tanks. If this will be a central part of your water system, plan carefully to position the storage tank near your house. Choose roofing that will not contaminate rainwater, and plan for a roof with quality eavestroughs that can duct water to the storage tank. Even in areas without heavy rainfall, efficient methods can collect and store abundant quantities of water. Collection methods, storage methods, and proximity to sources of airborne pollution will all determine the rainwater's drinkability.

Water Pumping Options

Regardless of where your water comes from, you will need a delivery system to bring it to your taps.

Electric Pumps

Electric pumps are the standard. In either a submersible or non-submersible form, an electric pump will pull water from the source and push it into your house. Piston pumps use less power than jet pumps. Many pump options are available, including models designed for renewable energy power systems.

Wind Pumps

It takes much less wind speed to pump water than to generate electricity, making wind pumps a suitable option in many regions. Because they will move water only when there is wind, such systems require a storage tank for calm periods.

Hand or Foot Pumps

If your well or reservoir is close to the house and is not overly deep, a hand or foot pump is quite viable. Manual pumps can be used to supply water on demand or to fill raised tanks for gravity feed systems. Old-fashioned hand pumps are often easy to find and inexpensive to restore to working condition. Modern hand pumps and foot pumps are more efficient, though similar in design.

Gas Pumps

A noisy, inconvenient solution, gas pumps move large quantities of water very quickly. If you have to move water a great distance or have no access to electricity or wind, gas pumps can be used to fill reservoir tanks.

Ram Pumps

These pumps use no external power once installed. Instead, momentum from falling water (in a pipe) is used to pump water higher than the distance it fell. These are great if a stream is nearby.

Gravity Feed Systems

Gravity feed from raised storage allows you to pump water when it's convenient — by hand, or with wind, electric, and gas pumps — and provides quiet distribution on demand. Raised water storage can be created inside or outside your house. Interior storage requires additional planning for weight loads and the installation of trustworthy tanks. Exterior storage requires protection from freezing.

Sewage Options

We tend not to think much about what to do with our own sewage; it's regarded as an impolite topic to consider. But we all create it and should be responsible for making proper disposal and treatment choices. As contamination from our own waste is becoming a more crucial issue, more and better treatment options are being conceived and used. Research well before making any decisions.

Municipal Sewage Treatment

Most urban and suburban lots are serviced by a municipal sewage system, in which wastewater from a building enters a network of underground sewage pipes that route it to centralized waste treatment facilities. These facilities vary tremendously in their approaches to treating waste before releasing back into the environment. If you are concerned about treatment methods in your area, talk to municipal officials or visit the waste treatment plant. Pressure the government if you feel waste is being handled poorly or irresponsibly. It is possible to use alternative waste treatment methods even within a city, but you will probably face a struggle to receive approval. Remember, even in city buildings, composting toilets and other strategies are possible.

Septic Systems

Septic systems are the most common sewage treatment option for rural residences. These systems use a large buried storage tank into which liquid and solid wastes are deposited. The top layer of liquid drains off into weeping tiles that distribute it into the ground. Because septic systems release untreated liquids directly into the environment, the success of the system depends on what's being put into the tank. Conscientious use of a septic system can be gentle on the environment, but thoughtless use can deposit dangerous contaminants into your soil and groundwater. Septic installation is expensive, especially where problematic soil conditions exist. Soil percolation tests and a permit are generally required before building can proceed.

Composting Toilets

Composting toilets change human waste into usable compost, offering you a degree of self-sufficiency in waste management. Many brands of composting toilets are available, as are instructions on how to make your own. Not all brands are created equal, and there are many capacities and styles to choose from. Installation often requires a storage unit below the toilet itself, so if you choose this system, be sure to plan your house appropriately. Composting toilets do not handle gray water, so they must be used in combination with a separate gray-water treatment system.

Outhouses and Leaching Pits

A well-constructed outhouse can be pleasant, long-lasting, and relatively odor free. It is a reasonable option if you are willing to travel from your house to your facilities. It can also function as a backup for your main sewage system, and you can use it to lighten the load on other systems during the warm months when you are outdoors anyway.

Easy to construct, a leaching pit, or French drain, is basically a hole in the ground into which wastewater — gray-water, not sewage — can be ducted. From the leaching pit, bath and sink water can filter back into the soil. Again, what goes into a leaching pit enters your water table. A leaching pit may not be allowed by local officials.

Other Waste Alternatives

Much study and research has gone into new ways to treat waste. Many experimental systems exist and have proven to be very effective. Constructed wetlands use aquatic plants to feed on waste. This system often resembles a small canal system in which each stage is populated by different species of waste loving plants. A biological filter systems uses a pump to spray black water, sewage, over containers of foam cubes that harbor sewage-eating bacteria. A gray-water recycling system can be a simple arrangement that stores water to irrigate a garden or a complex system akin to greenhouse hydroponics. These alternatives to standard methods of waste treatment are worthy of your research and support.

Electricity Options

Humans have survived, often quite comfortably, for thousands of years without electricity. Indeed, much of the world's population still gets by without easy household access to electrical power. In this spirit, we include electricity options!

Grid Power

Modern homes are designed with grid power in mind. Little special planning is required for it during your design process. Grid power is convenient, relatively abundant, and reasonably priced for the time being. You may be offered a choice between underground delivery or pole delivery. The choice is largely an esthetic one.

There are many good reasons to hook up to the grid, but we won't elaborate on them here. Instead, we will provide a reminder that convenient electrical power comes at a cost, both to the environment and to consumers. If you choose to evaluate those costs, you will perhaps be persuaded to consider other options.

Independent Power

There are many ways to generate your own power cleanly and safely. Independent power production methods take several forms and, unlike grid power, produce varying quantities of power. Photovoltaics — solar panels — and wind or water turbines are well tested, viable, and affordable. As grid power and grid connection prices rise, independent power generation is becoming an increasingly popular choice.

You will need to assess your building plans and budget. Most modern homes are built close to the road because of the cost of extending utility service any great distance. When you sever the electric umbilical cord, you are free to build in areas that would otherwise be impracticable.

At the planning stage, you will want to integrate your generating system into your home. Most independent systems use large batteries for storage of electrical power, and they require venting to the outside. Batteries should be kept close to room temperature. Placement of photovoltaic panels can be integrated into your design on the south face of your house and can double as a shading porch roof or window awning. If you will be using wind or water power, don't

GLEN HUNTER

10.5a

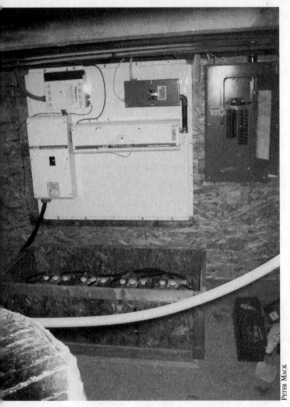

PETER MACK

10.5b

build too far away from your source, since costs for transporting the power will rise.

Check with your local utility company about the hook-up fees and charge for services. The money you don't spend for grid power hook-up could be used to purchase a small and serviceable independent system that you can upgrade or add to as time and finances allow. Switching to independent power is a big, rewarding commitment. There are many excellent sources of information available to you, and experienced people willing to help you out. Think about it.

No Electricity

It is possible to lead a relatively comfortable life with no electrical power at all. This choice involves greater adjustments than the move to independent power, but you can't beat the cost!

Kerosene or propane for lighting, wind or hand pumps for water, solar heating for hot water, wind-up radios — the choices exist. Even if you plan to build for no electricity, it is advisable to wire it now or include some provisions for wiring, should you decide to add solar panels or go onto the grid later. Wire mold baseboard or conduit through the floors, walls, and ceilings will allow you to add wiring later without having to tear your house apart.

10.5a - b: *These photovoltaic panels (right) and solar hot water collectors can generate enough electricity and heat to fully supply a home, or offset costs for fossil fuels, even in a northerly climate. The guts of any renewable energy system are the charge controller (top left), battery bank (bottom) and inverter (centre). The system feeds into a typical breaker panel (right) for distribution around the building.*

Interview with Orville Thertell, Licensed Electrician

Orville's list for getting an electrical permit:

1. Find a contractor.

2. Contact the electrical safety authority.

3. Find out who the local inspector is, and get his/her views on wiring a straw bale house, since he/she represents the governing body for electrical work.

4. Draw up a set of plans and present them to your local inspector for feedback and approval.

5. Once you have the feedback, make any necessary changes and then install according to plan.

6. Don't forget to book any necessary inspections before proceeding to the next step.

What were your first thoughts when you were contacted by a contractor to do the electrical work in a straw bale house?

I stated that I'd be interested, but first wanted to research the topic and get more technical assistance on how electrical work has been done in the past on straw bale houses. I became quite involved and was very interested in being part of this project. I bought the book, *Straw Bale Building*; also did a lot of research on the internet. I am open-minded, and enjoy a challenge.

What process did you use when wiring your first straw bale house?

We distributed lengths of electrical wiring around the site. I prefer R-2000 plastic airtight boxes because they prevent air leaks. We attached the electrical boxes to a stake to pierce into the bales, to hold the electrical box intact until plastering. As the bales are stacked, the wire is fed up through the bales. The electrical boxes and light switches are set at the required height and are held in place by the stake. The wire goes up in a zig-zag configuration to weave up through the bales. The wire is set back in the wall several inches.

Another method is to carve a vertical channel into the bales from the electrical box up to the top plate, and then the wire sits in the kerf.

Is it more work running wires in a straw bale house compared to a conventional house?

There is far less drilling involved, since the wires are simply fed up through the bales. We had to drill through the top plate where the wires would emerge, but it is far less labor-intensive in terms of installment from the electrician's point of view.

Do you have any tips for electricians when working on a straw bale house?

I highly recommend the R-2000 electrical box for any house. They have an airtight seal, and there are far fewer leaks with them. They also come with a half-inch flange that works well for plastering, so they're a good fit for a straw bale house.

When you are contacted to do the wiring on a straw bale house, you should do a plan and design your layout so that you can take all of the wiring back to ceiling boxes so that only one wire has to weave down through the bales to each outlet. ☞

10.6a: *Scrap plywood makes a good anchor in the bales for an electrical box*

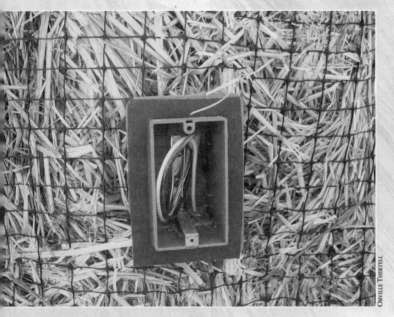

10.6b: *R-2000 box with flange for plastering.*

Can you think of any improvements to doing the electrical wiring?

I would design the stakes slightly differently next time. I would recommend they be 8" wide, rather than 6" like we used before, and 14" long instead of the 12" that we used. (Note: this length only works when the bales are on the flat). I would recommend that the stakes be cut at a 45-degree angle to help them go into the bales more readily. I believe the larger size will help to set the electrical box straighter.

Should electricians be wary of wiring a straw bale house?

No .... they should be cautious (as they should be when wiring any type of house!), and they need to pay attention to where they route the wiring. You want to avoid setting the wiring where there is a structural load, such as a header plate for a stairwell. Careful planning and frequent consulting with the plans is essential.

Do you have any preference for load-bearing versus post and beam?

Although I don't have any experience with post and beam, I would run the wiring straight up the vertical members, and thereby avoid having to snake the wiring up through the bales as much as possible. I don't have a preference for either.

Some people like 1110 boxes or utility boxes. Do you have any issues with them?

I wouldn't recommend them. I definitely prefer the R-2000 Nutek-type box due to its superior performance in preventing air leaks.

Could you give me your opinion on wire mold or baseboard wiring?

It is quite costly; the wire mold and wire way are far more expensive than using boxes, but ☞

there is less air loss than with traditional electrical boxes. But again, the R-2000 boxes don't have any air loss.

What kind of wire do you use? Do you have to use armored cable? Some people think that you have to use special wire since it's in the bale wall, which they think is flammable.

Ask your inspector what he/she would like you to use. I use NMD-90 wire.

There is no need to buy the more expensive wiring unless the inspector asks for it.

Would you recommend running conduit through the walls for the electrical wiring?

Although it would work fine, it is a lot of extra effort and expense. There is no need to run wiring through conduit unless you expect to require a lot of wiring changes in the future. It makes more sense to plan carefully ahead of time and wire for other potential uses. (Remember that you can always add additional wiring in internal stud walls).

Are you concerned about the risk of fire in a straw bale house?

10.7: *Using a post as a mount for an electrical box.*

Since plastered straw bale walls get a two-hour fire rating, I'm not worried about the wiring. As a volunteer firefighter and an electrician, I have no concerns with the risk of fire if all work is completed to code standards.

In your opinion, do you think wiring in a straw bale house is safer due to the fact that the wiring is set back so far in the wall compared with how close to the surface it is in a conventional house?

If the wiring is done to code standards, all wiring is safe.

— *Orville Thertell has been a licensed electrician since 1980. Self-employed, he works near Peterborough, Ontario. He has also been a volunteer firefighter for 14 years.* ■

10.8: *Baseboard wiring keeps all lines out of the walls. They allow access to wiring; the trade-off is cost.*

References

Canada Mortgage and Housing Corporation. *A Guide to Residential Wood Heating,* 1995.

Canadian Renewable Energy News: Practical Information Exchange for Energy Independence. P.O. Box 14, Pink Mountain BC, Canada, V0C 2B0.

Del Porto, David and Carol Steinfeld. *The Composting Toilet System Book: A Practical Guide to Choosing, Planning, and Maintaining Composting Toilet Systems.* Chelsea Green Publishers, 1999. ISBN 0-966678-30-3.

Fine Homebuilding. *Energy-Efficient Houses,* The Taunton Press, 1993. ISBN 1-56158-059-7.

George, Steve and John Lowe. *Basic Wiring Techniques.* The Solaris Group, 1993. ISBN 0-89721-251-7.

Gipe, Paul. *Wind Power for Home and Business.* Chelsea Green Publishers, 1996. ISBN 0-930031-64-4.

Grant, Nick and Mark Moodie, Chris Weedon. *Sewage Solutions: Answering the Call of Nature.* New Society Publishers, 2001. ISBN 1-89804-916-5

Home Power: The Hands-on Journal of Home-made Power. P.O. Box 520, Ashland, OR, 97520, USA.

Hyytiainen, Albert Barden-Heikki. *Finnish Fireplaces: Heart of the Home.* The Finnish Building Centre, 1993. ISBN 951-682-168-5.

Jeffrey, Kevin. *Independent Energy Guide: Electrical Power for Home, Boat and RV.* Orwell Cove Press, 1995. ISBN 0-9644112-0-2.

Jenkins, Joseph. *Humanure Handbook: A Guide to Composting Human Manure.* Jenkins Publishing, 1999. ISBN 04425890.

Lyle, David. *The Book of Masonry Stoves: Rediscovering an Old Way of Warming.* Chelsea Green Publishers, 1996. ISBN 0-931790-57-3.

Montgomery, Richard H. *The Solar Decision Book: A Guide to Heating Your Home with Solar Energy.* John Wiley & Sons, 1978. ISBN 0-471-05652-9.

Potts, Michael. *The Independent Home: Living Well with Power from the Sun, Wind and Water.* Chelsea Green Publishers, 1993. ISBN 0-930031-65-2.

Private Power magazine,<www.privatepower.ca>, Warren Publishing, 1-800-668-7788.

Schaeffer, John and Doug Pratt. *The Solar Living Sourcebook: The Complete Guide to Renewable Energy Technologies and Sustainable Living.* Chelsea Green Publishers, 1998. ISBN 0-930031-82-2.

Siegenthaler, John P. E. Modern Hydronic Heating. Delmar Publishers, 1995. ISBN 0-8273-6595-0.

Tickell, Joshua. How to Make Cheap, Clean Fuel from Free Vegetable Oil. Greenteach Publishing, 1998. ISBN 0-9664616-0-6.

Waterloo Biofilter:<www.waterloo-biofilter.com> 519 856-0759 <mwillson@mnsi.net>

Wehrman, Robert. *Basic Plumbing Techniques.* The Solaris Group,1993. ISBN 0-89721-250-9.

CHAPTER 11

From Designer to Draftsperson

As you approach final decisions about the size, shape, and features of your house, it's time to put pencil to paper and create some drawings.

Design versus Plans

The terms "design" and "plans" are often used interchangeably. They refer to two different kinds of drawings, however, and understanding the distinction can be important. Design is a spatial concept. It can refer to a floor plan, an elevation, or a model. In the design stage, dimensions and proportions only define the building's appearance and attributes. Materials choices, the sizes and dimensions of rooms and windows, the location of kitchen and bathroom elements, entrances, staircases ... all of these are components of a design.

But a design alone will not receive a building permit. Plans are the technical drawings that make the execution of a design possible. Plans include specific instructions for structural components, are fully scaled, and include all relevant dimensions. A good set of plans is literally an instruction book for the creation of the building.

Design Strategies

There are many different strategies for overcoming "blank page phobia." If you have already created cutouts of your rooms, you can start by translating them into individual forms on graph paper that in turn can be cut out and arranged like a puzzle. Alternatively, you may have a strong sense of the size and shape of the footprint of your house. If so, you can translate your outline onto graph paper and sketch in your interior rooms, hallways, etc. Perhaps you are very clear about the size, shape, and placement of one or two particular rooms. Draw these first and add the rest in relation to them. If you know how you want your house to appear from the outside, draw it from all four directions, to scale. The dimensions of these drawings can be translated into an outline for the floor plan.

PAT MARCOTTE

11.1: *Once you start thinking outside the conventional box, your straw bale walls will start to suggest all kinds of arches and curves!*

It's Like Lego!

The proportions of a typical block of Lego are very similar to that of a two-string bale. So, a return to your Lego-building days can result in accurate scale models of your home design! In addition to acquiring a good, three-dimensional understanding of your design, you'll be familiarizing yourself with many of the key rules for stacking bales. When it comes time to build the real thing, your Lego experience will serve you well!

Creating scale models of your design (whether out of cardboard, Lego, or any other material — we've heard of cheese being the

11.2: *A straw bale window seat makes a cosy spot for a child to curl up. Keep in mind the width of the walls when designing your plans.*

medium too!) can be very informative. The addition of the third dimension can make trouble spots quite obvious, and at the same time can suggest exciting possibilities you hadn't conceived on paper.

Disposable Drawings

Designing can be fun and frustrating. Draw and redraw. If something isn't working, change the perspective and work from a different approach.

Don't be afraid to take a break. Designing is a long process, so allow yourself time to create something you're happy with. Think of your initial drawings as disposable, and start over whenever you feel lost. Don't throw your drawings away though. Save them in a file, and go back to them every so often. Sometimes you'll surprise yourself with how right you were back when you first started, and you may be able to work those older elements into your newer drawings.

Add Detail Gradually

Your first drawings don't have to be accurate or beautiful. As you create a design that meets your needs and pleases you, you can gradually add detail. Make your outline reflect the width of your bale walls, and draw doorways and windows to scale. Add thickness to interior dividing walls. Consider the direction in which doors will open. Sketch in permanent fixtures like sinks, baths, and toilets, and add in counters, built-in shelving, closets, beds, desks, and tables. Think about where you can place items like stereos, televisions, or computers. In two-story designs, draw in your stairs and landings. Don't forget mechanical systems. Consider plumbing routes, heating devices, and passive solar features.

Dimensions

As you start to work with more accurate dimensions, you might want to carry a tape measure with you wherever you go. By measuring existing rooms, you can build a realistic understanding of what dimensions work best for you. Most people tend to overestimate the amount of room they will need. Only by knowing how your numbers translate into real-world space can you avoid over- or under-sizing. Consider how space will be used, not just the amount of space that's available.

The Building Code and Dimensions

Your local building code may have particular space requirements. Minimum and maximum square footages, ceiling heights, door widths and heights, minimum numbers of windows and their opening surfaces, and hallway and stair widths are commonly included in building codes. Become familiar with these requirements; you'll have to work within them.

Design for Efficiency

It is not difficult to design individual rooms to suit your needs. It is a real skill, however, to be able to join all these rooms efficiently. The least efficient spaces in a home are hallways. These take up a lot of square footage, and serve no purpose other than moving traffic. Try to arrange rooms to limit the number and size of hallways. If a hallway is unavoidable, make sure it serves several purposes (storage, art display, outdoor view, etc.).

Often, people trying to design efficiently forget to include adequate closets and storage spaces. Interlock closets and storage spaces between rooms. Build in shelving, cupboards, and counters. Observe how these elements have been incorporated in other buildings and other designs. There are clever storage strategies that take advantage of existing spaces in buildings (under staircases, over doorways, etc.)

Don't Strain to Be Original

If you understand what you want from your house, a unique form will necessarily follow. You don't have to come up with your own design from scratch. By copying and slightly altering an existing design that has many of the features you want, you can create a highly personalized living space. Even two houses built from identical

plans by different people can each look remarkably original. So don't shy away from plan books; rather, make those plans your own. The build-

PETER MACK

LAURA TAYLOR

11.3: *Many elements must come together in a kitchen. Consider how your bale walls and your cabinetry and counters will work together. A well-designed kitchen allows for a flow of movement and tasks that should function seamlessly.*

11.4: *Lighting is an important consideration that is often overlooked during the design phase. Natural lighting and electrical lighting should work together to make rooms functional at any time of day or night.*

11.5a

Ross Kembar, Architect

11.5b

Laura Taylor

11.5a - b: The simple addition of a uniquely sized set of windows can transform a wall — and the space behind it — into something individual and personal.

ing techniques you use and the choices you make about finishing and interior detailing will be as integral to the creation of a unique living space as the floor plan and elevations.

From Design to Plans

Once you create or find a design that suits you, it will need to be translated into detailed plans. Plans have their own language, a collection of symbols and drawing conventions that allow builders to understand plans from any designer, architect, or engineer. Typical elements include a scaled floor plan, elevations (exterior views), a foundation plan and details, floor framing and details, wall section and details, and roof framing and details. The floor plan and the elevations will be marked for cut lines, through which the house will be sliced to show cross sections of the various elements. Cross sections are shown for areas that are typical of the construction method to be used. Special exceptions are also shown in detail. It is important to become familiar with these symbols and conventions if you intend to draw your own plans or build yourself.

Do-It-Yourself Plans

If you intend to perform your own translation from design to finished plans, it is crucial to obtain a copy of your local building code. If straw bale is included in your code, homemade plans should be acceptable; if not, most other jurisdictions will not accept them. You may, however, draw up your own plans before approaching a professional who will be able to get code approval.

Everything in your plans should be drawn to an exact and consistent scale. Access to a drafting table or computer drafting program can be useful and could speed up the planning process. Try to avoid incorporating odd dimensions that will require excessive trimming of each piece of plywood or lumber. Sheet materials — plywood and drywall — usually come in 4-by-8-foot sheets. Lumber usually comes in 8-, 10-, 12-, 14-, 16-, or 20-foot lengths.

If you have previous building experience, some knowledge of drafting, or the time and patience to acquire these skills (many community colleges offer basic drafting courses), it is entirely feasible to draw your own plans. If you don't, it may be better to hire a professional.

Purchasing Plans

Prefabricated plans for straw bale homes are not yet common, though some architectural firms are producing them. Most commercially produced plans will need to be adapted for bale homes. A professional may be able to make adjustments for you, or you may be able to adapt them yourself. If plans are altered, approval by the original architect or engineer will no longer apply, unless you work directly with that person.

Architects

Architects perform a unique set of tasks from the artistic to the scientific. Primarily, they visualize and create plans for a built environment. An architect can take you from the early design stage to finished, approved plans that will meet code requirements.

Architects are licensed by a self-regulating professional body in their particular state or province. Once registered, an architect agrees to work within the established guidelines of that body and carries liability insurance to cover his or her work. An architect's stamp is usually accepted by building officials as a sign that the architect assumes legal responsibility for the plans in question.

Your area may support several architectural firms and individual practices; each will have its own specialty, fee structure, and style. You can set up an initial consultation with an architect — it should be free of charge — to discuss ideas, fees, and scheduling and to determine compatibility. Finding an architect with an interest or specialty in natural building styles like straw bale is a good idea.

Take your ideas and questions to the initial meeting. Even if you intend to use a professional to design and plan for you, it is worthwhile to play the Design Game before you make an appointment. Anything you take into the office will help you communicate your vision and goals more clearly.

It helps if you know why you have chosen certain options and not others. If you feel strongly about some aspects of your design, be sure to let the architect know. He or she might be able to tell you about options that make sense to you that you didn't even know existed. On the other hand, you might meet with strong disagreement.

Peter Mack

If so, you may want to work with someone else.

Ask to see pictures of buildings the architect has designed or planned; it may be possible to tour one or two. Remember, you are hiring someone to help you achieve your goals. As long as your demands are reasonable, you should expect them to be met. Consult with several architects and take time to evaluate them before choosing one.

11.6: *Allow yourself some design freedom, and include some elements like this octagonal stained glass window that will be highlights in your building.*

Good referrals are the best way to find good architects. You may want to talk to some previous clients to get their opinions on the quality of work and level of service. Check with a contractor or builder who has worked with that architect's design. He or she can tell you whether or not the plans were practical and economically feasible.

Regardless of the architect you choose — and it is perfectly valid and common to hire a professional — be sure you proceed at a pace that allows you to feel comfortable with the important decisions you'll have to make.

Budget, fees, and services. Determine how you will be billed, when you are expected to pay, and what services the fee covers. Know what you are purchasing. If you want finished plans, make sure you will receive all the relevant drawings and references required by your building inspector and financiers. Also, make sure that you can understand them. If you cannot follow the drawings or feel that certain details have not been adequately addressed, request clarification.

Be clear about how changes and modifications will be handled and billed. Building inspectors, hired carpenters, or even your own eagle eye may spot problems with the plans that will require changes; if your professional is not available to make or approve changes, you can experience long delays and incur extra expense.

Finally, you should be comfortable with the amount of support your architect offers. From site inspections and meetings with building officials to advice on materials and finishes, you should both be clear about the amount of involvement your architect will have in the project.

From the Engineer's Desk

11.7: *This straw bale research building at the University of Manitoba was designed by Kris Dick, and will be an important centre for alternative building materials testing.*

Design professionals face challenges from many directions. Working with alternative building materials adds new dimensions to those challenges. For me, as a structural engineer, it creates an opportunity to work with many interesting people on unique projects, to apply fundamental engineering principles to non-traditional ways of building, and to explore the use of alternative building techniques through engineering design and applied research. However, some aspects of doing things differently can expand the boundaries of a design professional's responsibilities, both explicitly and implicitly.

Choosing to build a home is one of the biggest decisions many of us will make in our lifetime. Many of us are generally unfamiliar with all of the services, permits, scheduling, and finances that are a part of construction. One of the services usually required is that of a structural engineer. It is from the perspective of a structural engineer working with straw ☞

Structural Engineers

The stamp of a structural engineer for straw bale home plans is a must in many jurisdictions. Structural engineers can work from completed plans or can often do the design and drafting work as well. They ensure that the plans, as drawn, are feasible, structurally sound, and meet code and safety requirements. The stamp of a structural engineer can help circumvent the concerns of a building official and allow you to get approval for your straw bale building plans. If you have drawn your own plans or purchased plans that require adaptations or minor changes, it may be better to take them to an engineer rather than to an architect.

Professional Draftsperson

Often known as an architectural technologists, a draftsperson has the skills and understanding to

PETER MACK, LIIKER HECHT DESIGN STUDIO WITH STONES THROW DESIGN

11.8: *You can blend other materials with your bale walls to good effect, like the stone base and wooden shelving in this sharply plastered wall.*

bale structures that I would like to discuss what you should expect from a structural engineer, and what the engineer hopes you as the owner appreciate regarding their role and responsibility in the project.

A good place to start is where most projects begin, with a request for services. The phone rings, and a voice on the other end says, "We understand that you provide engineering for straw bale buildings. We're building a straw bale house, the building inspector says we need a seal, the plans are done. If I courier the plans to you tomorrow could I get a stamp in a few days? …. We're on a budget, I hope this won't cost much …. I just need a seal." While totally understanding the caller's situation, and willing to help, the engineer must address professional and legal responsibilities.

Constructing a straw bale house places the building outside of structural systems that are specifically addressed in the building code. In Canada, this means that a straw bale building must be evaluated based on a more rigorous engineering analysis, one primarily applied to commercial structures. This analysis is done in accordance with Part 4 of the National Building Code of Canada (NBCC). Due to the nature of the building materials used for a straw bale structure, it cannot meet the more prescriptive requirements of Part 9 of the NBCC, reserved for traditional residential buildings. In the case of a nontraditional building, the plan examiner or building official will require that the plans be "sealed" by a registered professional engineer. For those components of the building that do not have a specific reference in the building code, an equivalency of the proposed components must be demonstrated. Since there is engineering input required, the engineer responsible must affix their seal to all of the drawings associated with their design. Once an engineer puts their seal on a drawing, they are indicating to the pubic and the jurisdiction having authority that they are accepting responsibility for that portion of the project, and more specifically, any liability associated with it. ☞

draw up quality plans but is not a licensed architect. A competent draftsperson has the training and knowledge to assist you with your design and your plans, from the initial stages through to completed construction documents, but he or she will not have the stamping powers of an architect or structural engineer. Still, a good draftsperson can be a valuable partner, and charges less than an architect.

Designer/Builder

Experienced builders can often draw up plans for clients, offering the advantage of minimizing miscommunication between designer and builder

Having the plans done before sending them to an engineer may or may not be a good approach, dependent upon how they have been done. There are industry standards for drawings that each engineer works to, and in some instances, there may also be certain details required by a local authority. By sealing a set of plans, the engineer is indicating the work has been done either by them or under their supervision. This is not to say that an engineer cannot review a set of plans done by someone else and seal them. The engineer must, however, perform an engineering review, request that any revisions be made, and when all is in order, seal them. If, upon review, there are numerous changes required to a plan set, it may be easier to have the engineering company make the changes. A change to one seemingly insignificant component often creates a ripple effect through an entire drawing set. If the original plans are in computer format, then it is a case of modifying the existing files to reflect the changes required. If the plans have been done by hand, then it may be a little more time-consuming to adjust the drawings. In some instances the engineer can create a separate set of drawings under their company name that can be appended to the plan set.

Involving the owner, engineer, building officials, and drafting personnel early in the design process can reduce time delays and minimize frustrations. Remember that, as the building season gets closer, all those involved typically get busy, resulting in unavoidable delays.

Naturally, with every service there is a cost. Every straw bale project is unique, requiring varied degrees of engineering involvement. Thus, it is impossible to estimate specific fees for engineering services. I would, however, ask the reader to consider the various roles and responsibilities of an engineer involved in a straw bale project and the value they bring to your project.

Some typical business costs, such as supplies, rent, support staff salaries, disbursements, and facility insurance, are reasonably straight forward to determine. The fees that are challenging to quantify are those related to the more intangible aspects of engineering service. When an engineer is requested to either prepare the design and plans, or review a design, there is an expectation that they will apply due diligence to the task. This expectation comes from not only their client but also the professional bodies through which all professional engineers must be licensed to practice. In the case of a nontraditional building designed in the absence of clear code guidance, the engineer must apply an analysis based on specialized knowledge gained and refined over time to meet a personal comfort level that allows them to take responsibility for their portion of a project. On occasion I have half jokingly said to people that for me this is a function of how high the acid rises in my stomach! It is difficult to place a value on years of study, experience, and a willingness to be legally and financially accountable for design decisions. As society becomes more litigious, one measure of cost might be to look at the amount of liability insurance design professionals pay. For example, at the time ☞

and the disadvantage of having fewer people's thinking applied to the plans.

Revising Your Plans

It is rare that a building does not undergo many changes throughout the planning process. Each person you add into the equation will have ideas and suggestions they believe will make the plans better. Remain open to suggestions. Be sure that your agreement with your design professional clearly outlines the provisions for revising the plans.

Show your plans to people you trust and get their input. Start making some preliminary

of writing, liability insurance has gone up fourfold in the last 18 months. It is important to recognize that while two structures may be identical on paper, they are not the same once constructed. They are built in different locations, and thus, from the engineer's perspective, each project carries with it separate risk and inherent liability.

Before choosing an engineer for your project you should assess their skill set. Structural engineers will typically have their own area of specialty. Do not be afraid to ask for references and to talk with previous clients of the particular engineer you are proposing to engage. The structural engineer will conduct the relevant analysis on your project, ensuring that all of the components meet or exceed a minimum standard for structural integrity, ensuring the structure performs as a building system. With straw bale construction, the structural engineer must be conversant with the behavior of load-bearing and infill straw wall systems. In my opinion this knowledge should extend past the structural behavior to include building envelope details related to moisture and vapor management. It has been said that a building is a stationary machine that has to manage all the environmental and end-use loads. Your engineer must understand all of the workings of your building to ensure that it functions well.

Depending upon the jurisdiction in which you build, there may be a requirement for the engineer sealing the drawings to provide site inspections at milestones during the project. Inspection requirements should, if possible, be established as soon as possible during the design process. I cannot emphasize enough the importance of working with your local building official up-front. While some people may think that building officials are there to make our lives a misery, I would suggest that their mandate is to ensure that we have a good final product. It is in everyone's best interest to establish a good working relationship. While the path to open communication may not always be a smooth one, ensure that your engineer is open to talking with the building official directly.

There are many aspects involved in building a straw bale home. I believe your engineer should bring not only the technical competence and expertise to your project but also an understanding of alternative building materials and an appreciation of the reasons why people choose alternative building approaches. From the other side, it is important that clients appreciate that providing engineering design services for structures that do not have clear code requirements places an added responsibility on the engineer. Unfortunately, one can sometimes get the feeling that engineering and plans are considered a necessary evil in order to build. If this brief article has done anything, I hope it has conveyed a message that engaging an engineer is not just a way to get a permit but is a worthwhile investment in your project.

—*Dr. Kris J. Dick, P.Eng., is the Principal of Building Alternatives Inc., and Adjunct Professor, Dept. of Biosystems Engineering, University of Manitoba. Contact: Building Alternatives, Anola, Manitoba, Canada R0E 0A0* <krisdick@mts.net> ■

11.9: *If you aren't going to aim for straight bale walls, you can design with other "curvy" materials, like this round wood stair railing.*

cost estimates. If you will be hiring professional builders, begin to set up meetings and use a draft version of the plans for your consultations. Your straw bale house will require construction details unfamiliar to many professional designers. Before you call your plans "finished," be sure that everyone involved understands how the bales are to be used, integrated with other structural elements, detailed, and finished. Don't give approval for a professional to create the final stamped set of plans; be sure that you are completely certain that they are right. Any changes made after the drawings are stamped require a re-stamping that will cost you. Rushing things at this stage will only cause headaches later.

When all seems right (and sometimes it takes a frustratingly long time before you reach that stage!), make up enough sets of the finished plans so that each key person involved in the project has one. Only the set submitted to the building official needs to be stamped.

Keep in mind that for you this is a very personal and unique experience. But for the design professional, it is a job. You must have reasonable expectations about timelines, costs, and revisions. It is best to outline all of these concerns at the beginning of the process to avoid misunderstandings.

The Thrill of a "Paper House"

It is exciting to see your house go from an idea in your head to a detailed drawing on paper. You can finally show off pictures! The project will take on an air of reality that may have been lacking during the design stages, because soon you will be building.

References

Bahamon, Alejandro. *Mini House.* Harper Collins, 2003. ISBN 0-06-051359-4.

Hilliard, Elizabeth, Ray Main, and Laura Hodgson. *Perfect Order: Simple Storage Solutions.* Soma Books, 1999. ISBN 1-57959-046-2

Institute for Research in Construction. NRCC38726. Canadian Commission on Building and Fire Codes, 1995.

Susanka, Susan. *Creating the Not So Big House: Insights and Ideas for the New American Home.* Taunton Books, 2001. ISBN 1-56158-605-6

Susanka, Susan with Kira Obolensky. *The Not So Big House: A Blueprint for the Way We Really Live.* Taunton Books, 1998. ISBN 1-56158-130-5

Wanek, Catherine. *The New Strawbale Home.* Gibbs Smith, 2003. ISBN 1-58685-203-5

Bale plan sites:

50 Straw Bale Plans, <http:/www.balewatch.com>

Plan and Budget for Building a Small "Starter" Straw Bale Home, <www.solarhaven.org/StarterStrawBale.htm>

Proven Straw Bale Home Plans: Cottages, Homes, and Small Houses, <www.strawbalehomes.com/stockplans.html>

Stock Straw Bale Home Plans, <www.strawboard.com>

Straw Bale House Plans, <www.ricestraw.com/baleraisers>

CHAPTER 12

Straw Bale Construction Plans

For your construction plans to be ready to use, they must be well detailed and very thorough. Bale details will be especially important.

When people ask if bale building is more or less difficult than standard framing, it is tempting to say less. The actual act of stacking and preparing bales is very straightforward. However, this doesn't mean that there is nothing to it. The key to strong, long-lasting bale walls is in the details. Construction plans for straw bale buildings must be detailed, accurate, and reliable. It should be obvious from your detail drawings that your building will be structurally sound, impervious or resistant to accumulations of rainwater and snow, and practical to execute with a minimum of materials and time-consuming fussing. Because very few owners, builders and inspectors have experience with bale walls, it is only from the detail drawings that all the crucial considerations will be met, making this a critical stage in your project.

Bale Details
Foundation/Bale Junction

Your foundation serves the purpose of supporting your building and all the loads imposed on it. Remember in the detailing phase that all those loads are transmitted through the bale walls and into the foundation. This means that the entire bale wall *and* the plaster skins

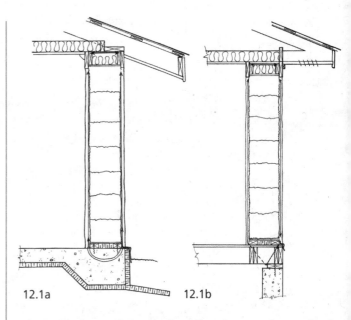

12.1a   12.1b

12.1a - b: *These are good basic wall sections. 1a shows a load-bearing wall on slab foundation with a framed roof. 1b shows a load-bearing wall on a perimeter wall or pier foundation with a truss roof. The arrowed lines show the path of the precompression wires. Notice the top plate bearing on the plaster and the plaster bearing on the foundation, with a flashing to protect the seam at the bottom. This kind of generous (24 inch minimum) roof overhang is a must.*

(which carry most of the loads) must be able to bear on the foundation dir-ectly (or indirectly, if the load path is appropriate).

There are many ways to successfully create a good junction between your foundation and your bales. The main points to be remembered are:

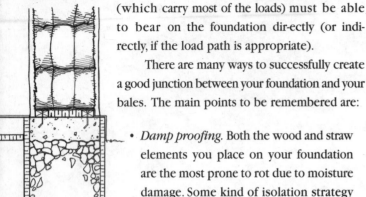

12.2a: *Rubble trench*

- *Damp proofing.* Both the wood and straw elements you place on your foundation are the most prone to rot due to moisture damage. Some kind of isolation strategy must be in place, which could include foam sill gaskets, poly vapor barriers, asphalt paint, tar paper, or any other long-lasting, waterproof material. Use wood species like cedar that are naturally more resistant to moisture damage. If you must use pressure-treated lumber, be aware that some types are more toxic than others.

12.2b: *Slab detail (with hoses)*

- *Elevation above grade.* Your foundation material is capable of handling sub-grade and at-grade moisture and exposure; your walls are not. Make sure any wood and straw are at least 12 inches above the finished grade.

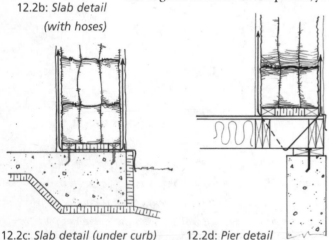

12.2c: *Slab detail (under curb)*   12.2d: *Pier detail*

12.2 a - d: *The same kind of thinking goes into bale/foundation junctions regardless of the kind of foundation being used. Bale curbs elevate the bales from the floor height, a base flashing keeps the seam dry, and both plaster skins bear on the foundation.*

- *Curbs or toe-ups.* These wooden runners serve several purposes: they help to elevate the bales above the finished floor level, in case of interior flooding; they provide attachment points for mesh, flashing, and trim; they provide guides for placing the first course of bales; they provide a channel under the wall for routing wiring; and they are good plaster stops.

- *Flashing.* The base of a wall is where all the rain running down the wall will accumulate. A flashing strategy must be employed to ensure that this moisture cannot end up running or wicking under the wall.

- *Anchor points.* The wooden curb rails must be anchored to the foundation, as do any posts and rough framing bucks. For load-bearing walls, the compression system for the bale walls also needs an attachment point or a route through the foundation.

- *Insulation strategy.* A great deal of your heating energy can be lost if your foundation is not properly insulated. Take care to prevent all thermal bridging at this critical junction, both above and below grade. If you can successfully integrate all of these considerations into a foundation detail, then it will serve its purpose.

- *Cantilevered floors.* A wooden floor system can be cantilevered past the edge of the foundation wall or beam so that the bales are centered over the foundation wall. This allows for a bit more room on the floor of the house without requiring a larger foundation footprint.

Bale Curbs

The bale curbs (also known as toe-ups) consist of two pieces of wood spaced apart to match the width of the bales. We use them on every type of foundation because they serve so many useful purposes. How you place these curbs will help to determine the final finish of the walls and will have implications at many stages in the bale raising. Here are some guidelines for curb design details in your plans.

Width

Make sure your curb rails reflect the real-world dimensions of your bales. Many designs assume a certain standard dimension for bales, but not all bales match these standards. Since a difference in spacing of an inch or two will make a big difference during construction and plastering, know the accurate bale dimensions prior to creating the detail drawings, and ensure that the drawings reflect these dimensions. It may be more difficult to draw a 19-inch spacing than a more even 18 inches, but it will save many hours on the jobsite if it's drawn properly in the first place. There are many ways to space the curb rails, and each will result in a different finish:

- *Directly in line with bales.* It is common to arrange the curbs so they are directly aligned with the inside and outside faces of the bales. In this case, the interior plaster will cover the wooden rail and finish directly on the floor. The exterior plaster will also cover the wood, and in this case it is very important that the curb rail be set back from the edge of the foundation by ¾ to 1 inch, so that the plaster skin is bearing on the foundation, not overhanging it. *Overhanging plaster is not able to transmit loads to the foundation directly,*

resulting in a wall that is not as strong.

- *Set wider than the bales.* The inside, outside, or both curb rails can be set ¾ to 1-inch wider than the bales. In this scenario, the plaster will finish on top of the rail, leaving the face of the wood exposed. The wood then acts as a finishing line for the plaster, and the exposed wood can be used to attach trim after plastering.

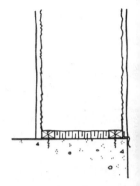

12.3a

- *Overhanging the foundation.* The outside curb rail can extend beyond the edge of the foundation, and with a bevel cut on the top and a drip kerf grooved into the bottom, it can be part of the flashing strategy. In this scenario, the wood must be properly treated to handle exposure to the weather, and the plaster must bear on this wood such that loads are still traveling into the foundation. This usually involves a rail of wider dimensions (2-by-6 or greater).

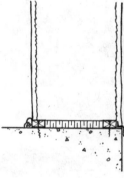

12.3b

Height

The most common curb rails are 2-by-3s or 2-by-4s laid on their flat side, providing a toe-up of 1.5 inches. If more height from the foundation is required, these rails can be placed on their edges, and larger dimensions of lumber can be used. In such cases, blocking should be run between the rails at regular intervals to tie them together, where compression wires will be run in load-bearing buildings.

In areas with seismic activity, the curb rails are typically larger in dimension, from 4-by-4 to 6-by-6. These become part of

12.3a - b: *Above, the curb rails are spaced to allow the plaster to bear directly on the foundation/floor. below, the curb is set wider to allow the plaster to finish on top of the wood, leaving a nailing face exposed for trim. The curb could also be outset on the outside edge, depending on the flashing detail.*

the strategy to ensure the wall maintains its integrity under earthquake conditions.

Insulation

Insulation materials to be used between curb rails should ideally combine three key properties: impervious to moisture, well-draining, and rigid. It is common to use rigid foam insulation here, but it does not allow for good drainage should water enter the wall. Pea gravel is also used, but it doesn't offer much insulating value. The best insulations are vermiculite, pumice stone, or foam balls. Drainboard insulations can also be used, but their effectiveness at draining is much poorer when used horizontally.

12.4a

12.4b

12.4a - b: Two volunteers fall victim to sharp rebar pins and clutch their shins in pain! The dark patch at the base of the rebar pin shows the serious accumulation of moisture that a pin can allow into the bale wall. It is next to impossible to seal the wall effectively against rising moisture around the pins.

Rebar Foundation Pins

Rebar foundation pins were used in earlier straw bale buildings to impale the first course of bales. We strongly discourage their use. A wall that is built without pins will not differ appreciably in stability or structural strength from a wall with pins.

Rebar pins are a nuisance to place during foundation construction and often end up being poorly embedded and floppy. They unfailingly do damage to knees and shins and pose a serious safety hazard. If someone fell on one they would certainly be hauled off in an ambulance .... or worse! They also make the important task of sealing the foundation from the bales virtually impossible and may provide a place for migrating moisture to condense inside your bale walls. Without pins, you'll save time, money, and eliminate a high embodied energy material that is simply not necessary.

If you live in an area where the use of pins is prescribed, you may want to express your disapproval, but you'll need to abide by the code until it is changed. Make sure you seal any pins you do use with a generous amount of tar or asphalt at the base.

If you are concerned about impaling your bales on something, drive some nails into the tops of the curb rails and leave them proud by 1.5 to 2 inches. This will provide plenty of resistance to slippage

Door and Window Bucks

There are as many ways of making door and window bucks as there are bale builders. Your design will have to take into account several factors.

Choice of Finish

How you want your building to look will be the biggest determining factor in the design of your bucks. Narrow bucks will allow for significant rounding or carving around windows and doors. Full-width bucks will result in squared openings, typically finished in wood. You can combine different widths for the top, the sides, and the sill to create different appearances. This is a place to be creative!

Size of Opening

Because both post and beam and load-bearing bale walls use some form of heavy beam at the top of the wall, most rough bucks need only be strong enough to handle the weight of the bales that rest on them. Structural loads from the roof will be carried into the wall via the beam or top plate (which can be beefed up over wide openings).

Therefore, heavyweight lintels are usually not required over the windows and doors, and small dimension lumber can be used. But in the case of larger openings (greater than four feet) it may be necessary to have a more substantial header on your rough frames. We often use a box beam in these situations.

Plaster Finish

The placement of your bucks will determine the finish of your plaster. Bucks set flush with the straw will be covered with plaster, and the plaster itself will use the installed window or door as a stop. Bucks set ¾ to 1 inch beyond the face of the straw will themselves act as plaster stops, leaving an exposed wooden face for attaching trim.

Moisture Control

Your rough buck can play an important role in moisture control. Bottom sills that slope downward a few degrees will help to shed water. Bottom sills that protrude beyond the face of the bales by two inches or more can act as a drip edge if a saw kerf is cut on the underside. Gluing or caulking all the joints in the buck will help stop water leaks from entering the bale walls. The bucks can provide attachment points for whatever flashings you decide to use.

12.5a - e: A buck must be designed that will create the kind of window opening you want. Combinations of flat and rounded elements will give different effects. The key is to ensure that upper and lower edges are well sealed and flashed against leaks, since this is the most vulnerable point in your wall

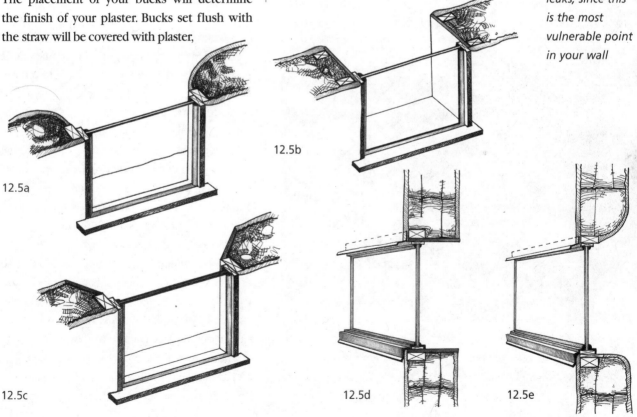

12.5a

12.5b

12.5c

12.5d

12.5e

Positioning in the Wall

One of the most common failure points for straw bale walls in wet and northern climates is below the window openings. Why? Too many builders set the window bucks back in the wall

SANDRA ZABLUDOFSKY

RICARDO STERNBERG

12.6a

12.6b

12.6a - b: *If the sills for a rough buck are notched into the uprights on the inside and front edges, then glued or caulked into the grooves, the rough bucks themselves become an excellent defense against moisture penetration. Give the rough sills a slight slope downward to the outside, allow them to extend well beyond the plaster and cut a groove on the underside to act as a drip kerf.*

HANK CARR

HANK CARR

12.7a

12.7b

12.7a - b: *A beautiful arched window opening requires proper detailing in your plans, and in execution. The framework, the straw and the mesh must all come together to create the desired effect.*

to achieve that southwestern look of the rounded plaster sill. This is a bad idea in places where it rains and snows! Setting bucks and windows to the outside of the wall (along with a good flashing strategy) helps to ensure that water running down windows is shed away from the wall, not ducted into it. It also gives snow nowhere to accumulate. *Only* if a window is extremely well protected by a porch or significant roof overhang should the window be set into the wall. The best strategy is to keep the window to the outside of the wall and save the wide sill for the interior. Door frames have more latitude, since there is no bale wall beneath. Be aware, however, that if the door frame is set in partially or fully, that water will need to be kept out of the junction at the base of the wall with flashing and/or caulking.

Lumber for rough frames is usually 2-by-6, and where sheet lumber is used, it is typically Oriented Strand Board (OSB). The frames must be built to be strong enough to handle the rigors of a bale raising, which includes the use of some temporary cross-bracing to keep them square. The rough frame bucks installed in the bale wall will provide a place to attach the actual windows and doors. Design and construction of the rough frame bucks are open to a certain amount of improvisation by the builder as long as the above principles are adhered to.

Some builders make floating rough window bucks which sit on the appropriate course of bales. Others prefer secured bucks, which have legs that are attached to the foundation or the curb rails. We prefer bucks with legs, since they can be put in place prior to the bale raising (i.e., not positioned at the whim of the bale stackers!) and are easier to keep securely in position through the bale raising and prior to plastering.

Bale Heights

Bale heights are an important consideration at the planning stage, especially for post and beam structures. Nothing is more frustrating than stacking bales into a frame that is just a little bit taller or shorter than an even number of courses of bales! Set your post heights based on the actual dimensions of the bales you will be using. It is best to make the finished height one to four inches shorter than the stack of bales, since they will do some settling on their own and are easier to work with if placed tightly into the frame, not loosely.

Bale heights can also be taken into account when you are designing window and door openings. Rough bucks or windows that correspond to bale heights will help solve annoying stacking difficulties, especially if you decide to use floating bucks.

Roof Plates for Load-bearing Designs

The top plate plays an important role in load-bearing designs, acting as a lintel over window and door openings and providing the stiffness required to transfer the loads of precompression

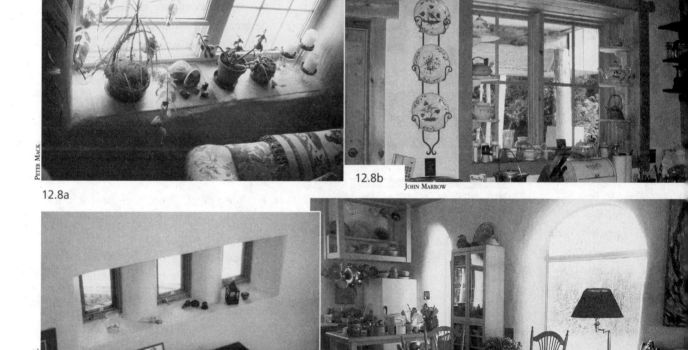

12.8a

PETER MACK

12.8b

JOHN MARROW

12.8c

TINA THERRIEN

12.8d

JOY ALLAN

12.8a - d: *Whether you want your window openings to be completely squared, a flat sill with rounded sides, or completely rounded, the buck underneath all that straw and plaster must form the desired shape.*

evenly over the top of the wall. As with window bucks, there are many ways to create a top plate for a load-bearing wall. A good top plate should do the following:

- *Provide adequate structural support.* Remember that the top plate needs to be just strong enough to transfer loads into the bale walls. It is only over wide openings that it plays a large structural role. Therefore, it is best to size the top plate

12.9a

12.9a - b: *Top plates can be built many ways. Our favorite is 9a, in which a small box beam is placed on the bales, and lightly larger lumber is fastened to the sides after compression is complete. 9b is similar, but uses wooden I-beams to create the box.*

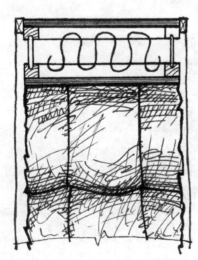

12.9b

on the smaller side and simply double or triple up on the rails over openings than it is to use vast amounts of lumber around the entire wall. When beefing up a top plate over wide openings, be sure to extend the extra lumber beyond the width of the opening below by 12 to 18 inches.

- *Provide precompression support.* When precompressing the walls, the top plate must be able to distribute those point loads evenly over the top of the wall without significant bending or twisting. The top plate should also provide a route for the compression wires or straps that allows them to run on, or close to, the surface of the wall. Depending on the top plate design, this may require drilling holes or cutting channels to allow the wires or straps to sit tight against the bales. Otherwise they will be in the way during plastering. Blocking should always go across the top plate wherever a compression wire or strap will be run to prevent the force from buckling the sides. Place blocking to correspond with the roof framing.

- *Provide a plaster stop.* Regardless of how you'd like to finish your plaster at the top of the wall, your top plate can provide the guideline. Some designs leave the faces of the top plate exposed for trimming, others bury them in plaster, but either way be sure your design creates the opportunity for the finish you'd like.

- *Provide water protection.* The top plate is a good defense against water penetrating the core of your bale wall, which is where it will do the most damage. Top plate designs should fully cover the top of the wall, and joints in materials should be caulked and/or overlapped. We often incorporate a strip of vapor barrier plastic over the top of the plate, covered by the top piece of plywood.

- *Provide a tie-in for the ceiling barrier.* The junction between the top plate and the ceiling is one of the greatest potentially leaky spots in a bale building. We incorporate a strip of vapor barrier plastic behind the rail of the top plate and make sure that a tail is left protruding from the top plate so the ceiling vapor barrier can be caulked or taped to it. This barrier will also run behind the plaster at the top of the wall, sealing the inevitable crack between the plaster and the top plate.

- *Concrete option.* A concrete top plate is formed in place on top of the bale wall. Wooden forms remain to provide an attachment point for stucco mesh and/or trim. Rebar is used and the thickness of the roof plate is determined by the openings it is has to span. A concrete roof plate provides a tight seal against the top of the bale wall. Its weight consumes some of the dead load capacity of the wall.

Precompression Details

Whatever system of precompression you use for a load-bearing structure, it will take some planning to ensure that the placement of attachment points is accurate and useful. Always plan to have precompression points within one to two feet of every inside corner, and keep the spacing to approximately four feet between points. Where wide openings are planned — sliding doors, large windows — precompression points should be located as close to the opening as possible,

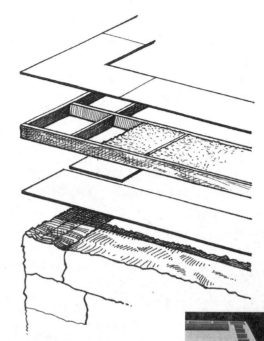

12.10: *The corners of the top plate receive an L-shaped piece of plywood on top for extra stability and to ensure squareness.*

without interfering with the buck frame or the plastering finish.

You must avoid precompression points that run through a window or door opening. You can plan for more attachment points than are necessary and then choose the ones that are appropriate once the walls have been constructed and doors and windows have been placed.

Post and Beam Details

Post and beam designs must be carefully adapted for use with straw bales to ensure that the two elements integrate well. First decide where to place the framework. It can be set interior to the bale walls, buried in them, or set exterior to them.

12.11: *The top plate for a load-bearing building is usually a simple affair: two side rails, some blocking, and a plywood base. It will be built on the foundation prior to the bales being raised. The cavities will be filled with insulation and the box topped with plywood once it is in place.*

Internal frames, left exposed inside the building, can add to, or detract from, the finished appearance of your home depending on the materials you've used. Internal frames can be created completely within the bale walls (ensure enough space is planned for plastering behind them), flush to the face of the bales, or set back into the bales.

In many internal frame scenarios, the plaster must make a seam with the post. Because the plaster won't make an airtight seal at this junction — due to shrinkage during curing — a vapor barrier (with diamond lath covering it) is attached to the back side of the post and extended two inches over the straw before the straw is installed. The vapor barrier is thus keyed into the plaster and creates a continuous air barrier even when the plaster shrinks from the post. The same procedure can be used to tie the ceiling vapor barrier into the wall around the beams. Some caulking applied after the second coat of plaster has cured will further help to minimize air leakage at the post/plaster seam.

Buried frames allow for a seamless plaster finish inside the house but can require the time-consuming and often inaccurate notching of bales to accommodate the frame members within the wall. If the bales can be placed to minimize or eliminate notching, it will save a great deal of time and effort. Frame systems with members that are the full width of the bales can avoid bale notching.

Frames built outside the wall envelope make for simpler roof construction, but the foundation of the building must be larger to accommodate the frame, or individual piers must be poured for the posts. Exterior posts will be exposed to the elements and may require treatment to prevent early decay.

Roof Plates for Post and Beam Designs

For post and beam designs, the roof plate is simply a plywood baffle, or barrier, under which the top course of bales comes to rest. It provides protection against pests and moisture (from possible roof leakage), a point of attachment for stucco mesh, and a plaster stop. Often this plate is caulked to the beam. If this plywood barrier is cut ¾ to 1 inch wider than the bales on both sides, it becomes a good plaster stop and provides a good edge for abutting the finished ceiling material inside and the soffit material outside. Don't forget that this plywood baffle will also be

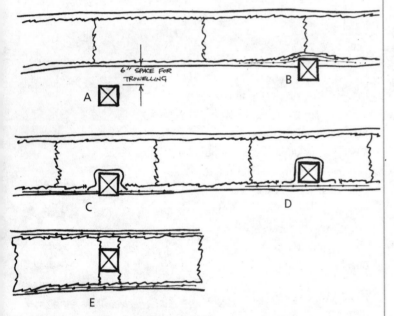

6" SPACE FOR TROWELLING

12.12: *All of these options for post and beam junctions are viable. A shows the post set far enough from the bales to allow for plastering. B, C and D show the post set into the bale wall at various depths. For these options, a vapor barrier runs behind the post and over the face of the bales, covered by mesh, to prevent air leakage from the plaster/post seam. E shows the post buried in the wall, with stuffing to fill in the gaps and mesh spanning over the stuffed areas.*

required on the underside of the trusses if the bales are to extend up into the gables.

Wherever possible, avoid having to cut or stuff bales around roof or ceiling joists, or into awkward angled spaces. These areas always create problems during bale stacking and plastering and are best avoided. Bales like to come to rest against flat surfaces; if you have angles to deal with, try to do so with the attic insulation or with other materials. If not, you will add more time and more possibilities for air leaks in your wall.

Plaster Finishing Considerations

At the planning stage, it's a good idea to think about the kind of finishing details you want for the plaster. Bull nose finishes require no pre-planning and tend to look somewhat random unless the plasterers are top-notch. Nailer strips and the wider top plates must be accounted for during the planning stage. The finish at the floor can likewise be affected by your choices of curb design — plaster can end on the floor/foundation or on the curb itself.

Ceiling and Floor Insulation

Regardless of the type of insulation you choose for your ceiling and floors — bales, batts, loose blown, or rigid — don't skimp on quantity. Your ceiling insulation should at least match the R-value of your bale walls — R-40 or more. Your floor should be insulated adequately for your climate and foundation style (heat does radiate and conduct downward, too!). Otherwise, the benefits of your highly insulating straw bale walls will be lessened.

Asking Questions of Your Plans

It is a good idea to ask yourself a series of questions as you scrutinize your plans. The world's best authors have editors and proofreaders; your plans will benefit from a similar third-party reading. Friends and family may be able to help a little, but someone with building experience will be most helpful. It may even be worth it to pay a professional builder to review your plans. If you can find someone who has had some experience building with bales, all the better.

Run your plans through a philosophical checklist to be sure they fulfill your original intentions. Is the house the right size? Does it contain the kinds of rooms you wanted? Does its appearance suit your esthetic sense and the landscape it will occupy? On a more practical note, do some budget estimates. By this point, you'll be able to do an accurate tally of all required components, including lumber, doors, windows, roofing, concrete, and interior finishing. Give your plans to professionals who can generate estimates for materials and labor.

Check your plans for buildability. Do all your measurements pan out? Will the intersections of different components be possible to construct as drawn? Do measurements make sense — lengths,

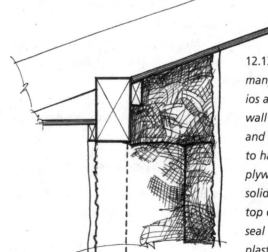

12.13: *There are so many possible scenarios at the top of the wall when using post and beam. The key is to have a baffle of plywood or other solid material at the top of the straw to seal it and provide a plaster stop.*

widths, and spans? Where there are interruptions in wall or roof directions, can the transitions be achieved without undue hassle? Will gravity pull water into the building? Will your finishing components — plaster, drywall, wood, etc. — be well detailed, with accurate starting, finishing, and attachment points? Have you planned adequately for the installation of the bale walls? Sufficient roof overhangs, raised curbs, and flashing? Does the height of your

12.14: Don't let the square page fool you into making everything square. Bale walls can be curved, sculpted and oriented to create unique spaces. Some of this can happen spontaneously on site, but it's usually best to plan for it ahead of time.

walls correspond to even bale heights? Do you understand how you will achieve directional changes with your top plate? Do your window and door bucks correspond with bale heights and your desired finish?

With carefully considered drawings prepared, your troubleshooting scrutinizing process can begin in earnest.

Making Changes Can Make Problems

Changes and corrections made to plans must be executed carefully. Every alteration can have implications that affect the whole building, so if you change or correct one dimension, you must follow through and make sure that the rest of your plans are adapted to this change. Consider how changes you make will affect the spacing of framing members, the dimensions of rooms, the foundation, and the roof. If you've spent time trying to make the most effective use of materials, don't forget that changes to your plans may result in odd sizing for lumber and sheet materials.

The Detail That Got Away

Most plans are bound to contain some contradictions, problems, and minor inconsistencies. A thorough study can help to reveal most of these errors. What details escape notice will have to be dealt with during construction. When you are satisfied that you are ready and able to begin construction, it's time to submit your plans for approval. Or, if you don't require approval, it's time to start building!

Have a Party

Finished and approved plans call for a celebration! You will be poised on the brink of your building adventure, and you'll have made it through the long and often difficult planning process. Blow off some steam and regenerate your excitement and enthusiasm before you grab your tools and start building!

Resources

Magwood, Chris and Chris Walker. *Straw Bale Details: A Manual for Designers and Builders.* New Society Publishers, 2002. ISBN 0-86571-476-2

CHAPTER 13

Building Permits

Difficulties in pursuading code officials to accept the use of straw bales in construction is the single largest hurdle facing the growth of bale building at this time. However, if you go about the process in a well-considered manner, obtaining a permit is not necessarily a barrier.

About Codes

If you are committed to building with bales, you will be able to get a permit for a soundly designed structure. It may be issued with a minimum of concern and hassle, or it may take several months — or more, in rare cases — to meet the demands of code officials. With each new project that gains approval, however, a greater precedent is set for the acceptance of straw bale construction.

What Is the Building Code?

Building codes are fascinating, and no two are the same. Most municipal authorities require that builders obtain a permit to construct or renovate a building. This is issued when a project is deemed to meet all the necessary provisions of the applicable building code.

Both the United States and Canada have national building codes. States and provinces fine tune these codes to suit their own purposes.

Local governments — charged with the authority to implement, regulate, and enforce the codes — can fine tune them even further. Regional variations to the codes usually address specific climatic concerns such as seismic activity, snow loads, depth of frost penetration, as well as zoning or property use issues. Considerations such as minimum and maximum building size, appearance restrictions, and water and waste management are also decided regionally. A building permit, once issued, provides information to the municipality for the assessment of property taxes.

Straw bale building is not currently prescribed by any national building codes, although some state and regional prescriptions do now exist in the United States, including all, or parts, of Arizona, California, Colorado, and New Mexico. Some European countries are also beginning to set standards. As the demand for straw bale structures grows, more national, state, provincial, and regional building codes will begin to adopt provisions for straw bale construction, and the process of obtaining permits will be greatly simplified. Until then, most straw bale builders will have to apply for permits on a case-by-case basis.

Same Code, Different Interpretations

The building code is enforced by individual code officials, all of whom have varying levels of knowledge, experience, and comfort with new ideas. The exact same building code can receive quite radically different treatment depending on the personality of the official involved.

We have all received both good and bad service from public officials in our lives, and working with a building inspector is open to the same range of service. Depending on where you live and your local inspector's level of interest in alternative building practices, you may be dealing with somebody who has never heard of bale construction before or with somebody with a high degree of awareness and interest. Chances are, though, your path to getting a straw bale building permit will likely involve some educating of your building inspector.

Get to Know Your Code

Most states and provinces publish their building codes in builder-friendly editions or make the relevant sections available through the municipality. The time you take to familiarize yourself with the code can be worth its weight in gold.

From a Skeptic to a Believer

During a class at the 1994 Annual Business Meeting of the International Conference of Building Officials (ICBO) in Indianapolis, I experienced a major change in my views of code interpretation. The instructor, Mr. Brent Snyder of ICBO, brought to our attention the preface page of Volume I of the newly formatted 1994 edition of the Uniform Building Code (UBC).

He asked us to read the first paragraph. He pointed out that this was the mission statement of the UBC. The second sentence of this statement really caught my attention: "The code is founded on broad based principles that make possible the use of new materials and new construction systems." This simple statement brought me up short. I realized that I had an obligation to look at all systems with an open mind.

In December I was given the task of hosting the Colorado ICBO Chapter meeting slated for August, 1995. I was even given the theme of alternative building systems. So I asked several members, "What kind of alternative systems are you interested in?" The answers were usually, "Oh, you know, those tire houses and straw houses." I had heard of tire houses, but straw houses? You've got to be kidding, I thought. Fate and chance were going to play a role in my search for these systems in the months ahead. A trip to Cortez, Colorado, to visit my son brought me into direct contact with my first straw bale structure. My son was helping to build it!

What I saw impressed me. "Where did you find out about this?" I asked. "From Out On Bale in Tucson, Arizona," was the reply. Bingo, I had a contact, a starting point.

Back in Pueblo I used the phone to locate Out On Bale and was advised by a friendly person there to contact Matts Myhrman and David Eisenberg. I left a message for either of them to call me. A call from Matts quickly indicated to ☞

You might find that there are special provisions for alternative or experimental building systems in your code, or perhaps there is an owner-builder clause that removes liability from the municipality and places it back on you. These options are easy to research — call your local building department. Knowing your local code will help you appear knowledgeable and responsible when you enter into discussions with your inspector and can go a long way to helping you receive favorable treatment.

Dealing with Officials

Approaching Inspectors

Often, the liability-driven nature of the building inspection profession will prevent you from getting any direct answers from your inspector until you present working plans. If you are reluctant to proceed through the planning process without some positive indications from your inspector, you must be sure to ask answerable questions (i.e., don't ask if straw bale homes are permitted, ask what provisions exist to allow for alternative building materials). Otherwise, it is usually best to proceed with your plans and work things out with your inspector over the plans themselves.

If you approach your inspector early, inquire about his or her familiarity with bale construction. Ask if he or she is aware of other bale structures in the region — you should already know the answer! Ask which code provisions affect straw

me that I was dealing with a very knowledgeable and professional person. Matts was very interested in being part of the program in Pueblo. He even suggested I meet him at a seminar he was doing in Carbondale, Colorado, in mid June, just weeks away. In spite of the favorable impression I had of Matts, my skepticism about straw as a viable building material was still high. I told him I'd see him there and we'd iron out the details for the program in Pueblo.

The program was outstanding. Over 52 building officials from across Colorado listened intently as Matts and David put on their program, which was very well received. The next day we had a hands-on program and built a straw bale wall. In the minds of those who participated, straw bale construction took quantum leaps. Its validity as a building material passed the test. I had learned that the word "alternative" was a misnomer. Here was a material that was environmentally acceptable and would offer an R-factor of as much as 50. I was hooked.

I saw it as a material we could use in our often frustrating search for affordable housing. Here was a material that doesn't require a lot of expertise to install and isn't labor intensive either.

One of my children, after hearing me expound on the virtues of straw as a building material, said "My old red necked, conservative dad is turning into an environmentalist!" I would rather they call me a practical man. But it's a fact that our infatuation with timber is reaching crisis stage. An average single family home uses 55 mature trees in its framing and trim lumber. I feel, as Building Official and Code Enforcement staff, we have, as our mission says, a real responsibility to look at these emerging alternative systems.

— Clint Tawse, Pueblo, Colorado, Building Official

■

bale design — again, it helps to know already. Ask if he or she would like any information about straw bale design and research. Expect noncommittal answers. There is very little chance a code official will say, "Yes, by all means build with straw bales. I'd have no problem with that." Still, you may observe enough about his or her personality and openness to make it easier for you to go ahead.

Being Open and Friendly

It is best to maintain an open, friendly attitude toward your building inspector. Remember, it's his or her job to allow building, not to prevent it. Ideally, inspectors are there to assist as you build the home you want. Begin with this attitude, rather than with a confrontational one. Try to avoid criticizing conventional construction, since inspectors are closely connected to conventional practices. Express a general familiarity with the building code. Stress the many positive reasons for choosing straw bale, and let your inspector know that you are willing to be a reasonable working partner in achieving code compliance for your straw bale plans. While there is plenty of opportunity to go over the head of your inspector, this should only be a last resort.

Make Mine Straw!

Shortly after taking my first building department job, I had the fortunate opportunity to attend what I consider the best meeting ever held by the Colorado Chapter of the International Code Council. It was the summer of 1995, and one of our more enthusiastic and colorful members, Pueblo Colorado Building Official Clint Tawse, had the task of doing a segment on alternate methods and materials.

This usually implies dreary dissertations on engineered wood products or the latest plumbing gizmos. But not this time. Clint had the audacity to parade true alternative pioneers Matts Myhrman of Out On Bale, David Eisenberg of the Development Center for Appropriate Technology, and Dennis Weaver (actor and earthship advocate) past a bunch of hardheaded and wary inspectors. Prior to this meeting, I had never even heard of straw bale construction. By the end of the two-day session, I was even given the opportunity to build with it. One touch and I found that it left an indelible impression branded permanently on my soul.

Straw bale is the alternative to all of the alternatives. With so many choices available, it remains at the pinnacle. What other material can claim the insulative superiority, ease of construction, aesthetic qualities, and environmental friendliness that straw does? Where else can you find something that is locally packaged as a waste product where disposal can result in the achievement of the American Dream of homeownership? So with all of these wonderful qualities, why does it seem so darn hard to get a building permit?

Straw is an anathema, at least as far as the building industry is concerned. There is simply too much of it available to control, standardize, and monopolize. As a result, there is not enough financial impetus to research, draft, and argue prescriptive requirements for inclusion in the model building codes. Without the endorsement of codification, we are forced to qualify its existence one building department at a time. ☞

The Straw Bale Precedent

As more bale buildings are erected, precedent makes it more likely that permits will be issued. Being prepared with facts, figures, and contact names and numbers — especially of other inspectors who have approved straw buildings — is important. While the existing straw bale building codes have no legal status outside their jurisdictions, a building inspector provided with such information may be more willing to proceed, using the terms of those codes as a starting place for understanding bale construction. If you should happen to find a building inspector who is enthusiastic about straw bale,

you have a valuable resource on your hands. Ask if he or she is willing to be used as a reference for other bale builders in the same area.

The Architect and Engineer's Stamp

You can address many of the building officials' concerns by presenting plans that have been stamped by an architect and/or an engineer. This approval often removes some of the weight of liability from the building official's shoulders and places it on the professional. Your building inspector may require professionally stamped plans before approving a bale design, in which case you don't have much choice but to commission

I often see land advertised in straw bale-friendly publications as having "no building codes." I am not surprised that straw proponents are disheartened with slow and onerous local approval processes. Unfortunately it is the price of pioneering. Today, it is hard to fathom that it took nearly 100 years of practice with 2-by-4 stick framing before it was included in a building code. It takes a lot of trial and error before a process is perfected, and straw bale construction is certainly no exception.

One way or another, you will have to interact with your local building inspector. Think of it as an adventure to a foreign country. You might want to read up on the local customs and language before going. That means knowing and understanding the local building code and alternative methods approval processes. Compile and organize as much governmental and academic data as possible. Be prepared to address moisture management, load transference, lateral stability, fire resistance, and termite control. Most important, be prepared with a good attitude. You may be surprised how helpful the local building officials will be when you try to speak their language. If you are uncomfortable with building codes, consider bringing along an interpreter. That might be a local architect or engineer with straw bale experience or somebody who was successful with a straw bale approval in another jurisdiction. Most areas have professional building code consultants who might assist. Consider contacting the individuals and organizations listed in this book for advice. Don't be discouraged; you are not the first person to obtain a permit for a straw bale building!

My next house will be straw bale!

— *Thomas Meyers, Colorado Code Consulting, LLC, 811 Fourth St., Berthoud, CO 80513*
303.895.9988, <tmeyers99@hotmail.com>

■

them. You don't want to learn about this requirement on the day you submit your plans! If stamped plans are required, have them prepared before you make an application.

Good Plans Are the Key to a Building Official's Heart

Comprehensive, clear, and accurate plans are the key to impressing a building inspector; the merit of your plans will determine his or her final decision. Be sure to provide references for all aspects of your design that can be related to the building code. Especially on home-drawn plans, these references prove that you have done your homework and don't intend to circumvent the code, even unknowingly. Plans should be large, legible, and contain explanatory notes or supplementary drawings where details vary from standard practice. Many aspects of your plans are likely to be straightforward adaptations of the conventional building practices familiar to building officials. As the unusual element in your plans, bale wall details should be presented clearly and precisely and contain references to existing standards and tests where applicable.

Safety is a key issue for building inspectors, so include references to safety oriented clauses — sizing and placement of indoor and outdoor stairways and handrails, entrances and exits from the building, smoke and carbon dioxide detectors, etc. Make note of the span charts

An Interview with Bob Fowler

Q: Why have you been willing to support the efforts of the straw bale construction community to reintroduce this building method?

A: There are probably a dozen reasons. First, I have an adventurous spirit and see the need for finding more sustainable ways to build. I also have a farming background and know the properties of straw and the disposal problems straw in the field presents to farmers. So I appreciate that these problems can be turned into assets. As an architect and an engineer, as well as a builder, I find straw bale something I can really get excited about. Not just for the fact that you can build very good-looking buildings with it, but for the environmental reasons, the energy efficiency, and the affordability of it.

Q: The straw bale construction revival has been unique in that it is a very popular older building material that lacks the large quantified base of data we have for most other building systems. As a building official who has been supportive of this way of building, how do you respond to this?

A: When someone comes in with a material that has a documented history, but no certified testing data, my suggestion is that we let them build an experimental structure, within our code jurisdiction. This is an opportunity to raise the level of comfort of the building officials. I'd also encourage doing a house, rather than a nonresidential structure. A residence will be a better demonstration of the technology, and there are so many good things about straw bale construction that I'd prefer a house were built to be lived in. People are more likely to be influenced by a beautiful straw bale home, because they will be able to relate to a home better than other buildings. ☞

used for major framing components — floor joists and roof. If you are using manufactured trusses, be sure to note this on your plans. Approved drawings from the truss company can be supplied later, as long as you inform the inspector.

The role of the building inspector is not to prevent you from building but to ensure that your building is structurally sound and meets all safety objectives. Rarely does a building inspector completely reject a viable set of plans. In most jurisdictions, building is encouraged because you will be adding to the permanent tax base. Ample evidence now exists to prove the safety and viability of straw bale construction. Getting approval is a matter of providing enough of this evidence to satisfy your particular inspector.

Other Submission Documents

Don't assume that just submitting a set of plans is enough to get a permit. Some bale builders get so focused on the plans, they forget all the other components of the application. Site maps and surveys, water tests or wells, septic permits, driveway allowances, zoning, property deeds, and many other documents will likely be required as part of your application. More straw bale plans have been turned down the first time because they were lacking some of these factors than because they were straw bale plans. Most municipalities have a package that contains all this

Q: What suggestions would you have for people when introducing the idea of straw bale construction to building officials who have never heard of it?

A: I think a wide variety of approaches is necessary. It's an education process. Let the building official know that this isn't a crackpot idea but a tried-and-true building method that's been used for years. Give the officials adequate material and don't push too hard. They see a lot of snake-oil artists and you don't want them to think you're pushing them into something. Give them time to review the information, put on a program to show them photos or books or videos. Use as many approaches as you can to educate them about it. You have to elevate their level of comfort.

Q: What suggestions would you have for those building officials?

A: Keep an open mind. We all need to understand that we have to embrace different methods of construction. We must find low-cost sustainable methods to build housing. Here is an opportunity to use a waste product. Express your concerns, ask your questions. Take the time to really look at it and learn about its history. I'm convinced that if you do, you'll get excited about it, too.

— From an interview by David Eisenberg, with Bob Fowler, FAIA, RE, C.B.O., originally published in The Last Straw, *no. 13, Spring, 1996 p. 4. Mr. Fowler was the chief building official for Pasadena, California, at the time of the interview, and was a past chairman of the board of the International Conference of Building Officials (ICBO), board member and vice-president of the World Organization of Building Officials (WOBO), and founding chairman of the board of the International Code Council (ICC). He was killed in a motorcycle accident in August 2001 — a huge loss — though he left behind a legacy of inspirational work, vision and leadership.* ■

information; make sure you get it early and meet all its requirements.

The Hassle Factor

Don't be discouraged by a negative response to your plans to build with straw. Be prepared to persist; many permits have been issued after an initial rejection of the idea. There are answers to all of your building inspector's questions and concerns, but you will have to make the effort to supply them. Remember that getting approval from your building department is not a one-shot, win-or-lose affair. It can be a process of change and exchange, in which modifications are made until both you and the building official are satisfied with the results.

Rejections and Appeals

In the rare case when approval from a local building official is not forthcoming, there is an appeals process, one that will vary between jurisdictions. Often you will find a higher authority who is willing to recognize the validity and importance of building with bales. The process might be short and informal, requiring only a call to a state or provincial bureaucrat or politician, or it may be long and legal, involving a quasi-judicial appeals process. Either way, if your plans are valid, the chances that you will be allowed to build are weighted in your favor and grow more favorable with each new approval for a straw bale design.

If you find yourself involved in an appeal, find out as much as you can about the process: who will hear your case, what your role in the hearing will be, and whether or not you would benefit from representation from a lawyer or building code consultant. There are professionals who specialize in representing clients before appeals boards, and their knowledge can be worth the expense. Whether or not you are professionally represented, make sure you have professional quality information and a demeanor to match.

Approval Can Take Time

Whatever you do, don't rush your building inspector by imposing your own deadlines and time frames. Approval can take one day or, in extreme cases, a year or more. Even if the inspector has no problem with straw bale construction, other adjustments to your plans may be required. Be patient and courteous during this process. Building inspectors wield a fair bit of authority and can choose to seriously delay your project. Maintaining a positive attitude is your best defense. Gaining permit approval can be a bit nerve-wracking, but it shouldn't deter you from putting your plans into action.

A Note on Straw Bale and Codification

Many efforts have been made to have straw bale construction included in building codes. As time goes on, these efforts are likely to meet with greater and greater success. Success creates both benefits and disadvantages to bale builders. Inclusion in the building code allows owner-builders to use the code to create their own plans with some confidence that they will receive approval. The elimination of architects and engineers from the planning process removes a significant cost from straw bale projects. On the downside, straw bale building is still at a very young stage in its development. While codification could make approvals simpler to obtain, it also poses the risk of freezing the technique before adequate experimentation leads us to sound standard practices.

Were building codes flexible in nature, immediate codification of straw bale would be an undeniable asset. However, codes tend to simplify, overprotect, and narrow options. It remains quite likely that as techniques, approaches, and our understanding of how bales work as a building material change for the better, they will outstrip the provisions of any existing codes and require a willingness on behalf of code officials to change and update their regulations.

Building codes in North America are currently undergoing substantial changes that may have positive effects for bale builders. Existing codes are largely prescriptive, meaning that they prescribe actual techniques, materials, and practices. But the next round of building codes are going to be performance based, meaning that performance parameters will be established, and any building system that can be shown to meet them should be accepted. With the available testing data for bale walls, meeting performance requirements will be much simpler than trying to fit bale building into the existing prescriptions.

We look forward to the day when straw bale construction is an accepted and widespread practice. We're also glad to still have some of the freedom made possible by the case-by-case nature of project approvals. Let the learning continue ....

An Interesting Comparison

When we think about materials and their acceptance, we should consider the reality in which we already operate. Joe Lstiburek of Building Sciences, Inc., a building consultant of the highest regard, has put the situation into perspective by describing the realities of using wood as a building material. He points out that wood, were it being introduced today as a new building material, could never get into the building codes. It has nearly every problem a material could conceivably have. There are hundreds of species. The strength and durability depends on the species, as well as some of the environmental conditions that occurred while it was growing. The strength depends on factors including the orientation of the grain, the age of the wood, how it was dried, moisture content, and the size, location and frequency of knots. It burns, it rots, and insects like to eat it. It is dimensionally unstable, it splits. And yet, in spite of all these problems, it is the material of choice in this country for residential construction, even though there are huge environmental problems associated with its profligate use. Of course it is a wonderful material. And there are reasons it is so widely used. But if a new material [like straw bale] is introduced with any one of the problems that wood has, it is nearly impossible to get it accepted into the codes.

— David Eisenberg's "Straw Bale Construction and the Building Codes: A Working Paper" is an excellent document concerning the ongoing process of making straw bale building viable. This excerpt from the website version of the Working Paper offers a profound perspective on the codification of bales. The printed version can be ordered from the Development Center for Appropriate Technology, PO Box 27513, Tucson, AZ 85726-7513, or you can view DCAT's excellent website at <www.dcat.net> ■

References

Appendix - The new California Code

Straw Bale Codes:

The following straw bale codes are available in Acrobat.pdf format for download from the DCAT website, <www.dcat.net>.

- Austin Straw Bale Code (20K)
- Boulder Straw Bale Code (16K)
- California Straw Bale Code (20K)
- Tucson/Pima County Straw Bale Code (24K)
- Tucson/Pima County Earthen Code (52K)

Eisenberg, David. "Straw Bale Construction and the Building Codes: A Working Paper." Development Center for Appropriate Technology, 1996. Available PO Box 27513, Tucson, AZ 85726-713 USA.

Eisenberg, David and Peter Yost. "Sustainability and the Building Codes," Environmental Building News, September 2001 (Vol. 10, No. 9) page 1.

King, Bruce, P. E. *Buildings of Earth and Straw: Structural Design for Rammed Earth and Straw Bale Architecture*. Ecological Design Press, 1997. ISBN 0-944718-1-7.

Lerner, Kelly and Pamela Wordsworth, eds., *Building Official's Guide to Straw Bale Construction*. California Straw Building Association, 2000.

Straw Bale Building: An Information Package for Building Officials in Ontario. Ontario Straw Bale Building Coalition, 2004. <info@strawbalebuilding.ca>, <www.strawbalebuilding.ca>

Bale Building Associations:

Architects/Developers/Planners for Social Responsibility/ADPSR, <www.adpsr.org>

AUSBALE, info Austrian StrawBale Network/ASBN, <www.baubiologie.at>

California Straw Building Association/CASBA, <www.strawbuilding.org>

Colorado Straw Bale Association/COSBA, <www.coloradostrawbale.org>

Development Centre for Appropriate Technology/DCAT, <www.dcat.net>

Ecological Building Network/EBNet, <www.ecobuildnetwork.org>

Irish Ecobuild Network, <www.irishecobuild.com>

MidAmerica Straw Bale Association/MASBA, <jc10508@alltel.net>

Northwest Eco-Building Guild/NWEBG, <www.ecobuilding.org>

Ontario Straw Bale Building Coalition, <www.strawbalebuilding.ca>

Straw Bale Association of Nebraska/SBAN, <www.strawhomes.com/sban>

Straw Bale Association of Texas/SBAT, <www.greenbuilder.com/sbat>

Straw Bale Building Association of Wales, Ireland, Scotland and England/WISE, <www.users.globalnet.co.uk/~straw>

CHAPTER 14

Do-It-Yourself (DIY) and Building Professionals

Your role in the creation of your straw bale home can vary from the purely administrative to the hands-on building of the entire structure. How you choose to employ yourself and others in the process requires careful consideration.

Some people know for certain that they want to build their own home. Others are equally certain that they want no part in the hands-on building. Still others take a middle path and hire professionals for particular aspects of the work or act as their own general contractor.

DIY

Most people can acquire the skills and learn to perform the tasks required for building their own houses. Even tasks that may seem unappealing can be undertaken if you are motivated by necessity, desire, or ambition! Books, manuals, and codes are readily available as reference material for every aspect of house building. Choose sources that reflect your perspectives and values. There is no point in following a guidebook written in a spirit that conflicts with yours.

For any given aspect of construction, you must understand why you are performing a task; to follow instructions without comprehending

their purpose is a recipe for error. If you can grasp the theory, its specific application in your building will follow much more easily. You do not have to cram an encyclopedic amount of information into your head at once — not many people can absorb and retain that much new

14.1: *Sometimes renting equipment and machinery, like this mini-excavator, can save an owner-builder money. But be sure to weigh up the extra time it can take to learn to do things yourself.*

information. Learn enough about each stage to know what specific planning is required, then set about each task individually and in the right order. Don't be afraid to tackle a job you're unsure about. Often it is only when you get your hands on the materials that you will understand what's required. You might make a mistake or two before it all comes clear, but if you wait until your theoretical understanding is flawless, you may never get your house built.

Professional Advice and DIYers

Often, the best way to learn how to do a particular task is to seek advice from an experienced professional. Many professionals have spent years learning the hard way, and the information they are able to convey is invaluable. While some may be willing to share their knowledge freely, you should never expect them to do so. Offer to pay for consulting time, and take them your plans and a list of specific questions. During your consultation, take notes, make drawings, and ask for clarification when you don't understand. Try to spend more time listening than talking, and avoid getting into arguments. By keeping the consultation positive and focused on an exchange of information, you will get the best possible return on your investment.

While time and money spent in consultation may seem to be expensive at first, a few big mistakes made by you can cost much more in the end. Even if you strongly disagree with the advice you are given, contradiction can pave the way to clearer understanding. If a professional advises against a given practice or idea, it is usually because he or she has had a bad experience with it and is trying to help you avoid a similar pitfall. You are always free to seek more than one opinion if you find yourself unconvinced.

Remember that professionals make their money by doing things in their own time proven way. They may discourage new approaches and techniques and will always present their own options in the best possible light. While they may be right according to their own practice, there is always more than one right answer. You need to find the professional whose attitudes and opinions are closest to your own.

Task Hiring

Some specialized tasks may be better left to professionals. While we encourage you to attempt as much of your project as you want, if you feel like you're in over your head, it may make sense to hire. Specific experience and proper equipment often allow professionals to do a job faster, more efficiently, and with fewer errors than you can, and you may find the cost is less than you expect. Let your own interests, skills, time allotment, and budget determine if you want to hire or not.

Building professionals cover the spectrum from highly skilled, enthusiastic practitioners to scam artists. Your hiring decisions will be based on a combination of factors, including the personality of the person you are considering. Do you get along with this person? Does he or she seem easy to talk with, open, honest, and forthright? If you are bringing particular values to the project — ecological awareness, attention to detail, or esthetics — does this person share or respect your values? Is he or she easy to reach, organized, and punctual? If a gut feeling attracts you to a particular professional or warns you away, listen to your instincts.

Experience is another important factor you will need to consider before you hire anyone. Someone with experience usually makes fewer errors, works faster, and uses materials effectively. But not always. On specialty projects like straw bale homes, someone who has performed the same set of standardized tasks hundreds of times may not be who you need. You need someone who can think, plan, and act to achieve particular goals. Ask to see pictures of the professional's work, or go and visit projects he or she has completed. Make sure you understand what kind of experience he or she has had and that it meets your needs.

Estimates and Contracts

As an owner-contractor, you should always try to obtain written estimates prior to hiring a building professional, and obtain a written, signed contract before work is undertaken.

Cost estimating is often a point of contention between owners and the professionals they hire. The owner wants to know the exact final cost of the task. The professional knows that there are usually enough variables in a project to make perfect estimates impossible. Furthermore, the professional also knows that quoting too high may scare away a prospective client; quoting too low may mean working for too little or having to charge extra after the fact.

You are best served by knowing, as accurately as possible, what the real cost of the task is going to be. This means you shouldn't always go with the lowest quote you receive. Allow other factors to enter into your decision: the professional's reputation, honesty, and thoroughness in the provided quote will all give you clues as to the accuracy of the price. Some professionals quote low just to get the job, and then end up charging you just as much (or more) as the more expensive initial quotes.

You will need to have multiple sets of plans, since each professional will likely require a set in order to accurately price a job. Be sure to give professionals enough lead time to work up quotes, and yourself enough time to properly research and consider them.

The contract you sign with a professional should be as comprehensive as possible. It should contain the scope of the work (i.e., a description and comprehensive list of the task(s) to be completed), a time frame, a price quote, and a list of requirements and understandings to cover both your needs and the professional's. The contract should also include a clear agreement on how cost over-runs are to be handled. Payment terms should be clear, as should warranty commitments. If you plan to use materials other than standard building supply yard fare — for cost or environmental reasons — be sure to specify these in the contract, along with who will be responsible for obtaining them. How will delays be handled? Make sure you allow yourself an option that releases you from the contract if the work cannot be performed on time.

Be prepared to meet with many people before you make a hiring decision. Try not to approach this process in an adversarial way; the people you hire will ideally be active and enthusiastic partners in the building process, helping to keep your project on time and on budget.

General Contractors
Owner as General Contractor

If you are going to hire all or most of the labor for your project, you will be fulfilling the role of general contractor. In commercial construction, general contractors oversee entire projects, for which they hire other individuals or companies to complete particular tasks.

General contracting can demand as much of your time as a full-time job. You must juggle the needs and schedules of many different professionals and are responsible for seeing that all work is done correctly and on time. It takes organizational skills, planning, and crisis-control abilities to keep a project running smoothly. The process can be rewarding, however, and allows you to be closely involved without requiring that you actually undertake the construction yourself.

Organize a project meeting; it will allow all parties concerned to meet and discuss your project. You will likely have to pay for the time the meeting takes, but the benefits to your project can far outweigh the costs. Plans can be reviewed and issues raised and solved with input from all parties. If the foundation builder understands what the carpenter needs, and the carpenter the bale raiser, etc., a much better project will result. You may be surprised to find out that professionals often don't meet onsite, but simply pick up where another tradesperson left off. The meeting, therefore, will give everyone a chance to confer, make sketches, and form a more complete understanding of the project. If an architect or engineer helped draw up the plans, be sure to invite him or her to the meeting. Try to work out a rough schedule and make lists of what each

The Owner as General Contractor

Basically, I think general contractors earn their money. General contracting is hard work, and you need lots of time to be able to do a good job. It was important to me that everybody I hired to work on the project was totally aligned with our goals and ideals. If a tradesperson wasn't supportive, I didn't want them on the project. You have to find people whose attitudes match your own. If any crews are resentful or aren't getting along with you, it can make it unpleasant to be at the building site. But you can't stay away; it's your house! So a good working relationship is a must. Right from the quoting process, you can tell if you're dealing with someone who's going to be thrilled to be involved. You can tell by the questions they ask and their language and attitude. It's not just the price to be watching for. We have a friend who is Cree, and he taught us that you leave your energy in anything you do. So make sure you like a person's energy before you hire them, because they're going to leave it behind in your house. The guys who did our post and beam frame always gave us updates and let us know their needs and schedules. You need that kind of relationship or you could really screw up. When it works, it's very exciting.

I had prior knowledge of other building types, having self-contracted a conventional home. But that didn't prepare me for the specifics of putting up the bales. I'd read a book and seen a video, but had no hands-on experience. As a result, I missed entire aspects of the process. Quilting the stucco mesh was a process I didn't even have in my schedule, and it took as much time as raising the bales. If you have the time to do it yourself and learn as you go, that's fine. But if you have a tight schedule, it's good to have someone knowledgeable to oversee the bale raising process, even if you're using volunteers. I also wasn't prepared for how much time it would take to call and arrange volunteers. Phoning and asking for help is not something I'm good at, and it was hard to do.

There is always the problem of running out of money. Don't forget to add in taxes when doing your budgeting! That extra percentage makes a big difference. Wood prices can change, too. Wood went up almost 40 percent ☞

professional requires of the other. Keep the meeting short and focused, and be sure everybody leaves with what they need to know.

If you are incorporating nonstandard materials in your project, be sure everybody knows what materials are to be used, where they can be sourced, and how they function in the building. Otherwise, most professionals will price, source, and buy materials based on their own experience and habits.

Building professionals usually work on a first-come, first-served basis; make sure you book your work early. In areas with harsh winters, building projects are crammed into a short, fran-

tic season, so trying to hire somebody mid-season can be difficult and frustrating.

Hiring a General Contractor

A general contractor's job is to provide you with a finished home that meets your expectations and demands. General contractors hire the appropriate professionals to build your house, on schedule and according to a determined budget. It is up to you to be sure your general contractor understands the requirements of your straw bale building. While you will be consulted during the construction process, contractor built homes are frequently a hands off option. Because the job

in the six months between getting the quotes and delivery. You've got to manage your money well, and know when to hold back and when to pay in full. You don't want to pay for a job that isn't done right.

When you're building a unique house, you've got to expect that something's going to happen that you didn't foresee. You'll have to make decisions on the fly. I was always trying to visualize what was coming next, and anticipating what would be needed. Mistakes can often be turned into design opportunities and decorative bonuses.

It's a great feeling to be so involved in the building of your own home, making decisions and knowing where things are and why. In the end, I'm thrilled to have this house.

— Anne-Marie Warburton acted as general contractor for her family's two-story, 2,500-square-foot post and beam home in the Hockley Valley, Ontario, Canada. The house was built by professionals, and the bale walls were raised by volunteers. The project was completed with a conventional bank mortgage and received regular home insurance ■

14.2: *The Warburton home.*

involves a great deal of trust and responsibility, you want to select your contractor carefully.

Working with Professionals

Even the most enthusiastic professional is, at the end of the day, working for you in order to make money. While your project is of the utmost importance to you, a professional cannot always be expected to match your enthusiasm and eagerness. Other people who are similarly enthusiastic and eager to have their projects completed are likely to be in line for that professional's services too, and their needs are being balanced against your own. You need to have realistic expectations about hours of work and responsibilities.

Many professionals rely on work from large contracting firms for most of their income. Your project may not take precedence over a contractor's. You are unlikely to build again — in the near future, anyway! — but a contractor will be hiring continually, year in and year out. You shouldn't

From Timid Newcomer to Power Tool Aficionado

I'll never forget arriving at my first straw bale related jobsite. We were to whack down a barn to provide the posts and beams for the house. I arrived a day later than the first work crew, so everybody else was already dirty, grubby, and experienced. I felt severely inadequate, unprepared, nervous — that is, until I took my first crack at a wall with a sledge hammer! Soon I, too, became an expert, guiding the newcomers and doling out jobs.

From that first act of demolition, I was present for every possible aspect of the straw bale project, my work schedule permitting. I especially loved the gut-slugging jobs, such as hauling heavy beams and digging impossible holes in the ground. At the straw bale work sites I've been involved in, all ages, abilities, and genders are welcome! There are jobs to be done, and whoever wants to claim them, does.

Eight years later, I have left my full-time position of teaching elementary school to become a full-time straw bale builder. It doesn't seem like that long ago that I was shown how to properly use power tools for the first time in my life, and now I find myself in the position of directing others on a jobsite (and I especially have to emphasize safety equipment with those who are quite comfortable with power tools!).

I am now as comfortable using a power nailer or skilsaw as the food processor in my kitchen— interestingly, I once heard on a radio talk show that the skilsaw was invented by a Quaker woman, who thought of the invention while watching her spinning wheel go round.

All these years later, I am still the mixer for our plastering crew. People often ask me how I got stuck working at the mixer all day long. In fact, I choose to be there .... I take great pleasure in knowing exactly how to make a good mix, and it feels good for my five-foot-one-inch frame to haul heavy bags, watch my mix form, and then pour it into the waiting wheelbarrow or stucco pump. We now have a new pump which has a mixer attached to it. It is mostly a one-person job, unless we are doing an earthen plaster or lime putty plaster job, in which case a few people need to be on hand to feed the mixer. The new pump is a diesel machine, which can also run on biodiesel, so I look forward to switching over! ☞

be given compromised service, but the reality is that you might be.

Be clear from the start about your expectations. Arrange to inspect or receive regular reports on the progress of any work being done for you. If you are unhappy with the quality of work or the pace at which it is proceeding, voice your concerns and try to work out a solution. Your hired help should be told how to deal with unforeseen needs for changes. Make sure you can be reached if you are not onsite to make critical decisions, or give someone the authority to make decisions on your behalf.

Building Professionals and Snowflakes

Every single builder has specific beliefs, methodologies, and materials by which they will swear. (This may be doubly true for straw bale builders!) In order to stay sane and keep your own goals intact, listen to the advice you are given, but don't feel you need to defer to it all. It's better to have a plumber mutter about your being crazy than

Most of my favorite tools have lost their shininess, and have chunks of plaster stuck on them permanently .... as a matter of fact, I myself find myself getting a little crusty in this job from time to time, but the enthusiasm of a bale raising is always enough to rejuvenate me.

The best part of working on the straw bale construction projects I've been involved in is that I've been able to have valid input into decision making and problem solving. The wall raising is reminiscent of the old barn raising projects of the past, with huge shared meals and festivities afterwards. I've seen volunteers from 10 to 84 years old, men and women alike, people of all kinds of abilities come together and help out.

People often ask me if I miss teaching .... I tell them that bale building is way less work! And frankly, it doesn't always seem like work. Many of our new close friends are former clients for whom we have built. I don't know very many other tradespeople who could say the same. For now, at least, this is what I choose to do. I foresee a future of delving more into building clay ovens and pursuing my newest passion, blacksmithing. But for now, I'm content to look over a set of plans with a cup of tea from home, see a project through from the early stages to finished plaster, and to cherish the teamwork that occurs on a straw bale jobsite.

— Tina Therrien is a full-time partner in Camel's Back Construction, based in Warsaw, Ontario. ■

14.3: *Proper safety equipment and a smile are prerequisites in a mixer.*

CHRIS MAGWOOD

to be talked out of a system you are convinced is right for you! Keep an open mind but a firm one. The opinions of professionals are like snowflakes — every one is unique, and every one will eventually disappear. Be sure you have what you want before the professionals go away!

Loose Ends, Deadlines, and Construction Madness

Even if you are remarkably well prepared at the outset of your project, the construction process is fraught with unforeseen obstacles. Expect a strange kind of chaos, complete with noise, debris, and time warps galore!

Adapt yourself to the pace of building. Sometimes, weeks can go by and it will seem as though nothing has changed. Other times, work will progress so quickly it will make your head spin. Schedules shift, expectations need to be modified, budgets get challenged. All of this is normal. Your only defense is to try to remain calm and focused. At the end of all the madness, you will have a house to live in. When it all gets to be too much, remind yourself why you started this process, and remember what you can expect once it is completed!

References

See References from Chapter 13, Building Permits, pg. 150.

CHAPTER 15

Budgeting

Budget considerations have been guiding your choices throughout the design and planning stages. All along, you have been getting approximate figures and ballpark quotes for materials and services. Now that your plans are complete, you have the ability to (finally!) prepare a realistic budget.

How Much for One of Them Straw Houses?

It's the question that everybody in this business dreads, and it's also the most frequently asked: How much does a straw bale house cost?

It is impossible to answer this question accurately. Contractors in conventional construction can give standard per-square-foot costs with a high degree of certainty, because they build homes from standard plans and basically do the same things the same way every time. But if you are building a custom home — a category into which all straw bale homes currently fit — the answer is not so easy. If you consider all the elements of a home, from foundation excavation through to the knobs on kitchen cupboards, it is an astoundingly complex mix. The choices you make along the way can have dramatic impacts on the final cost, such that

two homes of the same size (and even the same exterior appearance) can have radically different price tags.

In our practice, we have built for as little as Can$40 per square foot, and for as much as Can$250 per square foot — quite a range! A reasonable average for the homes we have built is Can$95 per square foot. But how will you know what your building will cost?

Hitting a Moving Target

There is never a single point during the planning process when you can fix an exact budget for your project. Once your plans near completion, however, you have a chance to use them as a guide for estimating both materials and labor costs. Make many copies of your set of plans, and start shopping them around. It is wise to get at least two — preferably three — quotes for each major material and labor requirement. Make sure you get written quotes, so that there is a paper reference that can be filed and found.

It can take some time to receive all these quotes. Be persistent without being annoying as you give people friendly reminders. As the quotes begin to come in, your budget will start to become clear. If you find, as the numbers add up, you have missed your budget target by a significant amount, you will have to go back to your plans and start making adjustments. This can be disheartening, but it is better to catch such a problem early than to run out of money before there's a roof over your head!

If you need to reassess your plans to lower the costs, talk to all the people involved and get their advice on how to achieve more manageable costs. This includes your designers as well as the suppliers and subcontractors, all of whom may have very simple, straightforward ways in which to adjust your plans to be more affordable without having to completely reconfigure the building. The people quoting you prices will do so based on the exact specifications of your plans, but there are often many cheaper options in materials choices and labor approaches. Many times, we've found that somebody will tell us, "Well, if you wanted to do it this way, we could do it for a lot less." Consider such advice carefully. Sometimes it's a practical and useful suggestion; other times it can be quite contrary to your initial reasons for building (remember Chapter 6?). Explore these options with several people before altering or scrapping your plans!

You may discover that you have apparently created plans that will allow you to build for less than what you budgeted. Congratulations! This is every homebuilder's dream. Don't change your plans, however. When the project is over, you'll be able to spend a bit more on detailing, furnishing, and landscaping.

It Always Costs More Than You Think

The building project that is completed without going over budget is rare. Although it is relatively easy to get quotes for all the major components of your project, allowing you to create a budget estimate, there will always be unforeseen costs, delays, and problems. Leave yourself with plenty of budgetary breathing room, at least 10 to 15 percent of your total budget, so you can deal with the inevitable.

Preconstruction Costs

Your project's preconstruction costs will not be evident from your plans. They include:

- the price of property and interest on your property payments
- building permit fees
- driveway allowances and access roads (fees and construction costs)
- septic permits and installation fees
- service and utility hookup fees
- municipal development fees and taxes

Depending on your location, these fees can total several thousand dollars and take quite a bite out of your actual construction budget. Don't just guess at these figures; your municipality should be able to give you very accurate figures for these expenses.

Some preconstruction costs are more evident, but may not be able to be accurately budgeted for. Anything that requires digging or drilling into the ground can be unpredictable in terms of final cost, including:

- wells (and water testing)
- septic systems
- excavation of your foundation

Each of these activities must be completed before you actually begin construction. These jobs are most often done on a per-hour or per-foot basis, so it's not until the job is finished that you will know the final price. Experienced drillers and diggers will have a good idea of what the costs might be, but there are always surprises under the ground!

Other Hidden Costs

In addition to materials and labor, don't forget to consider other possible hidden costs. These might not be immediately evident from looking at your plans, and they may be things that nobody will mention to you, including:

- **The purchase or rental of tools.** Working without the right tools is frustrating and slow, so think your way through the construction process and make a list of what you'll need. From shovels and picks to carpentry tools and plastering trowels, the list will be extensive and expensive. Used and borrowed tools can help lower these costs. Budget for unforeseen specialty tools you'll need to buy or rent.

- **Tarps** to cover materials and bale walls from the elements. You probably know that your bales and walls will need to be well covered, but so does plywood, lumber, insulation, generators, and many other onsite supplies. Invest in enough good quality tarps to cover everything that will need them.

- **A generator** for your power needs. Whether you are building on the grid or off, there is often the need for a generator onsite, and it needs to be powerful and reliable (there's nothing worse than a whole crew sitting idle while somebody tries to coax the generator into life!). Check the costs of purchase and rental; if you need it for a long time, it's likely cheaper to buy one. You can always sell it when you're finished if you have no further need for it.

- **A truck, van, or trailer.** Building requires the ability to move stuff around, and a utility vehicle of some description is really useful. Such vehicles can be sold when you no longer require them, but you will need money to purchase, license, insure, and service them.

- **Onsite toilet.** Rental toilets are convenient but they can also be expensive if the project is a long one. An outhouse requires an early outlay of time and money, but you get some building practice, and an outhouse is not a bad backup in case of future plumbing disasters.

- **Proper clothing.** Construction is hell on clothing. There are two tactics you can take: buy high quality stuff that's meant to last, or buy piles of second-hand stuff that you can treat as disposable. Two areas you won't want to be cheap with are footwear and cold/wet weather gear. You rack up a lot of miles on foot when you're building, and comfortable safety boots are a must, and if you're working in an inclement climate, warm and/or waterproof work wear will vastly improve your efficiency (not to mention your health and safety!).

- **Construction insurance.** You may want to consider taking out a policy that covers both you and your project in case of mishaps. Make sure hired help has coverage, e.g. workers' compensation. Rates can vary tremendously, so get a number of quotes, and be sure you are covered for the risks that concern you most — personal injury, fire, accident, damage from wind, rain, etc.

- **Sales taxes.** It is a rare material or labor quote that includes the sales taxes. So if you add up all the figures, don't assume that's how much you'll pay! Depending on your location, sales taxes can add a significant percentage to both material and labor costs, and many people forget this factor to their detriment.

- **Delivery fees.** These, too, often don't show up on price quotes. Be sure to clarify if delivery is included, and if not, find out what the charges will be (and then add the tax!).

- **Inspection fees.** Architects, engineers, building officials, electrical and plumbing inspectors may need to visit your site, and might charge you for the visit.

- **Time-sensitive quotes.** Some materials quotes, especially for lumber, will only be valid for a set period of time, due to volatile market prices. Be sure to find out if such conditions apply, and if so, keep an eye on the dates to ensure your quotes are still valid.

- **Cost of living.** Even though it would be nice if the world left you alone while you're engrossed in building, basic living expenses must still be covered. Food, rent, and any regular payments for bills must be accounted for during the building process. If you are taking time off work to build, these expenses can take quite a bite out of your budget.

Materials

Materials costs are often the biggest budget entry, especially for owner-builders. This is true whether or not you buy all new materials or include some recycled materials. We talk to a lot of people who assume that they will be able to make do with recycled building supplies, and therefore significantly reduce their costs. The next chapter, Going Shopping, addresses some of the important considerations when buying used building materials. But when you are budgeting, it is best to base estimates on average prices for new materials, unless you already have the recycled materials. A great number of material supplies simply can't be found used (used plaster, straw, caulking, nails, concrete?). You might, in fact, come in under budget if you find used materials or materials at bargain prices, but your figures will be realistic in case you don't.

Many building supply yards will have a catalog that can help you with your materials estimates. These do not usually include prices for supplies — like lumber — whose costs fluctuate. You will have to get a quote on such items in person or over the phone.

Big-ticket items are easy to price out. More difficult to estimate are all the soft supplies. How many nails, screws, brackets, tubes of glue and caulking, and other such materials will your building need? One thing you don't want to do is underestimate the cost of all these soft supplies; add as much as ten percent of the estimated cost to cover these unseen supplies.

Labor Estimates

Obtain a written estimate from every professional you hire. Ideally, those estimates will be guaranteed and not subject to increase. However, in the real world of building — and in the sometimes shady world of estimating — oversights are made, and problems can occur that will change the price. It is highly unlikely that the price you are quoted will decrease, so leave room in the budget for each and every quote to go up.

Be suspicious of especially low quotes. There is a good chance that suspect numbers are being used to secure the job, and that the price will rise later to reflect real costs. We have found it better to go with professionals who have a good local reputation, and whose quotes seem realistic, than to just go with the lowest quote every time. Base your labor decisions on your own personal reactions to people you are negotiating with; it is better to work with someone you like and trust for a few more dollars than someone you don't for a few dollars less.

A well-negotiated labor arrangement will include provisions for dealing with cost overruns and this can help you plan for a contingency fund. Your labor arrangements should clearly state how cost overruns will be handled (i.e., when and how you'll be notified, steps for resolution), and put a cap on them. Even with people you really like and trust (including good friends), a written contract is valuable for the clarity it brings to a situation. Don't forge ahead without one.

You can always change your labor budget — you may be able to take on the tasks yourself that you had intended to hire out, or find friends with special skills who may be willing to help you out.

Labor Costs versus Tool and Equipment Costs

For specialized tasks — plumbing, wiring, heating, roofing, concrete form work, etc. — weigh the cost of acquiring or renting the appropriate tools and equipment against the costs of hiring experienced labor. A friend who runs an excavating company has the slogan: If you think I'm expensive, hire an amateur! This is not always the case, but experience and equipment can make a complicated job go quickly and smoothly.

To Finish or Not to Finish

Many owner-built homes never see completion — at least in the first decade! Money and time often run out first. If you think you can handle living with bare ceilings, no trim, unfinished counters, or other uncompleted elements, this may not be a problem. If you find this thought abhorrent, then reserve plenty of money to ensure that you will not run out before completion.

Know What You Can and Cannot Live Without

Apportion your spending so that key elements of your home can be finished even if the project stalls. Plan to have working plumbing and heating. It's no fun to have to boil water in your well-appointed kitchen in order to take a bath! Know your priorities and make sure you buy what's required to achieve them before spending elsewhere. It's no good to be sitting on $10,000 worth of custom cabinets in an unserviced shell!

Budgeting Your Own Time

If you are going to build your own home, you will not need to account for the exact dollar figure of your labor, but you will want to be able to budget your time. There is a huge difference between a six-month project and a two-year project, and it helps to figure out which yours is.

If you've never done a task before, it's very difficult to calculate how long it might take. This is where it is worth establishing ties with other owner builders (even if they haven't built with straw bales). Other people who have gone through the same process can help you figure out some reasonable timelines based on their own experiences, and may have some good input on improvements they would make the second time around.

If you don't know any owner-builders, check at your local building supply yard. The managers will know who has built, who did a good job, and who didn't. They can put you in touch with the right people. And they might turn out to be a good source of information, too, having watched a great number of owner-builders go through this experience.

An Inexact Science

Unfortunately, budgeting is an inexact science. It is impossible to account for every contingency and glitch that may arise. The further afield you move from conventional construction, the more variables enter your budgeting equations. The only certain advice is spend plenty of time figuring out your budget, and leave lots of room for error. Don't let the momentum of having plans and being ready to start building detract you from the important phase of budgeting.

Studying Other Budgets

No two houses ever have the same budget, even if they are built from similar plans using similar materials. But studying the budgets of other homes can help you to approximate your project's place on the budget scale. Below, we present the budgets for three different bale houses, all built recently. While we wouldn't suggest that you pick one and base your own budget on it, you can compare the various categories of expenditure and create some ideas for how your own budget might compare in each area.

15.1: *The Soltan residence.*

Budgets

The Soltan house

Karen Soltan's house was built on 100 acres just outside of the city limits of Peterborough. Karen shared the role of General Contractor with Jim Gleason on the 2045 sq. foot saltbox home which was built in 2002. Dale Brownson and Karen designed the house together with energy efficient considerations. Special features include radiant floor heat with a dual purpose boiler, an interior bale wall housing carved in niches and a bookcase, arched doorways, and a solarium. Camel's Back Construction did the bale work and plastering.

Location	Peterborough, Ontario
Year Built	2002
Style	2 storey salt-box, load bearing main floor, modified post & beam second storey
Size	2045.3 sq. ft
Number of bedrooms	3
Number of bathrooms	2
Custom features	Carved-in niches; interior bale wall with arched doorways & carved-in bookshelf

Engineering and Design Fees	....	**$2,751.50**
	Engineering fees for stamping set of plans	$1,551.50
	Design work, consultation and construction drawings	$1,200.00
Site Preparation, Driveway Excavation and Foundation	....	**$24,315.75**
	All excavating, packing, purchase & installation of septic bed and tank, compaction, compaction test (Note: the driveway cost couldn't be omitted from this tally)	$16,033.95
	Excavation: More driveway costs, rough grade	$8,281.80
Foundations	....	**$13,845.92**
	Concrete House Pad	$13,845.92
Roof	....	**$11,843.22**
	Steel, engineered trusses	$9,089.04
	Soffit, fascia, eavestrough	$2,754.18
Straw Bale Walls	....	**$22,690.76**
	Straw Bale (spelt), 554 bales, locally sourced, organic	$1,332.00
	Bale work - raising and bale prep	$8,320.00
	Plastering - 2 coats exterior and interior	$11,700.00
	Plaster pump rental	$1,200.00
	Hemp fibres	$138.76
Custom Windows	....	**$11,997.95**
	Custom windows by Sunset Windows, aluminum clad cedar, low argon filled	$11,997.95
Construction Fees	....	**$114,278.35**
	Construction Materials: lumber, insulation, cement, some bale prep materials, nails, screws, brackets, etc.	$32,180.27
	Construction Labour	$82,098.08
Electrical	....	**$5,607.00**
	House wiring, phone jacks	$5,607.00
Water	....	**$6,260.57**
	PEX pipe, some fixtures, drains, connect to septic	$6,260.57
Other Mechanicals	....	**$14,361.52**
	In-floor radiant heat (installation of tubing & manifold, including labor)	$6,210.00
	Propane boiler (radiant floor and domestic hot water)	$8,151.52
Total	....	**$227,952.54**
Cost per square foot	....	**$111.45**

The Magwood Residence

15.2: *The Magwood residence.*

Greg Magwood's home is a two-storey, load-bearing structure, totalling approximately 2,200 square feet. The design was intentionally simple — a large rectangle — to keep costs low and construction simple. Rather than relying on complicated design for beauty, the building materials themselves were used to enhance the feeling of the space. Sculpted bale walls, hempcrete window sills, exposed log joists and wood floors enliven the space. Contracted by the owner, the building sits on a pier foundation, with a small basement space in one corner acting as a mechanical room. An off-grid PV system, and heat is provided via a woodstove and a propane-fired radiant floor backup. This house features a large dojo room for martial arts training, and three bedrooms. The house is an excellent example of keeping costs low without sacrificing beauty or comfort.

Location	Madoc, Ontario
Year Built	2003
Style	2 storey load bearing main floor, modified post & beam second storey
Size	2200 sq. feet
Number of bedrooms	3
Number of bathrooms	2
Custom features	Arched entranceway, bale benches, internal clay plaster finishes
Engineering and Design Fees	Includes engineer, septic engineer and building permit $2717.91
Excavation, Foundation and Fill	Includes site prep, block basement section, piers, drainage, fill $8970.31
Septic and Well	.... $7296.37
Lumber	Includes framing lumber, strapping, T&G flooring, trim $8228.00
Roof Trusses	.... $5790.82
Roofing Steel	Includes fasteners, drip edge and ridge cap $2658.48
Bale Walls	450 bales @ $2.25 (incl. transport), mesh and flashings $2050.34
Plastering	Includes materials, pump rental, skyjack rental $3746.10
Insulation	Includes foundation, under raised floors, attic, window/door frames and caulking . $6191.02
Electrical/Solar	Includes all wiring and upgrades to existing PV system $9036.92
Electrician labour	.... $1324.67
Plumbing Materials and Fixtures	.... $2231.13
Plumbing Labour	.... $2464.04
Heating/Hot Water	Includes DHW tank, radiant floor tubing, propane hook-up, woodstove and .. $5996.82 professional installations. Radiant floor system requires another $2500 for completed hookup.
Windows	Manufacturer remainders $5216.08
Heat Recovery Ventilator	Includes parts and labour $2587.50
Drywall and Finishes	.... $3377.07
Drywall Labour	.... $1300.00
Cabinets, Lights, Fixtures	.... $1716.85
Construction Labour	Includes consulting and regular paid laborers $6500.00
Tools and Rentals	.... $3107.84
Miscellaneous	Includes all receipts not otherwise attributed, most for less than $25 total $2222.45
Total	.... $94,730.72
Cost per square foot	.... $43.06

The Hunter/Sokolowski Residence

Glen Hunter and Joanne Sokolowski built an off-grid, passive solar, straw bale home on 100 acres of land near Peterborough in 2002/2003. Glen and his father, Ronald, acted as General Contractor for the 2,650-square-foot home. Paul Dowsett of Scott-Morris Architects created a modern style home and incorporated the passive solar elements — a wall of windows faces south to let in the sun in the winter, but an overhang keeps the sun out in the summer. The overhang sits on a cupola with windows on all four sides that draw out the heat in the summer. There had never been hydro service on the land, so Glen and Joanne chose solar

15.3: *The Hunter/Sokolowski residence.*

and wind with battery and generator back up for electricity. Hot water is provided via a solar thermal system with an on-demand propane boiler for backup. This heat is used in the radiant in-floor heating system as well as for domestic hot water. The house is one level with no basement. It will eventually have three bedrooms and two bathrooms, but will retain the very open, loft-like feel with modern styling and details.

Architect	All architect fees, plans, revisions, etc.	**$15,484.20**
Permits and Approvals	....	**$1,021.39**
	Driveway Permit Fee	$150.00
	Building Permit Fee	$250.00
	Septic System Fee	$325.00
	Electrical Inspection and Permit	$296.39
Site Preparation	....	**$27,825.29**
	All excavating, packing, purchase & installation of septic bed and tank, grading and topsoil	$15,699.95
	Drilled well and casing	$3,303.09
	Excavating and gravel for 810m driveway	$8,822.25
Foundations	....	**$26,524.19**
	Footings - Insulated concrete forms, rebar, lumber and plywood for freestanding concrete footings, labor, pump truck for concrete	$18,537.84
	Poured, tinted 35.5 m3 concrete floor, insulated	$7,986.35
Framing and Roof	....	**$62,383.75**
	Custom fabricating, welding and installation of post shoes and brackets for post and beam	$1,825.00
	Parallams, lumber, roof trusses, joists, strapping, hurricane clips, all nuts, bolts and hardware for post and beam	$43,768.95
	Engineer Stamp for post & beam	$535.00
	Crane and boom truck rentals for installing post and beam and custom roof corners	$1,816.30
	Roof - plywood, Gavalum metal roof, trim, flashing, chimney and cathedral support, ice and water shield and labor	$14,438.50
Straw Bale Walls	....	**$22,229.78**
	Straw Bales, 600; used approx. 450	$900.00

Transport bales to house site	$624.02
Bale work - raising and bale prep	$6,250.00
Plastering - 2 coats exterior and interior	$9,575.00
Plaster pump rental	$1,000.00
Materials - mesh, hemp fibres, accelerator	$957.00
Cement, brick sand washed and trucked in, and twine for straw bale walls	$2,460.88
Gavalum base for walls	$462.88

Custom Windows **$53,300.45**

64 Custom fibreglass windows by Thermotech including installation	$53,252.15
Galvalum window sills	$48.30

Doors **$5,022.98**

Solid wood Madawaska red cedar doors - front doors are French doors, 1 exterior, 4 interior with sandblasted glass	$2,864.60
Glass and stain for doors	$609.00
Hardware for 12 doors and locks for 4	$1,549.38

Interior Finishing **$15,655.79**

Ceiling Insulation (Roxol)	$4,133.64
Vapor barrier for ceiling insulation, tape, drywall supplies, tools, lumber, electrical supplies, nails, screws, stain, paint, staples, foam, silicon, etc.	$8,937.15
Custom kitchen drawers, cupboards, pantry and countertops	$2,585.00

Electrical **$49,400.41**

Solar and Wind system including 8 85 Watt BP Solar PV modules, one Whisper H80 wind turbine on an 80-foot tower, 8 Surrette Big Red batteries, Xantrex control and conversion equipment, 48-volt deep well submersible pump that is built for use with solar systems, installed by Generation Solar	$39,486.16
Honda Generator	$2,553.00
Wiremold system for running all wiring. The wiremold looks like wood baseboards and runs on top of plaster walls with electrical and telephone wiring inside.	$2,785.46
Various electrical - wiring, switches, plates, plugs, etc.	$105.79
Lighting - 18 5-centrepiece hanging kitchen lights, 12 pot lights, 1 outdoor fixture and 3 fans	$4,470.00

Water **$17,821.55**

All plumbing work - running lines from well to house, all plumbing within house, installation of tank, one finished bathroom, one roughed-in bathroom, kitchen, laundry room	$6,875.00
Solar thermal system preheats water on custom-designed mounts from Peterborough Green-Up	$5,456.20
Bathroom and kitchen fixtures - tub, sink, Terrazo shower stall, toilet, all taps	$5,490.35

Other Mechanicals **$27,542.24**

Installation of telephone line ot house - over 810m	$2,436.39
Installation and fill of propane tank, all lines outside and inside house for hot water and stove	$4,186.42
Radiant in-floor heating system installed	$12,099.00
Appliances - energy-efficient refrigerator, gas range, dishwasher, front-loading washer	$5,095.00
Rentals - scaffolding and generator (before purchase), genie lift	$3,725.43

Total **$324,212.02**

Cost per square foot **$122.34**

CHAPTER 16

Going Shopping: Materials

Your finished plans will enable you to make a shopping list for all the materials you'll need to build your house. As with any kind of shopping, prices and quality will vary widely. Good decisions about materials purchases will help you create a building of excellent quality that's within your price range.

Some people collect building supplies for years before they actually construct a house. Others place a giant single order just before they're about to build. It all depends on your budget and personal style.

Bargain-priced Materials

If you have adequate storage for all your bargain buys, it is possible to shop first and design later, allowing your existing materials list to shape the house you will build. If you shop first, you may be able to realize some significant savings, since you can spread out your investment over an extended period of time. There are many sources for bargain building supplies.

Scavenging

It is remarkable how many excellent building materials get thrown away. Dumpsters, construction sites, demolition sites, and neighborhood trash collection sites can be full of useful stuff.

You can probably find lumber or plywood, doors, windows, toilets, sinks, furniture, and just about anything else that goes into a house, though your scavenged items may need a little repair or come in odd sizes or shapes. A clever scavenger will make note of piles of materials sitting in people's yards and garages and offer to clean up in exchange for keeping the materials. This kind of activity can net you large quantities of good

16.1: *These timbers were all reclaimed from old buildings. Sometimes, this can be a great strategy for finding affordable framing materials.*

materials. Municipal dumps and landfill sites often have special areas set up for construction waste, much of which can be salvaged.

When scavenging lumber, remember that in many jurisdictions you will be required to use grade-stamped lumber for structural elements. Much scavenged lumber will not be grade-stamped and will only be usable as nonstructural elements in your house.

A patient collector can assemble a goodly number of building supplies, though it would take a long time to scavenge enough material to build an entire house. Whether you save a few hundred dollars or several thousand, the effort may well be worth it. Ecologically, scavenging building materials has a double benefit, because you reduce the demand for more new material and save old materials from filling up landfill sites.

We caution bargain hunters against being tempted by the plethora of used windows out there. This is not an area to skimp in. Much of the your home's heat loss will occur through the windows, making quality windows a great investment. Be sure any used windows are in top shape by checking for condensation between the panes of glass, seals that are intact, frames that are not dented or twisted, and hardware that works. Try to find out why the windows were removed; often the reason should make you think twice!

Salvage Yards

Demolition companies often run salvage yards full of beams, bricks, blocks, banisters, balustrades, balconies, windows, doors, bowling alley floors, all at prices that might interest you.

Garage Sales and Flea Markets

Some people enjoy making regular rounds of local flea markets and garage sales where it is often possible to find excellent new and used building supplies. At garage sales, quantities will usually be small and consist of leftovers from other people's building projects. Prices are often low, since people want to get rid of these bulky and useless items.

Larger flea market vendors are usually aware of market values and don't often offer outstanding bargains for building supplies. Still, materials will be cheaper than if you buy new. If you develop a friendly relationship with vendors, they may start filling your requests or sourcing items they know you need. Give these vendors a list of what you want; over time they might find most of what you need.

Classified Ads

Check out the dedicated classified papers. They offer free photo and text ads and generally have a healthy smattering of building materials, netting you all kinds of useful supplies. Do your hunting the same day the paper is released; otherwise, you'll miss out on the best of what's available. Advertised materials are often new or in very good shape and in sufficient quantities to make the ad worth placing for the vendor. You don't have to just read the ads: place your own want ad listing the required supplies; it can bring a flood of calls and lots of good materials. People who respond may not have considered selling their goods before, and their prices might be great. If you keep a rotating list in the "Wanted" section, you might get regular finders calling you with materials.

Used Building Supplies Stores

The sharp climb in the cost of building materials over the last decade has given rise to many used building supplies stores. Some are connected with charities, such as Habitat for Humanity, and often work in cooperation with demolition companies and/or use the same scavenging methods outlined above. These stores stock a wide range of useful materials that are easily removed from old buildings. Lighting and plumbing fixtures, windows, doors, trim, and hardware can all be found in good shape at good prices. You are unlikely to find any remarkable bargains, but you to pay about half the price of new materials. Used supplies warehouses will often take lists of your needs and let you know when they have found certain items. The more frequently you buy from a particular store, the better are your chances of getting first pick of newly arrived materials.

Building Supply Yards

Most building supply yards are members of a chain that offers one-stop shopping for building materials. Sales can net you some excellent finds, as can spring and fall clear-out specials. Chain stores are usually quite competitive. Their advertising flyers can alert you to good prices on common building supplies.

Remember that building supply yards stock items required by mainstream builders. You probably won't find environmentally friendly options or anything slightly outside the norm at a typical building supply yard. Advice, too, will tend to pertain to conventional building practices.

Building supply yards do offer convenience for contractors and builders. They stock full inventories of common products and will deliver to your site for any sizable order. You can take your finished plans to a single outlet and place your order for everything you need — except for bales! Quite often, you will be offered a discount for a large purchase, and you may be able to arrange for credit directly from the supply yard. Some have knowledgeable staff who may be able to advise you on purchases and construction techniques. Most supply yards charge higher prices than do comparable specialty shops. Item for item, it is usually possible to find lower prices in other places but not under one roof. For some builders, the one stop convenience of a building supply yard is worth the extra cost.

Lumber Mills

Small-scale lumber mills are experiencing a widespread resurgence as affordable milling technology develops and the clearcutting techniques of giant lumber companies become unsustainable. Portable mills can be brought to your site if you have sufficient trees; quite often, you can get milled lumber for your project in trade for additional lumber from your property that the operator can sell later. There is a good chance that you will find several small mill operators near your site. Prices from small operators are almost always lower than from building supply yards, and you can question the operator about his or her harvesting techniques if you are concerned about sustainable forestry.

Lumber quality can vary greatly, depending on the operator. In areas where grade-stamped lumber is required for construction, the operator can hire an independent lumber inspector to approve and stamp your wood. In general, small operators take pride in the quality of their lumber and mill better wood than do larger companies. Be sure that lumber purchased this way is dry enough to use before you start construction; otherwise it may shrink, warp, mold, and twist once you have it in place.

Specialty Shops

A specialty shop exists for almost every construction need. It will likely stock a wider selection than a building supply yard can, and sales staff will give more detailed and knowledgeable advice. Watch for sales and remaindered items at these shops. Some may also sell used items or factory seconds, so be sure to ask about their availability. Prices at specialty stores will vary; most will undersell the building supply yards, and some will price higher. Often, the higher prices will get you a higher quality product and better service. Specialty shops are frequently independent and locally owned, so more of the money you spend there will stay in your community.

Farm Supply Stores

Farm supply stores and cooperatives can be very good sources for many building supplies at good prices. They will likely stock framing materials, steel roofing and siding, sheathing, plumbing, wiring, and tools. Many of the bale-specific supplies you will need are most easily sourced at farm supply stores.

If you join the cooperative, you will receive a discount on your purchases. If you become a member, or even a regular customer, you'll be able to get plenty of good advice for finding items you need or the names of professionals worth hiring. Farm supply stores can provide a welcome relief from glitzy showrooms and high-pressure sales techniques.

Look Around Before You Buy

Regardless of where you shop, take some time to become familiar with the pricing of certain items. You can't recognize a bargain unless you are aware of a baseline price for comparison. Lumber, for instance, is sometimes quoted by the board foot to allow comparisons between different sizes (a board foot is 12-by-12-by-1-inch, not 12-by-12-by-¾-inch). Read widely through

flyers, catalogs, and classified ads and visit several building stores. After a while, your ability to assess quality and price will allow you to make better decisions.

There's Always a Better Price

Even after the most thorough research and dedicated shopping, you often find a better bargain after you've made a purchase. Don't despair. You can only choose the best combination of quality and price available to you at the time of purchase. If you calculate the savings you could have made, it will only drive you crazy!

New versus Recycled Materials

For cash outlay, recycled materials always win out over new. However, lower prices often come with other costs. You may have to spend more time locating, assessing, and picking up used materials. Many used items will need a little resuscitation — or maybe a lot! — before they are ready to use. Sanding, straightening, repairing, refinishing, de-nailing — all of these can add time or money to your project. This may not matter if you are not under a strict deadline or if you are able to do all your repairs prior to actual construction.

When you buy used materials, you forego any warranty. If you feel better with a guarantee, it may be worth it to buy new items that will be subjected to heavy use or play a critical role in your house. Consider your willingness and ability to provide service and repair to your home when you are deciding what to buy new or used.

Cost versus Quality

It is not always best to choose materials by cost alone. Cheap but inferior materials often cost more in the long run (roofing, windows, toilets, generators, and water pumps come to mind). A mid-price item may split the difference between quality and price in a satisfactory way. Consider the relative importance of each item and its strength, durability, reputation, and warranty before you buy. Critical items like windows are worth a significant investment. Windows will help with heat retention for as long as your house stands, giving you a good return on your investment — heightened efficiency and lower operating costs. Consider, too, the costs and ease of replacement or upgrade for any item in your home. Professionals can guide you in your decisions, but your own satisfaction is what counts in the end.

Tools

Proper tools can make a big difference to your project, affecting not only the speed at which you can work but the quality of your finished product. Buy quality tools that you'll use a lot — hammer, tape measure, level, tri-square, handsaw, power saw, drill, screwdriver, and pliers. For other tools, first assess how useful they will be after construction. Buy or rent larger tools as your budget determines. Used tools are also an option. You may need specialty tools for some aspects of construction. Decide which tasks you intend to perform yourself and try to locate the necessary tools and equipment before it's time to start. Valuable days can be lost if you don't. Like anything else, tools are of differing quality and come from a variety of sources and at different prices.

It will be helpful to have four to six ends of scaffolding onsite for the entire project. Many people rent this and then find that buying it would have been cheaper. Save the scaffolding rental for the plastering stage, when you want it to surround the entire building.

Shopping for Bales

To find bales, you can approach farmers directly, inquire at or order from a farm supply store, farm equipment dealer, or cooperative, or place a want ad in a rural newspaper. Average prices can vary from Can$2–$5 per bale. (See Chapter 2 for bale buying tips.)

Bale Building Supplies

Some of the bale-specific materials and tools you'll need will require nontraditional sourcing.

Stucco Meshes

Chicken wire was a popular choice for wire reinforcement mesh, but we discourage its use. Wavy and impossible to stretch tight and flat against a wall, it is much too labor intensive. If metal wire mesh is required, welded galvanized fencing uses much heavier gauge wire than poultry netting but often costs about the same. The use of welded fencing can save a lot of labor time because it requires less stitching or quilting of the mesh. Welded fencing with 2-by-2- or 2-by-3-inch holes will work well.

When we use mesh on a building, we much prefer to use a plastic mesh. Our current favorite is Cintoflex D by Tenax. This mesh comes in 10-foot-by-330-foot rolls which are easy to handle and install (it can be cut with scissors or a utility knife instead of wire cutters!) and yet provides the same kind of reinforcement. As an added bonus, it is not prone to rusting that will eventually deteriorate even the galvanized metals.

Expanded metal lath —also known as diamond lath or plaster lath — is heavier than chicken wire, and comes in flat sheets rather than rolls. It is more expensive and can be more difficult to work with, but its extra strength is useful in corners and around windows. It's found

16.2a

at building supply yards or stucco specialty shops. It's not typically used to cover a whole building, but to provide extra reinforcement in key areas: door and window openings, corners and over wood.

Staples

In order to attach your stucco mesh, you will need thousands of staples and some good quality staple guns. Air-driven staples hold better and are faster to install. Sometimes the air pressure from the compressor must be reduced to avoid the staple severing the mesh. Buy your staples in case lots, rather than single boxes.

Precompression Materials

If you are building a load-bearing structure, your precompression system will require materials. Wire systems use 9-gauge galvanized fencing wire — also known as merchant wire — available in bulk at farm supply outlets. The saddle clamps you'll need are also available there or at hardware stores. Depending on your system, you will need tools to perform the precompression of your bales. Wire methods use Gripples and a Grippler tool, or fence stretchers — purchased from a farm supply outlet or fencing specialist or borrowed from a farmer — and a come-along, available at most hardware or farm stores. Load binders — from an automotive or trucking supply outlet — or a simple lever can serve as a come-along.

Bale Needles

Used to sew on stucco mesh, and sometimes retie bales, bale needles are a homemade item. Use your own ingenuity to source the materials and create the design. Needles should be several inches longer than your bales' width and have a hole or a notch capable of routing twine.

Baling Twine

Polypropylene twine can be used for retying bales and stitching or quilting stucco mesh. It can be purchased in large rolls at farm supply stores. Sisal/binder twine is not recommended as it is difficult to quilt with. In areas where baling wire is in common use, it can be used. Specialty wire-twisting pliers can speed up bale wire retying.

Line Trimmer

The most efficient way to trim and shape your bale walls is with a gas or electric-powered line trimmer or weed-whacker. Standard nylon string will work, but you will need a lot. Plastic blades or metal chain attachments, intended for heavier brush, work well.

16.2b

16.2a - b: *We really like using poly mesh, because a single person can handle a roll big enough to cover an entire house, and even young assistants can cut it with just a pair of scissors.*

Clippers and Hay Knives

Regular garden shears are useful for trimming and shaping walls, especially where weed-whackers have a hard time reaching.

Plastering Supplies

Depending where you live, stuccoed homes may be popular or rare. The availability of plastering supplies in your area will vary with the popularity of the finish. A specialty outlet catering to masons will stock the necessary tools and supplies. High-quality limes, mortars, and clays are critical to a good finish. Ask about favorite choices at a specialty store. You can also get advice on mixtures and application techniques from active practitioners. Be sure the ingredients you are buying are meant for stucco, and not just for poured concrete or mortar.

A wide range of stucco stops, edgings, and moldings are available. While it is possible to plaster a bale home without any of these products, they do help create a consistent finish. You can choose the ones that suit the style of finish you want.

Bale Beaters

Usually homemade, a bale beater is used to help align and straighten bale walls after they are erected. Any hammer-shaped object on a handle will suffice, as long as you can swing it and it applies its force over a reasonable surface area. They are usually the favorite tool onsite!

Bale Tarps

Farmers use heavy-duty, UV-resistant tarps — usually silver in color — to cover outdoor hay mounds. These make the best covering for your walls and your straw mound, too. More pricey than other tarps, they are designed to be rugged and long-lasting, and can more than pay for

themselves when the first wind and rainstorm batters your building site.

Buying Responsibly

While you are bound to give a lot of thought to price, quality, and convenience when you are shopping for materials, don't forget to consider other significant factors.

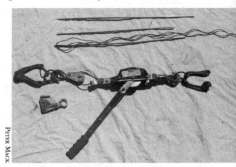

PETER MACK

16.3: *The come-along is a common tool, and when attached to a pair of fence stretchers (as in this photo) is a great way to precompress load-bearing walls. Bale needles (above) are home-made from stainless steel rod, with a hole drilled in one end. There's no need to sharpen the tip to a fine point.*

Sustainable Options

You can choose to support products and manufacturers that try to reduce environmental impacts. From sustainably harvested lumber to natural paints and stains, almost every product you could use is also available in a greener format. You may want to research your product choices and the production methods used to create them; often, the cheapest products come with nasty environmental side effects. Green products often cost more due mostly to economies of scale and lack of subsidies. Your purchase of

PETER MACK

16.4: *Bale bashers are home-made usually from scrap wood, and don't require a lot of fine carpentry skills to build! A variety of shapes and sizes allow the specialized bashing.*

green products helps ensure their continued production and increases the possibility of a more competitive pricing in the future.

Allergies and Toxins

Many of the manufactured products used in standard home construction contain chemicals and toxins that have undetermined effects on human health. Treated and glued wood products — pressure-treated wood, laminates, plywood, broadloom, and particle board — are of particular concern. Many finishing products, including paints, stains, and floorings, are also suspect. Research these purchases if you are concerned about their potentially harmful effects. Excellent replacements exist for all toxic items on your shopping list, but it may take some effort to locate them. Preliminary research has shown straw bale homes to be a healthy environment for those with allergies or chemical sensitivities.

Local Economies

The money you spend on your home can have a significant impact on your community. If you buy and hire locally, you will strengthen your local economy, which in turn will help you to thrive. Some regions have local economic trading systems, better known as barter economies. Whether formally organized or entirely spontaneous, this kind of trading can lower the cash costs of your building and encourage the development of stronger communities. Remember that barter tends to undermine government taxation, so you may want to keep records and claim income and expenses incurred through barter transactions.

Your Project Is Underway

With your first materials purchases and signed labor contracts, your building project will truly be underway. It is both exciting and scary to start spending money on your future home. Now you're ready to build!

References

Baker-Laporte, Paula Elliott, Erica Elliott, and John Banta. *Prescriptions for a Healthy House: A Practical Guide for Architects, Builders and Homeowners.* New Society Publishers, 2001. ISBN 1-89804-921-1.

Canada Mortgage and Housing Corporation. *Building Materials for the Environmentally Hypersensitive.* Canada Mortgage and Housing Corporation, 1995. ISBN 0-662-21107-3.

Chapell, Steve. *The Alternative Building Sourcebook: Traditional, Natural and Sustainable Building Products and Services.* Fox Maple Press, 1998. ISBN: 1-889269-01-8.

Chiras, Dan. *New Ecological Home: A Complete Guide to Green Building Options.* Chelsea Green, 2004. ISBN 1-931498-16-4.

Green Building: Project Planning and Cost Estimating. RS Means, 2002. ISBN 0-87629-659-2.

Hermannsson, John. *Green Building Resource Guide.* The Taunton Press, 1997. ISBN 1-56158-219-0.

Johnston, David. *Building Green in a Black and White World: A Guide to Selling the Homes Your Customers Want.* New Society Publishers, 2004. ISBN 0-86718-507-4.

Pearson, David. *The Natural House Catalogue: Everything You Need to Create an Environmentally Friendly Home.* Simon and Schuster, 1996. ISBN 0-684-80198-1.

Wilson, Alex, ed. *Green Spec Directory: Product Directory with Guideline Specifications.* Building Green, 2004. ISBN 0-929884-04-4.

CHAPTER 17

Construction: Before the Bales

We often joke about how small a component of straw bale construction the actual stacking of bales can be. Before you even touch a straw bale, your foundation must be built. And, if you are building a post and beam design, the framework must be raised and a roof assembled. If you keep several basic ideas in mind as you build, it will help avoid problems when it's time to install the bales.

We are attempting to give as much information as possible about the straw component of the building, but this is not a complete construction guide for your home. Depending on your design choices, the process of readying your project for the installation of straw bales may be quite fast, as for load-bearing walls on a simple pier foundation, or quite lengthy, as for a multi-story post and beam frame with a full basement. There are so many variables — design options, climatic and geographical considerations, and building code variations — that hard-and-fast guidelines governing the completion of the non-bale aspects of construction are impossible to prescribe. You will need to seek out accurate information, experience, advice, and common sense to ensure a smooth building process before you build your bale walls.

What follows are some key factors to keep in mind, focusing mainly on the specific interfaces each component will have with your bale walls.

Foundations

Building a strong, well-drained, frost-protected foundation that is square and level is very important. Many people panic when considering their foundations, and assume they should hire out the work to ensure it's done right. There are some good reasons to hire out foundations, especially if a lot of concrete formwork is required. But we have seen enough wonky professionally built foundations to know that hiring out won't always get your desired results. Regardless of who does the work, it needs to be done carefully. Nowhere does the line, "measure it twice, do it once" apply more strongly. The shape of your foundation will have many ongoing implications throughout the rest of the project, so do the work carefully, check it many times, refer to the plans often, and don't

ORVILLE THERIELL

17.1a

JOY ALLAN

17.1b

17.1a - b: *A properly laid curb rail is an important part of a good straw bale wall. The space between the rails must be insulated, preferably with a well-draining material.*

finalize anything (especially in concrete) until you're sure it's right.

Bale Foundation Details

Your foundation plans will have some bale-specific elements that may go unnoticed by professionals used to regular frame walls, or by yourself.

Load-bearing Tie-down Points

All load-bearing bale walls use some kind of tie-down point in the foundation for precompressing the walls. As shown in Chapter 13,

these differ for each kind of foundation. Any system that uses loops or hoses cast into a concrete slab or perimeter beam must ensure that these are well placed and secure, so they don't poke out of the finished foundation at the wrong place. We usually drill holes for our hoses into a scrap of 2-by-4 that is screwed to the formwork, keeping the hose from moving.

Sealing Foundations

Concrete can act as a wick, pulling moisture up from the ground and passing it on to wall elements. Wherever wood or straw will come into contact with concrete, gaskets made of tar, tar paper, plastic, or foam should be used. For post and beam construction, wooden posts should not sit directly on top of concrete piers. Spacers made from ice hockey pucks make an excellent and inexpensive barrier between wood and concrete!

Brackets and Anchors

For post and beam designs, various fasteners may need to be embedded in concrete within a few minutes of pouring. Make sure these fasteners are labeled, close at hand, and can be set to predetermined marks. Revisit them within 10 to 15 minutes of installation, to ensure they haven't changed position.

Curb rails or Toe-ups

On all styles of foundation, raised wooden curbs are placed under the bales to elevate the straw above the finished floor level. To attach these curb rails, anchor bolts must be embedded in the wet concrete at accurate locations, or concrete nails or screws can also be used within the correct time frame (while the concrete is still green, hard to the touch but not fully cured).

Curbs built on wood-framed decks should be built on top of the sub-flooring. If the curb rails are running parallel to the floor joists, the curb should be placed directly over top of joists to support the weight of the wall and provide adequate attachment points. This will affect the on-center spacing of the joists and may require doubling of the affected joist. Where the curb runs perpendicular to floor joists, solid blocking should be used under it.

Flashing

A properly designed flashing will prevent water that is running down the walls from seeping under the bales or under the curb, where it could wreak havoc. If your foundation has exterior insulation, the flashing may also be used to protect the insulation from damage. Check your building supply yard for prefabricated designs that may suit your purposes before you order custom bent flashing. Flashings usually don't get installed right away, but be sure your foundation is built to accommodate a flashing.

Vapor Barriers and Caulking

Vapor barriers and caulking help to prevent air and moisture migration. If your floor or foundation design incorporates a vapor barrier, that barrier should continue so it blends into the plaster on your bales. The barrier can be folded up and stapled to the wooden curb. Stucco mesh and plaster can be applied over this vapor barrier to create a seamless joint. Use high quality caulking on the joint between the foundation and/or floor and the wooden curb to help prevent air and moisture migration at this vulnerable point.

Your house will also have a vapor barrier between the ceiling and the roof insulation that should be cut to finish under the wall plaster. If you are building a post and beam design, be sure to have the vapor barrier continue from the ceiling behind the beam and into the plaster.

Plastering Considerations

Plaster is not a very common finish in many parts of North America, and so the detailing required for a good plaster finish is often not obvious or well considered. The following points should be taken into account at all stages in construction.

Mesh Connection

Reinforcement mesh for your plaster is often mandated by the building code and is recommended for certain kinds of plaster. If you are going to be using mesh — poly mesh, welded fencing, diamond lath, etc. — be sure your curb, top plate, and window and door buck design easily accommodate its attachment, usually with staples. Ensure that your stapler is easy to use and that there is enough material for the staples to grip properly. Consider renting or buying an air powered stapler for this job; it is faster, easier

17.2: A good base flashing will protect the wall from water seeping between the bales and the foundation. It is mounted so that the vertical face will be behind the mesh and plaster.

on the hands and wrists, and drives long staples deep into the wood.

Plaster Stops

Most bale builders are not professional plasterers and may not think about how to finish the plaster at the top and bottom of walls and around window and door openings. The most important thing to remember is that the plaster is approximately an inch thick on both sides of the wall.

17.3: *This lightweight frame uses many temporary braces to hold it plumb and square until the bales are installed and the plaster applied. These braces are important: make sure enough lumber is on site to create them.*

You want this thick coating to create a clean seam with the floor, the ceiling and/or beams, posts, doors, and windows. Always ask yourself, How will my plaster finish to this edge? What kind of look do I want to achieve? How can I achieve a leak-free seal?

The simplest way to achieve clean plaster stops is to ensure that the material the plaster is abutting will act as a stop. Making foundations, top plates and window bucks one inch wider than the straw itself will create clean wooden edges for finishing plaster. Tack thin strips of lumber or plywood into place to create temporary plaster stops for trim or other elements

that might be added later. Windows and doors themselves can be mounted ¾-inch proud of their frames, so that plaster can stop against the edge of the window or door itself. Flashings can also be designed and placed so they make clean, convenient plaster stops.

Regardless of the tactic you use in your design, take the detailing of your plaster into careful consideration. Your building will look and perform better for the effort.

Post and Beam Considerations

Reality Checks

In Chapter 12, different interfaces between bales, posts, and beams were detailed. When constructing your framework, be sure real-world conditions are consistent with your intended finish. Check that the meeting points between bales and posts are really going to work when the bales are put in place. Note how any brackets you use will affect the plaster and its ability to seal the wall against air leaks. Place vapor barriers and mesh carefully at post and beam seams before installing bales to prevent leakage at these points.

Cross-bracing

Plastered straw bales offer a great deal of stability to your post and beam frame, but before the bale walls are finished — including one coat of plaster — your framework will have to stand against wind loads without the help of the bales. A finished roof acts like a giant sail on top of your frame. Proper cross-bracing is essential. Cross-bracing can be either a permanent or temporary feature of your frame. Be sure any temporary bracing will not interfere with the placement of the bale walls. Cross-bracing should be added as each new part of the framework is built, not once the frame is standing. Never underestimate the power of the wind to topple well-fastened frame members if they are not adequately braced.

Attach all temporary frame bracing to either the exterior (to stakes driven into the ground) or the interior (to the foundation or subflooring), but not both. In this way, the bracing is not removed until the unbraced side of the wall has one coat of plaster.

Remember that your cross-bracing has the ability to deflect and alter the alignment of your framing members. Check them for being plumb and level regularly.

Door and Window Bucks

Prebuilding Bucks

Prebuilding all your door and window bucks will save a lot of time when you begin installing the bales. The joints in the box frame of your bucks can benefit from caulking when you assemble them. Be sure to build bucks with strength in mind and use screws rather than nails. Brace your bucks to keep them square using scraps of lumber or plywood. Braces should be placed so they don't interfere with installation of the bales, or the windows, or doors, and they should be kept in place until one coat of plaster has been applied, or the window or door has been installed.

Labeling

It's a good idea to clearly label the bucks as you build them, so there will be no question of which buck goes where. If you are working with a crew — or have a bad memory — note the direction of installation with arrows drawn on the buck. You don't want to have to pull down a straw wall to get a buck turned right side up!

17.4a

17.4b

Put corresponding numbers or marks on the foundation too.

Pre-installing

We most often build our window bucks with legs that continue down to the foundation, rather than using floating bucks. With legs, they are easy to keep in place, can be installed prior to the bale raising,

17.4a - b: *This rough window buck includes a sloped sill piece that will act as the finished sill and drip edge below the window. It is notched into the uprights of the buck and extends beyond the corner of the window, making an effective barrier against water.*

and are simpler to keep plumb with some temporary bracing. Door bucks already have legs down to the floor, so they can definitely be pre-installed. These frames take a real pounding during the bale raising, so anchor them and brace them strongly.

Top Plates

Load-bearing Top Plates

For load-bearing designs, a strong top plate is a must. You will already have determined the size and style of top plate you will be using, but when building it, you must ensure that the corners will meet in a strong bond and that any joints in the lumber are offset to avoid creating weak spots in the structure. L-shaped plywood corners can help to strengthen corners and ensure that they are square. Top plates can be constructed on the foundation before the walls are built. By using the foundation as a template, you assure a perfect match between the top and bottom of the wall. While the top plate is on the foundation, you can mark and drill holes for the precompression wires or straps that will correspond with those embedded in the foundation. Before moving the top plate sections aside to make way for bales, label the sections with directional arrows — N, S, E, and W — so that installation is simplified.

17.5: A simple 2x6 window buck is mounted on the curb rail prior to the bales being installed. It should be well braced to handle the bumps and thumps of the bale raising.

JOY ALLAN

Post and Beam Top Plates

Depending on how the tops of your bale walls interface with the framing, you will still need some kind of cap over the straw. Often, this is a strip of plywood attached over or under the beam, or to the underside of the floor or roof joists. Place this wood carefully and caulk, or otherwise seal, the joints between strips. Cut this cap wider than the bales (one additional inch on each side), so that it can act as a plaster stop and create a clean edge for abutting ceiling or soffit material.

Tarps

Load-bearing tarping

Preplanning your tarping strategy will save a huge amount of time and effort should you need to put it into place. One good strategy is to roll out a wide (10- to 12-foot) strip of poly or house wrap over the top plate prior to installing the top piece of plywood. This sheet can hang down on both sides of the wall, providing decent protection against all but driving rains.

Another strategy is to create some small roof trusses to go over your top plate. These triangles of scrap lumber or strapping can provide a tarp attachment point and the necessary overhang without interfering with work on the walls.

Regardless of how you attach your tarps, do it well. Strong winds often accompany the wet weather you are protecting against, so tie tarp ends down to heavy objects (concrete blocks, lumber, wheelbarrows, etc.); and don't rely on a few hand-driven staples.

Some builders raise scaffolding around the building perimeter and a taller section in the center of the building. An entire tarp tent is then created over the building site.

Post and Beam Tarping

Even if you are building under protection of a completed roof, your bale walls may still need tarp protection from windblown rain. You can attach and then roll up tarps to the underside of the roof framing, creating protection that can be dropped down into place very quickly. If you mount these tarps far enough away from the walls, you can continue working between tarp and wall even during rains.

Don't Rush the Job

You may find yourself frustrated by the amount of work you need to do before you can install your bales. And you will probably encounter delays, problems, and oversights that can dishearten you. Don't let problems force you into making rash decisions. It is better to miss deadlines and fall behind schedule than to compromise the integrity of your project just to speed things along.

Peanut Butter Problems

When construction problems arise, take a break and think about them. Ask for advice, make lots of sketches, or talk with co-workers until you devise the best plan of action. A good friend calls these problems "peanut butter problems" because she finds that the time it takes her to stop and chew a peanut butter sandwich allows her to come up with solutions that work!

Sometimes there is a simple solution to your problems, sometimes only a complete dismantling and rebuilding will do. Always keep your overall objectives in mind, and be sure that your solutions are in keeping with your goals. Ask yourself what the problem element is meant to achieve and what role it has in your building. Often, when you are clear about what needs to be achieved, a solution comes clear, too. Someday, your construction problems will become stories you tell for a laugh. Construction flaws that go uncorrected, however, can be an ongoing source of concern and expense.

References

Allen, Edward. *Fundamentals of Building Construction: Materials and Methods.* John Wiley & Sons, 1990. ISBN 0-471-50911-6.

Fine Homebuilding. The Taunton Press, 63 S. Main St., P.O. Box 5506, Newtown CT 06470-5506 USA.

Ching, Francis D.K. *Building Construction Illustrated.* Van Nostrand Reinhold, 1991. ISBN 0-442-23498-8.

DeCristoforo, R.J. *Housebuilding: A Do-It-Yourself Guide.* Sterling Publishing Co., Inc., 1987. ISBN 0-8069-6512-6.

Leger, Eugene. *Complete Building Construction.* Maxwell Macmillan Canada, 1993. ISBN 0-02-517882-2.

Lio, M. and T. Kesik. *Canadian Wood Frame House Construction}* Canada Mortgage and Housing Corporation. 1997. ISBN 0-660-167239.

CHAPTER 18

Raising Bale Walls

This is the moment that most of us have been waiting for: it's time to put the straw in place. As with any construction technique, there are many strategies that will help you to achieve the results you want.

The act of creating a straw bale wall is a joyous and celebratory one, and we have yet to be present at a wall raising where wide smiles are not the order of the day. Often, there are many people on hand, and the atmosphere is that of an old-style barn raising. Everything about straw bale lends itself to fun, creativity, and ingenuity. Each new building goes up in a slightly different way and can add to our collective knowledge of techniques and approaches. There are just a few hard-and-fast rules for stacking bale walls; the rest is a matter of creatively addressing some common concerns.

When you raise your bale walls, it is important to think clearly about your goals and how you can accomplish them. You will very likely come up with your own variations and innovations as you start moving and placing bales. This is precisely what makes building with bales so much fun! And it's even more fun if you share your insights and knowledge with others.

18.1: *Yes it's this much fun!*

The Golden Principles of Bale Stacking

Some aspects of building a bale wall will benefit from common construction practices. These in no way inhibit your creativity but rather ensure that you will have structurally sound walls.

Stack the Bales in Running Bond

Treat your bales as though they were bricks or blocks, making sure that the joints overlap with solid bale on the following course to create a running bond. If joints run parallel up the wall, you will be sacrificing structural integrity. Bales are not consistent in length like bricks or blocks, so perfect running bond is not really a practical pursuit; keep it as a guiding principle, not absolute law. In post and beam situations where bales will be packed into, and held stable by the frame, running bond is less important.

Start Each Course From the Corners and the Buck Frames

You will find it easier to achieve running bond if you begin each course at the corners and work toward the center of the wall. This can lower the number of custom bales needed, since you'll use only one near the middle of each course, rather than one at each end. Too many half-bales above one another can form a fault line in your wall by creating a poor running bond. Stagger bales at the corners so a strong overlap is created. Once a pattern is established, running bond will be simpler to maintain.

Don't Overpack or Overstuff the Walls

Your bales should fit comfortably against one another. Pushing them too tightly together or jamming in the last bale of a course will cause undue stress on your window and door bucks, forcing them out of square. You will also end up with a case of bulging corners. It is a slow, time-consuming process to fix bulging corners, so avoidance is your best defense.

Have a Cover-up Plan for the End of the Day or in Case of Rain

Have plenty of waterproof coverings available to completely protect your walls. Putting up tarps can take you quite a bit of time, so don't leave it until the end of the day when you're really tired and the sun is setting! You'll want to securely fasten your tarps to prevent them from disappearing in the wind. Such a broad expanse of material will act just like a sail or kite unless it is properly fastened. On larger buildings, choose smaller sections (i.e., between two doorways or tall windows) to tarp. This eliminates some tarping and smaller sections are more manageable.

Be Aware of Fire Hazards

We can't emphasize enough the importance of fire precautions at a straw bale work site. Your site will inevitably get covered in loose straw (unless you are pre-dipping your bales; see sidebar, Bale Dipping, p. 208) that is extremely susceptible to fire. Keep smokers well back from the site and provide sand-filled buckets for butts. Keep spark producing activities like welding and grinding far from loose straw. Be sure to rake whenever loose straw gets overly abundant and create a mound or two away from the walls. Always maintain a straw-free space between the walls and the loose stuff on the ground.

In case of an accidental fire, make sure you have adequate water on hand, as well as proper fire extinguishers. If running water isn't available, strategically placed drums and buckets will have to do.

Take Your Time

Bale walls go up very quickly. Because the work is fun and energetic, the tendency is to go too fast: the dreaded Bale Frenzy! Do your best to temper your enthusiasm with frequent checks to ensure you are progressing correctly. This will help ensure straight walls, square corners, and properly placed windows and doors. A wall that's raised in five minutes will likely need five hours of repair; a wall that's raised in two hours is finished.

Chris and Pete's Highly Unpatented Bale Stacking Methodology: Condensed Version

Here are the steps we follow when raising bale walls:

1) Inspect carpentry

2) Prepare corner guides

3) Mark and place door and window bucks

4) Inspect and mark electrical boxes.

5) Uncover and distribute bales

6) Retie partial bales

7) Place ceremonial first bale

8) Complete the first course

9) Continue stacking, one course at a time, placing appropriate bucks, wiring, fastening points, service entrances

10) Brace or pin as required

11) Complete walls to full height

12) Place top plates and compress (load-bearing designs only)

13) Stuff all the holes and voids

14) Trim, carve, and straighten walls

15) Install any required flashings and mesh

16) Stitch or quilt mesh

17) Cover up and celebrate

And Now, in More Detail:

Inspect Carpentry

So many elements need to come together for a successful bale raising. Check your foundation and curb rails, top plate, framing (for post and beam projects), rough buck frames, and all the other elements that will interact with the bale walls. Be sure everything is ready. For bucks that will float in the walls, mark the installation points on the foundation and mark the bucks clearly with arrows indicating the right side up and the right side out. For bucks that are attached to the floor and pre-installed, be sure they are adequately braced to the foundation or the outside, and well cross-braced. For load-bearing designs, make sure the routing for the compression wires has been inspected, and cut these wires to length.

Also, for load-bearing designs, be sure your top plates are ready to go on top of the walls. We usually have the ladders attached to the bottom piece of plywood, but leave the insulation, vapor barrier, and top plywood off until they are in place and the compression wires have been tightened. Be sure that your top plates have been

properly labeled, so they can be quickly installed in the correct order and direction. Similarly, the plywood for the top side of the box should be cut and labeled. The top plates should have any holes or channels for the compression wires prepared and marked.

18.2: *The boss has one last instruction for the carpenter before the bale raising.*

Set out the lumber that will be used as braces, ties, and supports during the bale raising.

Prepare Corner Guides

Bales do not necessarily want to be stacked perfectly vertical. A bale wall tends to want to lean outward further and further with every course. The only way to prevent yourself from having a

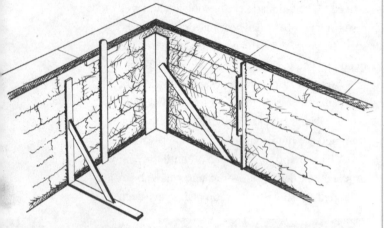

18.3: *A variety of devices are used to help bale walls go up plumb, square and level. From left: A plumb brace for long, straight runs of bale wall; A height stick, used to measure the walls during precompression; Corner guides are braced plumb in both directions (only one brace shown) at every corner on the building; A plumb stick with a level attached is used to check walls at various places.*

18.4: *Door and window bucks must be braced plumb and square. They will likely see lots of abuse!*

case of the leaning corners (which can be very slow to repair) is to use temporary corner guides at every corner. These are simply made of lumber screwed together to form a long, L-shaped unit approximately the same height as the wall. These guides are screwed into, or on top of, the curb rails (depending on the placement of the rails). Chris always fastens his corner guides to the inside corner, and Pete fastens his to the outside corner. Some workshop participants have split the difference and attached them to the inside and outside. Regardless of their position, these guides are then braced into place while being checked very carefully for plumbness using a four-foot level. Fasten them in place with screws, so they'll be easy to dismantle later.

Similar guides can be built to help ensure that long sections of wall go up straight. These can be braced to the ground or to the inside of the building. You can also build a wow checker by using a long straight piece of lumber with a carpenter's level. Make frequent rounds of the building with this tool and adjust the walls as necessary. The earlier you catch problems, the easier they are to fix.

With inside corner guides, the bales can be tied off to the guide to keep them from leaning outward. With outside guides, you want to ensure a loose fit between the bale and the guide. If the bale is too tight against the guide, it will likely bulge outward when the guide is removed.

Check the plumbness of your corner guides every so often during the bale raising, as they can get knocked out of line.

Mark and Place Door and Window Bucks

Door bucks can be attached to the curb or foundation in advance of the bale raising, as can any window bucks with legs that extend to the foundation. Be sure to brace these frames to the foundation or to stakes driven into the ground outside the building, and also screw in adequate lateral bracing. They are sure to take a lot of abuse during the bale raising, and if one frame gets knocked askew and the bales are stacked with it out of line, it will be very time-consuming to fix after the fact.

We don't often use floating window bucks; they are difficult to keep plumb and level, and often don't get positioned properly during the bale raising. But if you use them, mark their position on the foundation and directional arrows on the buck. Have lumber ready to use as bracing to keep them in line. Make note of the course number on which the buck should be installed.

Inspect and Mark Electrical Boxes

Your wiring should already be routed between the curb rails, with the boxes (preferably airtight, R-2000 plastic boxes with ½-inch flanges) mounted. The electrical inspector should visit the site before the bale raising to inspect the wiring, since it will be buried in the straw soon. With the nod from the electrical inspector, you can fasten the boxes to the wooden stakes that will keep them located in the bale wall. These stakes can either be long and narrow, fastened to the side or back of the box (See figure 10.6), or they can be flat pieces of thin scrap plywood mounted to the top, bottom, or side of the box. The stakes can be driven into the bales, or the plywood inserted between the bales vertically or horizontally. The electrician should leave you some extra wire length, as the wires will be threaded between the bales in a somewhat circuitous route.

For post and beam designs or where a rough buck is conveniently placed in a load-bearing design, the wiring can be routed up these wooden posts and the box solidly mounted to them.

On the foundation, mark the approximate position of the box, and whether it is intended for a plug (mounted low), a switch (mounted mid-height), or a light (mounted high).

18.5: *The R-2000 electrical box is fastened to a scrap of plywood which can be inserted between two bales to keep it in place. The wire is snaked up between the bales to keep it away from the surface of the wall.*

18.6: *The plastic wrapped behind the box stops air leaking in or out; essential with metal boxes.*

Keep an eye on the electrical boxes as the walls go up, ensuring that they end up in the right position. It may require removing bales if they do not.

Uncover and Distribute Bales

Ideally, your bales will be delivered on the day you need them and unload directly from the wagons or trailer and onto the foundation. Alternatively, unload them from the transport trailer that has been storing them onsite. Use your entire crew to cooperate in moving bales quickly and with a minimum of movement and effort.

Much time and effort can be saved during the wall stacking if you place your bales in well-planned stacks around the site. Each wall should have its own stack near at hand so that wall building need not be accompanied by long walks to a faraway mound.

HANK CARR

18.7: *A hay elevator can save a ton of work ... literally.*

Bales are all unique. If there are bent, broken, or loose bales, set them aside for use in retying to smaller sizes. Be choosy about your bales. If you think a bale feels or smells damp, don't use it. If there are bales that are bent out of shape, take the time now to force them back into their proper form. All of this will allow your wall stacking to go forward with as few disruptions as possible.

Retie Partial Bales

We used to leave the retying of bales to a dedicated crew of custom bale makers who would supply the wall stackers on an as-needed basis. This almost always resulted in bottlenecks. Everybody wants to stack walls, and nobody wants to retie bales.

So, we now dedicate the first half-hour or so of a bale raising to having everybody onsite retie at least a bale or two. We make a variety of sizes, using both halves of the bale. These partial bales are then added to the stacks around the site in an accessible way. With this strategy, the flow of the bale raising is not disrupted while two or three stackers stand idle waiting for one person to make a shorter bale. There will inevitably be a need for some further retying of bales, but by minimizing this you speed up the whole process.

Custom bale lengths can be achieved in two ways. The simplest is to cut the strings, remove excess flakes until the bale is the right length, and then retie the strings. Create a loop in one end of the string and feed the other end through this loop. Press down on the bale with your knee and cinch the string tightly before tying it off. Repeat for the second and, where appropriate, third strings. The leftover flakes can be used to make another partial bale or to fill all the small spaces in the walls.

Bale needles can also be used to retie bales to custom lengths. With the original strings still in place, thread the bale needle and insert it through the bale (do not allow the strings to twist around each other) at the appropriate length, just inside the original string. You will now have a string coming out both sides of the bale. Remove the needle and, using a cinch knot, tie the new string tightly. Repeat the process once for two-string bales, twice for a three-string bale. Then cut the old strings and you'll have a new shorter bale. By feeding two strings through the bale each time you insert the needle, it is possible to tie off two shorter bales if the strings are tied on opposite ends of the bale. Be sure that the two strings don't cross over one another inside the bale, or your two custom bales will be bound together!

For three-string bales, it may be necessary to build a bale press onsite to compact bales during retying. Simple to make and operate, these big clamps allow lots of force to be applied and ensure tight custom bales. For two-string bales, the time and effort required to make each bale in the press is overkill.

Ceremonial First Bale

This is a moment to pause and gather everybody together before the madness of the bale raising truly begins. Cameras will flash as the homeowners proudly install the first bale (remembering, of course, to start at the corner). We don't recommend the breaking of a champagne bottle against the side of the first bale. It's tough to get the bottle to break, and there are some moisture issues surrounding the practice!

Complete the First Course

Different crews can start installing the bales at the various corners of the building. Things will work best if the same crew stays dedicated to that area of the building throughout the entire process. Natural divisions in the wall will become obvious as the bales move from the corners toward the various obstacles they will encounter (window and door frames). Some crews will move faster than others, so let everybody have a chance to figure out their own turf.

Encourage the stackers to take their time, position each bale carefully, choose the best bale

18.8: *The whole crew takes some time to retie bales to a variety of shorter sizes.*

18.9: *The ceremonial first bale is laid by the owners.*

for the spot, and monitor their own work after each bale is laid. We like to call a halt to the proceedings after the first course is in place. This gives everybody a chance to pause and survey the progress. If things are being done improperly they can be corrected, and the whole crew

18.10: *A perfect fit!*

ORVILLE THERTELL

JOANNE SOKOLOWSKI

18.11: *Bale raisings are busy places, with many hands making the work go quickly.*

has a chance to see what everything should and should not look like.

The most common mistake with bale raisings is to have bales hanging out over the corners. It is usually best to set your corner bales in from the corner by a few inches, since they tend to miraculously grow as the rest of the wall is built. The first course is a good time to catch this problem, since adjustments are easy to make.

Continue Stacking

Once everybody has seen the appropriate stacking method on the first course, work can proceed to build the walls up to full height. Work is bound to happen at different rates around the site, but it's best if the crews do not get too far ahead or behind of each other. You can reassign a person from a fast-moving crew to help out with a slower one, or get the fast stackers to take a break while others catch up.

As the ends of bales are slightly rounded, two small spaces will be created as bales are laid end to end. If not stuffed, these spaces will have less insulation value and eat tremendous amounts of plaster. We've found it is best to neatly lay a hand-twisted bundle of loose straw in these spots before each bale is laid. Fill wider gaps with untied flakes. Then do an inspection. Fuss and fiddle until everything is just right. We often try to place the cleaner cut side of the bales (laid on the flat) toward the inside of the building to minimize indoor trimming later on.

Continue stacking, one course at a time. Keep placing bales in running bond. If you limit yourself to one course at a time, it will enable you to monitor your progress. Course meetings can bring everyone together, give you a rest, and allow you to make sure all plans for the next course are implemented.

Using a wide, flat bale beater, pound each bale down after you've placed it. This often encourages the bales to sit better on one another and means there will be less precompressing to do for load-bearing buildings and less natural settling in post and beam frames.

Certain items will need to be inserted into the walls during the stacking process. Each crew should be well aware of the wall items for their section, and these should be accessible and well labelled. These will include:

Bucks. Floating window bucks will need to be installed at the proper height and in the proper direction. Make sure all the required bracing lumber is at hand, and that the crew takes its time with the level to ensure that the buck sits plumb and level. Standing bucks will already be installed, but encourage the crew to periodically check that they are remaining plumb and square, and to stop and fix things if they are not.

Wiring. The wiring can be snaked up between the joints in the bales one course at a time, until the appropriate height is reached. You can make some measuring sticks for each crew that will indicate the correct height for plugs, switches, and lights. This way, the heights will remain consistent (otherwise, tall people will mount them higher than short people!). Make sure the boxes sit squarely and tightly in the wall. There will be some room for adjustment later, but the better they sit at this point, the easier it will be later.

Fastening Points. Most bale walls will require some attachment points, for hanging kitchen cabinets, electrical panels, and other site-specific items. There are numerous ways to insert wooden fastening points in the wall, from driving in stakes to building ladders that get sandwiched between courses to nailing strips mounted on stakes. These mounting points are not necessary for strength, as a simple drywall plug in the finished plaster is more than adequate to support anything you'd hang on the wall, but it can be more convenient to have some wood embedded in the wall so a screw can get a bite without having to drill and install plugs.

Service entrances. Passages through the wall may need to be created for electrical service, gas

18.12 : *A quick tap with the beater settles new bales into the wall.*

18.13: *Use levels often.*

lines, air intakes, plumbing vents, hose bibs, exhaust fans, and chimneys. Research the requirements for each of these entrances beforehand

18.14: *A metal electrical box has been vapor barriered, meshed, and is being attached to the wall using galvanized wire run through the mesh and the screw holes in the box. Wire pins hold everything snug against the straw.*

and determine specific conduit requirements or clearances that must be maintained. It is easy to run conduit between bales or to create plywood boxes that act as a chase through the wall. Some lines can just be run directly through the bales. Hose lines or other plumbing lines should always run through conduit to prevent leaks or pipe sweating from soaking the bales. Your bale crew should know where each of these entrances is to be placed on their wall.

Brace or Pin as Required

We have not used internal pins (metal rebar, wooden stakes, bamboo) in our bale walls in years, and would recommend that you avoid them. We definitely don't use the rebar pins embedded in the foundation. Hazardous, expensive, time-consuming, and able to allow moisture up into your bales, there is no compelling reason to use pins.

Driving pins or stakes into the bales to pin the courses together is something we avoid. In our experience, the time, effort, and material that goes into this type of pinning does not result in a better wall. In fact, many times we've seen perfectly straight walls get banged out of line while the pins are being hammered in, only to then be stuck out of line because the pin makes it difficult to straighten things out.

Much more effective as wall stabilizers are external guides, either temporary or permanent. The guides can be as

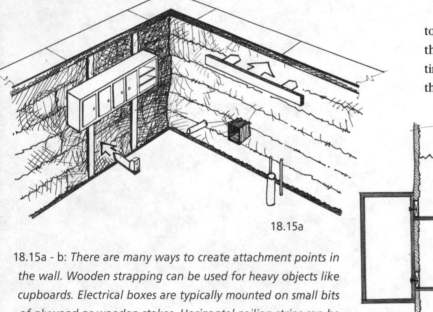

18.15a

18.15a - b: *There are many ways to create attachment points in the wall. Wooden strapping can be used for heavy objects like cupboards. Electrical boxes are typically mounted on small bits of plywood or wooden stakes. Horizontal nailing strips can be buried under the plaster or, if attractive wood is used, left proud of the plaster. Services enter through conduit or plywood boxes placed in the wall.* 18.15b

simple as 1-by-2-inch strapping, bamboo, or saplings placed on either side of the wall and then cinched together using baling twine and a needle. These will keep the walls bound together and straight and yet still allow for adjustments. They do not slow down the process nearly as much as driving internal pins, and fewer are required for greater stabilizing effect.

18.16: *This plywood panel mounted to the wall allows conduit for wiring to pass through the wall, and will provide a mounting place for the electrical panel.*

Just Plug It

A recurring question from people considering building with bales is How do I hang things on my walls?

There has been plenty of advice offered on this topic, most of which involves the placement of wooden nailing strips on or in the bale walls, which are then plastered over to lock the wood into place. A slight variation on this theme comes from brick and stone homes, where the wood is embedded between courses and allowed to show through into the home, providing a visual element as well as an attachment point. This works easily and well with bales. Another common solution is to drill into the plaster and knock a piece of wooden dowelling into the wall.

But since I'm not always the best at preplanning (or accurately preplanning, to be more precise!), I had always been curious about the strength of the common drywall plug when tapped into a plastered bale wall. I have seen people hang outrageous loads on drywall walls using only these little plastic plugs, and we all know a thickly plastered bale wall is a lot stronger.

So, when it came time to mount some bookshelves on a temporary display wall, we simply drilled holes into the plaster, dabbed some caulking into the hole (we don't want to create air leaks into our walls, do we?), and tapped in the plastic drywall plug. The shelves held their load of straw bale books with no problems. But where would the breaking point be?

18.17: *Two little plastic drywall plugs hold up this man!*

Enter my ever-enthusiastic and adventurous partner, Peter Mack. As we were breaking down the display, he decided to test out the brackets by bringing his own great weight to bear on the issue. As the photo shows, he was amply supported, and, being an amply sized young man, I now feel amply confident that some simple plugs can be used for most hanging/fastening needs.

I'll still try to give the kitchen installers some visible, accessible strips of wood to ease their jobs when installing cabinets and counters, but for just about everything else, the plug'll do!

— *Chris Magwood. A version of this article appeared in* The Last Straw, *no. 45, 2004.* ∎

Whether you leave these external pins in place when you plaster will be a matter of personal preference or code requirement.

18.18: *Sometimes bales simply refuse to rest snugly against a post. Tie them to the post temporarily; once the first coat of plaster is on they won't move and you·can cut the strings.*

18.19: *The bales are all in. Note the rolls of mesh hanging under the rafters waiting to be pulled down and stitched to the wall.*

If you have guides on your inside corners, you can tie off each course of bales to them, which will help to keep the corners cinched in and straight. Send the bale needle and twine through one corner bale, around the guide, and back out through the other corner bale. Tie tightly using the same loop and knot as you would for retying a bale.

You can also make temporary or permanent connections to posts and buck frames in numerous ways. The bales can simply be tied to such framing using a needle and twine, which can be left in place or removed once the wall is stable. More elaborate connections can be made with diamond lath nailed to the frame and pinned into the top of the bale, or with doweling drilled through the frame and pounded into the bale. In general, we have found such elaborate strategies to be overkill.

Where straw bale construction is covered in building codes, there are sometimes prescribed requirements for the pinning of bales, one course to the next. Be sure to follow any applicable pinning arrangements. Let your best judgment determine how much pinning you do, unless prescribed by code.

Complete Walls to Full Height

You'll probably be surprised by how quickly the walls can be raised, even by a crew that is being careful and taking its time. With some monitoring of the progress and a few repairs here and there, your walls will often be to full height within a day or two, even on larger buildings.

Along the way, you may have planned for some creative bale stacking, or you may have decided to improvise onsite. Bale benches, buttresses, shelves, and other unique features can be built in as the walls go up.

Bale walls, especially for load-bearing buildings, are often a bit wavy and tenuous by the time they reach full height. Don't worry too much about this, since the compression on the top plate or the jamming in of the last course of bales in the frame will bring about some stability. Just be sure that the walls are not in danger of falling on somebody, and everything will be okay soon!

Celebrate again .... you have something that looks like a shaggy house!

Place Top Plates and Compress (Load-bearing designs only)

Once your walls are full height and you are happy with their attitude, lift the top plates into place one section at a time. Be sure to attach

Merchant Wire Precompression

In our ongoing search for good precompression methods, the key factors we consider are cost, efficiency, availability of suitable materials, effectiveness, and user-friendliness. Here's our favorite system, to date.

For precompressing, we've found 9-gauge fencing wire, sometimes called merchant wire, to be the least expensive and simplest to use. We route a wire through the foundation and over the top plate to create a loop around the wall. Where the two ends of the wire meet, we create a closed loop on the top wire, securing it with a saddle clamp. (A farmer who attended one of our workshops could tie a knot in the wire that also worked effectively.) The lower wire is fed through this loop and pulled back down on itself.

The first fence stretcher is attached to this end — it will tighten on the wire under a downward force. The second fence stretcher is attached to a lower portion of the same wire — it will tighten under an upward force. Between these two stretchers, we attach a come-along or a load binder — or even insert a metal bar that can act as a lever — and apply force.

The beauty of this system is that the wire is strong enough, once bent through the tied loop, to maintain its position even without clamping. This allows us to move quickly from wire to wire around the building without having to clamp and unclamp for each adjustment. When the roof plate is level, a saddle clamp is added to the adjusting wire to ensure that it holds its position when we're finished, or the wire is simply twisted to hold it in place.

Measure the top plate height from the foundation in several places and make note of the high and low spots. Adequate precompression cannot usually be achieved with a single application of force at each point. Your first round of the building will be used to lightly draw down the top plate to stabilize the building and locate the top plate accurately. The lowest height ☞

18-20: *Wire is passed through the foundation and over the top plate.*

18-21: *A loop is created in the upper end of the wire with a saddle clamp.*

18-22: *A come-along is clipped to a fence-stretcher in readiness for pre-compresion.*

minus one-half inch is a good target at this stage. Achieving level is not the goal of this first round of tensioning. Be sure that you are not drawing the building out of shape by applying too much force on one particular side. Use your wow checker to ensure that the walls remain straight.

Round one of precompression gives you a chance to assess the performance of all elements in your chosen system and to familiarize yourself with your tensioning devices and fasteners. Check for any binding of your strapping materials and for places where the strapping is showing signs of early fatigue. If you can arrange for precompression to occur at two points on the building simultaneously, the overall time required for precompression will be halved, and it will be easier to apply offsetting forces on opposite sides of the wall. During the second round, you can apply most of the compressive force to the walls. You may not be able to apply maximum force at each point immediately. Each strap may need to be visited two or three times in order to reach maximum compression. If you cut a measuring stick to the desired height of the walls, this will be more accurate and convenient than a measuring tape, especially if the stick has a cross-piece that allows it to hang from the top plate. You can then compress until the stick touches the foundation.

Defining maximum compression is difficult. Prescriptive standards do not exist in current straw bale building codes, and due to the variable nature of straw bales, it is ☞

18-23: *Close-up of fence stretcher.*

18-24: *The steel bar method is fast and low-tech. Note the clamped loop in the top wire.*

18-25: *A downward force is applied to the bar or come-along drawing the top plate down.*

impossible to predetermine an exact compression figure that would apply to all structures. Variables such as bale quality, wall height, expected live and dead loads, size of openings in the wall, and system of precompression will all create unique conditions and requirements. It is typical to expect 1 to 3 percent compression.

It is important to remember that the point of precompressing your walls is not to squeeze every last bit of squish out of the bales but only to ensure that no further settling will occur before the plaster is applied. Precompression is not a matter of brute strength; balance and equilibrium are what is important.

Compression round three will allow you to achieve a completely level top plate if you tweak your straps in various locations to align the top plate. A few tickles with a sledge hammer may help at this point to ensure the top plate is also level in its other plane. When you are satisfied with the level of your top plate, fasten your straps securely to prevent slippage and trim any loose ends or major protrusions that might interfere with plastering. Once your building is precompressed, you might add some diagonal straps to provide cross-bracing, especially if you are building in areas with seismic activity or extremely high winds. ■

18.26: *The tension wires are pulled with a come-along and fence stretchers. The height stick hooks over the top plate, providing you with a reference for both vertical plumbness and overall wall height. Notice how the walls are protected by a sheet of plastic over the top plate.*

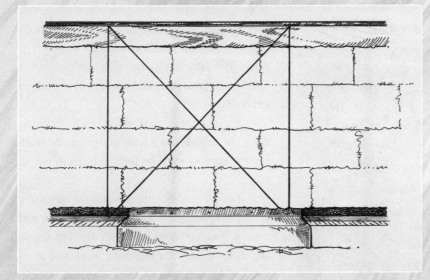

18.27: *The same kind of wire used to compress the walls can be run diagonally to provide excellent cross-bracing. This is particularly wise in seismic zones.*

18.28: *Leave voids over windows and doors until after the top plate is on and the walls have been compressed.*

intersecting pieces firmly, using screws in the splices to ensure a strong connection. Measure the diagonals from corner to corner to ensure that the top plates are square and pull them into

18.29: *The top plate that was carefully laid out on the foundation is now raised onto the walls.*

18.30: *Top plates need to fit together snugly and up against the corner guide which is checked for plumb.*

shape if they are not. If your temporary corner guides are a little taller than the bales, you may be able to use them as locating devices for the top plate, since they are plumb to the curb rails below.

Chapter 8 outlines several different systems of precompression for load-bearing walls. All the elements required for your precompression system should already be in place, including the right kind of top plate, and fastening points or conduit through the foundation.

Route all your wires, cables, straps, or other tensioning devices and fasten them appropriately. You may find anywhere from ½ to 4 inches of easy compression in your walls. This can be achieved relatively easily with a mechanical device.

Stuff All the Holes and Voids

It is very important to the long-term performance of your walls that all the gaps are well stuffed. Even if you have been filling these as you've been building the walls, there will still be some left to finish. If you've left the stuffing to the end, it will take several people dedicated to the job to get it done.

You don't want to stuff too much straw into the gaps, or else you'll start to deform the wall, but the stuffing must be tight enough to stay in place.

Believe it or not, there is a right way and a wrong way to stuff! The wrong way is to just push a bunch of loose straw into the gap, resulting in loads of extra trimming work and areas that will be difficult to plaster. The best thing to do is grab a handful of long straw and fold it over on itself twice. You'll now have a tight wad of straw in hand that can be inserted into the gap. Once there, it will present a neatly folded end to the surface of the wall and will expand to fill the gap.

The best way to stuff voids is with a cob mix. For this, mud and straw are kneaded together to make a sticky mix that will plug the holes well and can be worked with the palm of the hand to create a flat and even surface for the plastering. Mixing cob is a lot of fun: a job that kids and adults are happy to do!

Trim, Carve, and Straighten Walls

Your bale walls will continue to be adjustable until you apply the first coat of plaster. Homemade "persuaders" of many shapes and sizes have been employed in this task, as have feet, knees, arms, and hands. Work with a partner on opposite sides of the wall when you're straightening. By mutual consultation, you can arrive at a straight wall. Anybody who's ever had the pleasure of thumping a bale wall with a giant sledge will attest to the fun that can be had at this stage of the process!

Your bale walls should be well trimmed before they are plastered. Loose, uneven ends of straw will make plastering very difficult, so aim for as smooth a surface as possible. You can use several tools for trimming. A heavy-duty line trimmer or weed-whacker works well; light-duty models will die a premature death on the straw bale site. The more powerful the whacker, the faster the job will go. Gas or electric models will do, but exhaust fumes can be bothersome and bad for the health when working on the inside of the walls, so we recommend electric versions. Regular trimming cord can be used, but be prepared to go through several spools of cord, since straw is much more resilient than the grass for which it was intended. A plastic blade or metal chain attachment can also work, though

18.31: *Cobbing into gaps is dirty and fun for people of all ages.*

you will have to be more careful using them near wooden or metal elements in your wall. These attachments can also carve curved window openings and perform other sculpting chores. In hard-to-reach places, or to trim close to wood and metal, use hand shears. A well-sharpened set can quickly and effectively do the job.

Not for the faint of heart, heavy-duty tools may also be used to sculpt bales, including chain saws and angle grinders with lancelot wheels or circular saw blades spinning backwards. Exercise extreme caution using these tools, and be sure others on the site know what you are

18.32: *Gently persuading the bales into line.*

doing. Do something else if you're tired. A chain saw can be used carefully to make big cuts for rounded window openings or to create channels for plumbing drains or other embedded elements. Be aware that chain saws can create sparks around loose straw. Use with caution and keep a fire extinguisher handy. The grinder can be used to carve into bales to create rounded openings, niches, and channels. Tape an old sock over the grinder before tearing into a bale wall, as the loose straw will get sucked into the electric motor and cause the premature death of the tool.

Remember to wear appropriate safety gear when trimming and carving bales. Proper respirators are needed since a good deal of lung-damaging dust will be created. Eye protection is important: flying chips of straw are every bit as dangerous as chips of wood or metal.

Bale walls can be beautifully adapted to suit many tastes. Whether they are intentionally bumpy, gently undulating, or perfectly straight, your bale walls will create a unique home. Even someone who builds with the exact same set of plans won't end up with a building that looks like yours. It is at this stage in the process that you create the overall look of the walls.

Some people adopt a take-it-as-it-is-built approach to finishing their walls; others carefully craft a particular texture and shape. You can adopt different strategies for the interior and exterior of the house or vary the look from room to room. Your walls should please your esthetics before you install the stucco mesh. You can continue shifting bales once the mesh is hung, but it

18.33: *Giving a house a hair cut.*

18.34a

18.34b

18.34a - b: *Shaping bales with a grinder is fun and tiring.*

is easier to rearrange the exposed and uncovered bales.

Flashing, Meshing, and Plaster Preparation

This is the most often overlooked aspect of building bale walls. There is a sense of elation once the walls reach their full height and have been tensioned, trimmed, and straightened. However, the preparation for plastering often takes longer than the bale raising itself. Be sure to schedule for this time, and if you are building with volunteers, arrange to have helpers at this stage too. All too often, everybody leaves as soon as the walls are up, but the job is only half-way done.

The preparation you do for plastering will directly affect the look and performance of your building. It's time to get fussy!

Flashings. A good moisture-resistant design incorporates flashing at areas of critical importance for water shedding, including the base of your wall and the top and bottom edges of windows and doors where walls are likely to be exposed to direct rainfall. Flashing can be purchased prefabricated or custom bent to suit your design. Attach them securely to your wooden foundation curb or window buck. Be sure that the drip edge will be clear of the walls once the plaster has been applied (i.e., there will be an extra inch of material there soon!). Never rely on caulking alone to seal out water; gravity and flashing must work in concert to shed water effectively. Consider caulking only as insurance on a good flashing job.

Stucco Mesh. Whether you decide to mesh your entire building or not will depend on many factors, including code requirements, engineer specifications, personal preference, and type of plaster. Even if you don't mesh the whole building (which is not necessary in most cases), it will be needed for plastering some areas of exposed flashings, wood, loose straw stuffing, and vapor barriers. So even on a building that is not being completely meshed, count on a fair bit of time for this job.

Mesh embedded in the plaster adds strength and offers adhesion to the plaster. In the days before reinforcement mesh, plasters were strengthened by the addition of chopped straw, horse hair, and other natural fibers. These served a similar function to mesh, enabling plastered finishes to last longer.

BARRY GRIFFITH

Given the symbiotic nature of the straw/plaster relationship, the application of plaster to a straw bale wall is quite different from its more common application over brick, block, or wooden walls. The ends of straw provide excellent grip for plaster and create a strong bond both during application and over the lifetime of the wall. Most current building code requirements for plaster application do not take into account the interaction between straw bales and plaster. Your building official may require that you meet

18.35: *This metal flashing protects the base of the wall. It requires proper meshing prior to plastering, otherwise the plaster won't stick.*

Prepping a Bale House for Plastering

Bale walls can usually be raised very quickly, but that's only one step in the process. Before plastering can begin, there are many, many detailing jobs to do. If they aren't done, the plastering will not go smoothly, and it will be difficult to get the results you wish.

As professional plasterers, we often arrive to plaster bale walls that the owner has prepared for us. And usually there are a number of details that we need to do (or redo) before we can begin.

We've compiled a list of wall preparation details that we recommend be completed before calling in a plastering crew (or attempting to start plastering yourself). Remember, if you are planning a volunteer bale raising, try to spread out your volunteers so that you have help getting the bales prepped too.

Pre-plastering prep work to be done by owners:

Bales stacked. Well, you have done your best .... you and your extensive list of volunteers have done a beautiful job stacking your bales so that your walls are looking as plumb as a nicely stacked bale wall can look! Take an appreciative look at your work and enjoy a celebratory meal together, but don't let those volunteers all leave .... you'll need LOTS of help for all of the work to follow.

GRANT CHAPPELL

18.36: This wall is meshed, masked and properly flashed. It's ready for the plaster starting to cover it.

Start with stuffing. Holes and gaps between bales need to be tightly stuffed with straw. We suggest that you stuff as you stack the bales .... otherwise, it's a mammoth job for someone to do after the whole house has been built. Stuff holes neatly and tightly .... if you don't stuff them tightly enough, you will have air leaks and insulation loss in spots on your walls, and plastering will be difficult over such voids. You can also stuff holes and low spots with a cob mix, using a high straw to clay ratio.

Window shaping. All window openings should be shaped as desired and covered with plaster lath or mesh (the windows can be sculpted with a weed-whacker or other tool if the bales are on the flat; if they are on edge, you may have to use a big bale beater-type hammer to hammer them into shape, or you might have to resort to tightly stuffing behind lath to get the desired shapes). Diamond lath is usually the best mesh to use, especially on overhead plastering spots (tops of windows). This is definitely one of the more satisfying jobs once you get the knack. If you have a particular shape of window opening in mind, you'll either have to carefully train your volunteers or do them yourself. If there are any wooden sills in your windows, don't forget to check that the barrier paper has been put on before you lay your mesh.

Weed-whacking/bale trimming. All walls should be weed-whacked and straightened prior to hanging reinforcement wire .... please wear protective glasses, and a respirator for this very dirty job! Generally speaking, it is better to do this job wearing long sleeves and pants, or you'll end ☞

up with itchy bits of straw all over you! It might be a good idea to have a few different volunteers (maybe just the owners?) do this job as it is quite a hot job, and can be unpleasant in the heat of the summer. On the other hand, it can be quite satisfactory to do this job, with a noticeable difference in the shape of the house as the shagginess of the bales is now looking nice with the new haircut.

Cover and mesh wooden elements. Exposed wood surfaces to be plastered that are wider than 1.5-inch should be covered with house wrap or painted with slip coat, then covered in plaster lath (diamond lath works best). If you can push some straw in behind the mesh, even better. This helps prevent shrinkage cracking of the plaster as it hits a different substrate.

Plaster stops and drip edge. Plaster stops must be installed around doorways, windows, and at the top of the bale wall where needed. These can be temporary strips of plywood, 1-by-2s, permanent flashings, or trim boards. Drip-edge flashing must be installed above windows and doors, and below windows if no other drip sill provisions have been made. Generally, plaster stops of ½" are ideal.

Electrical boxes. Electrical boxes properly installed ½-inch proud of the surface of the bales, with vapor barrier hats behind, and surrounded by, diamond lath well fastened to the box and the bale wall. Airtight masonry (or R-2000) electrical boxes truly are worth the bit of extra money they cost. They don't require site-made vapor barrier hats, and they have a flange that acts as a natural plaster stop.

Braces, cabinet reinforcement. Extra bracing, if required for installing cupboards, etc., should be placed in appropriate places on walls, preferably before reinforcement mesh is hung (you can imbed a 2-by-4 or 1-by-4 into the bales as you are stacking them, or you can install vertical 2-by-4s that run from the bottom to top plate (keep in mind that these will mean notching or custom-fitting bales around them).

Reinforcement mesh. If you have to use reinforcement mesh for your building, we recommend using a strong plastic mesh rather than metal fencing or chicken wire. It's much easier to work with. Reinforcement mesh should be hung inside and out, stapled or nailed frequently and securely to top plate and bottom curb. We recommend using air staplers for this job. They drive larger staples. If you choose to use a hammer tacker or hand stapler, make sure you have several heavy-duty versions. You should work in teams of at least two people for installing the mesh, and if you are using metal reinforcement mesh, you may need more workers. Pull the mesh as taut as humanly possible. You can either stop at the window openings or continue right over them, stapling the mesh to the framing and cutting out the parts covering the window later. The tighter you can get the mesh now, the less fiddling and stitching later! ☞

18.37:
The heaviest cabinets need wood strongbacks under the plaster.

all the plastering provisions in the local building code or that you at least use some kind of mesh reinforcement, such as:

- Plastic mesh. This is our favorite type of mesh. It is the most convenient to install because it comes in 10-by-330-foot rolls, light enough to be handled by one person, and may be cut with a knife or scissors. It is also less expensive than most wire meshes, but may be more difficult to locate, as it is not a commonly used product.

- Diamond lath or expanded metal lath. This is a heavy-duty, galvanized mesh that is commonly available. It is not used to mesh entire buildings but offers excellent support where there is no straw for the plaster to bind with (over wooden surfaces, vapor barriers, flashings). It can also be used to form consistent curves at windows, doors, and corners. This mesh is also placed around electrical boxes to help fasten them to the wall and keep them secure. Use a metal cutting wheel on a circular saw to cut this mesh, as it is long, slow work with hand shears. Using diamond lath over the entire wall would actually weaken the walls by interfering

Reinforcement mesh should not extend beyond the bottom curb or above the top plate. It should be neatly and tightly installed, with any extra mesh cut off. Little pieces of mesh sticking out in these places will remain forever sticking out of the plaster, looking ugly and allowing potential air/moisture penetration.

Pay attention to the mesh at the bottom of the wall where it sits on the flashing: it really needs to be fastened well here, so that it lies flat and flush with the bottom of the flashing.

Stitching the mesh. Reinforcement mesh needs to be quilted or sewn so that it sits flat against the bale wall. Stitches must be tight. No lengths of string should hang down on the wall; after tying off the stitch, cut off excess twine.

After all the other rather labor-intensive jobs involved in getting your walls ready, this is a much calmer, somewhat meditative one. Look for spots where the mesh is sitting far from the wall and place your stitches there. Watch for the needles coming back through the wall towards you; stand back far enough to make sure you don't get jabbed!

Windows. Your decision about whether to install the windows prior to plastering or afterwards will depend on the kind of finish you want. If the plaster is intended to finish against the sides of the window and/or cover a built-in flange, they must be installed first. If the windows will be finished with wood trim, they can be installed after plastering.

Flashings. The flashing at the bottom of the wall can be installed prior to stacking bales, but there is a chance the flashing will get a bit dinged at the bale raising, so most people install it after the bales are in place. It gets attached to the curb with screws or roofing nails. Make sure that the flashing is actually installed so that it will do its job .... think like water! If the flashing is sloped towards the house, it won't be helpful!

Masking. Windows, doors, and exposed framing lumber must be masked with plastic or cardboard. Use a quality tape to fasten covering to them; cheaper brands will come off, leaving windows exposed and vulnerable to plaster droppings. When you are masking your windows, you need to decide where the plaster will end .... leave a ½ inch bare for the plaster on the outside of the window frames if the plaster is to cover over them. It is difficult to remove tape from window frames if it is buried under the plaster! ☞

with the bond between plaster and straw, since it is difficult to push the plaster through the narrow holes with any force.

- Welded steel fencing. In seismic areas, or where prescribed by code, use a welded steel fencing. Typically available in 2-by-2-inch grid, this is a strong mesh, with wire gauges of 14 to 18. Use bolt cutters for cutting this mesh. It can be expensive to cover an entire building with this mesh, so adjust your budget for this choice.

- Chicken wire. We don't know why some people still insist on using chicken wire on bale buildings. It is difficult to handle because it won't stretch tight or sit taut over the straw; it's awkward to cut and it's not inexpensive.

It has been standard practice to cover any exposed wood with tar paper prior to meshing and plastering. We'd recommend against this. It's better to isolate the wood and plaster with air barrier or plastic. Another option is to paint the wood with a runny slip coat of your plaster. This puts a coating on the wood so it doesn't suck the moisture out of the plaster and gives the plaster a better surface for bonding. The

Flashing needs to be masked; again, set the masking tape back a ½ inch, but don't tape the flashing too far in advance of the plastering, as it can be difficult to remove after baking in the sun for a long time. Same goes for the windows! If you have a dedicated cleaner, you can skip masking the flashing. *Never* skip masking windows, doors and thresholds!

Finished floors need to be masked as well. Set the floor tarps back half an inch from the bale curbs.

Plaster will be spilled during the process. The time you take to mask will be paid back in time spent not chipping and scrubbing cured plaster from surfaces. Remember that the tape lines you create will define the edges of the plaster; if you want it straight, tape it straight.

Scaffold setup. Scaffolding should be erected 8 to 12 inches away from the walls, with the ladders on the outside, except for the top row. Scaffolding should be ample enough to surround house; sky jacks or scissor lifts can be more economical than scaffolding on large two- or three-story buildings.

Site. Trenches, holes, and excessively rough terrain slow things down. Have the site excavated, if possible, to provide a flat, level, safe terrain for scaffold placement.

Extra time spent on prep really pays off; the finished walls will reflect the effort. So, good luck, hang in there, and hopefully you've been able to cull a keen group of volunteers to help with all of these tasks.

— *Tina Therrien, The Last Straw, no. 45, 2004.* ∎

HANK CARR

18.38: *The quality of masking of windows and doors dictates the quality of the finish. Good scaffolding helps plasterers do their best work.*

18.39: *Mesh goes on quickly with an air stapler and is held secure by long staples. Note that the mesh is pulled tight enough that is lays flat even before it's quilted.*

best option of all is to staple some loose straw over the wood so that the plaster is not applied to two different substrates at all.

All mesh will need to be securely fastened to your top plate, foundation curb, and window and door bucks. It can be stapled or hung from nails that have been driven at an angle into the top plate at 6- to 12-inch intervals. If the staples shoot through the mesh, turn down the air pressure. Once attached, the mesh can be pulled taut at the bottom of the wall and fastened securely. In some situations the mesh will install better horizontally.

If you are using a mesh with large holes, you will need to double it over wooden, metal, and concrete elements, or else fasten heavier diamond lath over top. Be sure you allow the doubled or heavier mesh to extend into the straw wall by about six inches. This can be useful where you expect the wall to take some punishment, such as around doorways and exposed corners, and where cracking is most likely, such as at the corners of windows and doors.

Stitching or Quilting

Once the mesh is secured to the inside and outside faces of the wall, you will need to anchor it to the straw. If you don't, it can sag and poke through the plaster. The most common method of anchoring mesh is to sew it onto the wall using bale needles and twine. With one person working on either side of the wall, a bale needle can be passed back and forth and the stitches drawn tight to prevent the mesh from sagging or riding too far from the surface of the wall. Don't worry

18.40: *Each bale is dipped on two sides in a pool of thin clay slip.*

Bale Dipping

The dipped bale technique originated with Tom Rijven, a bale builder in France. Tired of the difficulty involved in applying the thin slip coat of clay onto the bales in preparation for the application of an earthen plaster, Tom decided to try dipping the inside and outside faces of his bales into a tub of clay slip prior to stacking them in the wall. Unorthodox, yes, but perfectly in tune with the adventurous spirit of bale building!

Many advantages quickly presented themselves. First of all, it was easy to achieve a precise and even penetration of the clay slip into the bales. Placed on the surface of the tub of slip, the bales float. By pushing down on the floating bale, the slip is forced into the straw to whatever depth the dipper chooses. The bale is then rolled onto the side of the tub, the excess slip is wiped away with a trowel, and the process is repeated for the opposite side of the bale.

The dipped bales do not need to be trimmed or weed-whacked, saving lots of time later in the process. With their edges coated in slip, the bales are ☞

about placing stitches at even intervals; rather, focus on placing them where they're required. You will quickly develop a pattern with your co-stitcher that will allow you to pass the needle while the previous stitch is being pulled tight.

Stitching is quiet, meditative work and can go quite slowly if the mesh was initially applied very loosely or if only a few people are stitching. It can take as long to hang and stitch the mesh as it did to build the bale walls, so be sure to plan for this extra time.

You may be able to avoid doing a lot of stitching if your mesh is tightly stretched between the top and bottom of the wall. Occasional loose spots can be pinned down using homemade bale staples shaped from galvanized fencing wire. Push them into the bales over the mesh to add localized tension. Use all the wooden attachment points you've located in the bale wall to help secure the wire; 2-by-2-inch pegs can be driven into the bales to provide extra anchoring points, if needed.

Cover up and Celebrate

Bale structures must be kept dry. The best possible protection is a completed roof. For post and

18.41: *Stitching with baling twine and a long needle requires two-person teamwork to get the mesh lying down properly.*

much more stable when being stacked, much easier to align and keep in alignment. And for load-bearing buildings, very little settling occurs because of the embedded slip coat.

A terrific bond is created between the plaster and the straw bales, because the earth plaster bonds firmly to the slip that is embedded deep in the face of the bale. As so much of the recent testing of bale walls has proven, this straw-plaster bond is one of the crucial factors in the strength of a wall, and by dipping the bales, this bond is guaranteed to be strong. And no mesh is required!

The final benefit to dipped bales is in the reduction in fire hazards. Not only is there no bare straw in the walls, but eliminating the trimming phase means no accumulation of knee-deep piles of loose, cut straw.

I was extremely impressed with the results of the dipped bale technique and see it as another important evolution of the technique of building with bales.

— *Chris Magwood* ■

18.42: *A dipped wall needs no further preparation prior to plastering.*

beam designs, the roof can be finished before the bales are put in place. For load-bearing designs, it will be completed after the walls are up.

18.43a

18.43b

18.43a - b: *Tarping: a crucial part of any bale building until it is plastered. Whether you are covering the whole building or just blanketing the walls, you'll celebrate the day you are able to take the tarps off permanently.*

Any protective covers at the tops of your walls should be completely waterproof. Polyethylene sheeting — as used for vapor barriers — is a good choice, but any waterproof membrane will do. This does not include most hardware store tarpaulins. If you only have cheap tarps, double them up.

Use tarpaulins and house wraps to protect the sides of your walls. Cheap tarpaulins are quite adequate for the short term, stapled to the top plate or fascia boards, or to truss ends if the fascia is not in place. They should also be well anchored at the bottom, stapled to the foundation curb or weighted with tires, concrete blocks, or heavy lumber.

It can take several hours to put tarps up well, so leave yourself enough time to do a good job. If you will need to work on your walls again, make the tarps easy to roll up or remove. Otherwise, make the arrangement permanent enough to resist high winds and driving rains.

Typar and Tyvek house wrap also make excellent bale wall protection, especially if you will not be plastering for some time. These materials come in rolls wide enough to match the height of a typical exterior wall and can be fastened easily with staples or thin strips of wood. They resist UV rays better than tarpaulins and are more water resistant. Sealed with appropriate tape or caulking, they provide enough of an air barrier to lend the bale walls some insulation value before the plaster coat is applied.

Celebrate! Raising bale walls is a remarkably satisfying task. Even though you're bound to be physically exhausted, stand back and admire your work. You have cause for pride. Be sure to put down your tools, brush the loose straw from your clothes, and enjoy the moment!

CHAPTER 19

Plastering Your Bale Walls

The job of plastering your bale walls is a considerable undertaking. Whether you do it yourself or hire workers, the choices you make at this stage will critically impact the way your house looks and performs.

The plaster coating that is applied to your bale walls provides the long-term structural support for the wall system and seals the straw against air movement, fire, pest penetration, rain, and snow. Your choice of plaster coating and its method of application will define the final visual appearance of your home and create the feel of both the exterior and interior walls. It is possible to achieve many different finishes, while creating a wall that will last for several generations.

Plaster

A Time-honored Finish

Plasters of various kinds have been used to finish buildings for centuries. The correct kind of plaster can provide a durable layer of protection from the elements, and a wide range of textures, colors, and surfaces are possible. From a rough, devil-may-care application to the most meticulous professional job, plaster finishing allows for all kinds of approaches.

CHRIS MAGWOOD

Examine a wide variety of plastered buildings — both modern and historic — and you'll soon develop a sense of the variety of finishes you can achieve with different plasters. It is possible to get very creative with your plaster, so

19.1: *Trowel goes up, plaster rolls on; good form.*

don't worry if you look around and find most plaster finishes boring.

A Workout for the Mind and Body

Plastering permits the use of a wider array of materials and techniques than any other element of your straw bale house. There is no single best combination of ingredients and application techniques. You will have to consider cost, climatic appropriateness, embodied energy, availability of materials, desired finish, building code requirements, your attitude toward plasterers, especially amateurs, and speed of application and curing.

Plastering is the most labor-intensive phase of straw bale construction. Whether you apply by hand or by machine, the physical effort required to plaster a building surprises many people. Be

19.2: *The very first smear of plaster starts the process of covering the entire building.*

prepared to put in a lot of effort yourself or to pay well for workers to make the effort for you. Plastering is the one area in straw bale building in which the amount of necessary effort and materials can exceed those of conventional construction.

What Is Plaster?

People are often confused by the terms that are used to describe the coating used to seal straw bale walls. Plaster is a generic, catchall term for any kind of goop that is smeared on a wall while in a wet (or plastic) state and that dries or cures to become a hard, brittle substance, capable of withstanding weather and structural forces.

Plasters are made up of two basic ingredients: an aggregate (usually sand) and a binder. It is the latter that distinguishes the four basic types of plaster used for straw bale construction:

- Earthen or clay plasters
- Lime plasters
- Cement/lime plasters
- Gypsum plasters

Acrylic and synthetic stuccos are not permeable, and should never be used on a bale building.

Each type of plaster offers its own particular advantages and disadvantages in straw bale construction. It is good to learn lots about the plaster you are planning to use, since a little education early on can prevent many problems during the application.

Four Basic Plasters

Not Straight Cement Plasters

You might notice that there is no category for straight cement plasters (a mixture of portland cement and sand) in this book. Straight cement plasters have no place on straw bale walls for several reasons. A straight cement plaster does not offer the permeability or breathability required to ensure that moisture can freely transpire from within the wall into the atmosphere. Without this breathability, the walls could experience moisture damage. Cement plaster is also very difficult to work with, tending to be quite crumbly and hard to stick to a vertical surface. Because it also comes with a significant environmental price tag, we avoid its use as much as possible. Usually, when bale builders refer to cement plaster they really mean (or should mean) cement/lime plasters.

Cement/Lime Plasters (Stucco)

The most widely used plasters in straw bale construction are cement/lime plasters. Mixed together, cement and lime produce a plaster that combines some of the stickiness, workability, and permeability of lime with the quick curing times and strength of portland cement. It is often the default choice because it is the most widely available and common form of plaster. Building supply outlets typically will refer to cement/lime mixes as masonry cement. Different companies make different blends of cement and lime in their masonry cement. Some have as little as 25 percent lime, others as much as 50 percent. Try to find mixes with the highest lime content. Some will be specifically intended for plastering or parging purposes, and are better choices than those intended for brick or block laying. Cement/lime plasters are also sometimes referred to as stucco. Make sure the material you select is intended for above-grade applications.

Durability

Cement/lime plasters create hard, durable surfaces and offer impressive strength. Cement/lime and straw bond well together and are very long-lasting.

Cost

Cement/lime mixes are widely available, and their cost is relatively low. In many places it's possible to find crews who specialize in plastering with cement/lime.

Mixing and application

There are plenty of available resources pertaining to the proper mixing and application of cement/lime that are useful for novice plasterers. Because cement is the same wherever you buy it, standard mix formulas can be used. There are likely to be many experienced cement/lime plasterers in your area, should you wish to consult or hire professionals.

While many cement/lime mixtures are available bagged together, it is also possible to mix portland cement and lime together onsite.

Code Compliance

Cement/lime plaster may be the only exterior plaster recognized by your building code. A great deal of testing has been done on cement products to ensure their suitability for various applications.

Embodied Energy

Cement is created from ground limestone, clay, alumina, and other minerals that are heated together in kilns and then ground to create a powder. The mining and burning of cement consume large amounts of energy and is not appropriate if you are attempting to build with a minimum of impact on the environment. (See sidebar, What to do About Cement, Chapter 9.)

Quality of Finish

Cement/lime plasters can create a wide range of surfaces, from very smooth to rough and stippled. A local masonry supply outlet can likely provide you with examples of different application techniques. Cement/lime plasters can support the use of pebble finishes, in which large aggregate is used on the top coat to create a variety of looks. You can also embed tile, stone, wood, and other elements in a cement plaster.

Cement/lime plasters respond well to the addition of pigments. White cement and/or white sand can be used in the top coat to brighten pigments. Lime washes can also be used, as can traditional paints, although paints are prone to cracking and flaking and can act as an unintentional vapor barrier.

Other Factors

Cement and lime are corrosive to skin. Care must be taken when you are working with the powder to ensure that correct breathing apparatus is worn. Curing times for cement/lime plasters are short and predictable; usually they are hard to the touch within 6 hours and hard enough to support another coat within 24 hours.

About Lime Plasters

Lime plasters have a very long and proven history going back thousands of years. The qualities that made lime the literal cornerstone of many civilizations — its durability, strength, and permeability — make it well suited for straw bale walls. There is much to be relearned about working with lime plasters that has been forgotten in the past century as lime was replaced by the simpler-to-use portland cement.

There are two basic kinds of lime used in plasters: hydrated lime (the most common) and hydraulic lime, both available bagged similarly to cement and masonry cement. Hydrated lime powder is mixed with water and sand and does not start to cure until the wet mixture is exposed to the air, when it starts to cure by recombining with CO_2 in the atmosphere.

Hydraulic lime powder begins to cure as soon as water is added, in a chemical reaction with the H_2O, similar to portland cement. This is an important distinction to understand when researching lime plasters, as the two are handled quite differently because of their different curing styles.

The reason lime plasters are so suitable to straw bale walls is their excellent permeability. A lime plaster, though hard to the touch and able to withstand the elements, is porous enough to offer a rapid rate of transpiration for humidity in the bale walls.

Durability

Properly applied, lime plaster is very long-lasting, since it returns to being limestone. One only need to see some of the buildings made by the Romans to understand the durability of lime plasters. Lime plasters are suitable for exterior applications in any climate.

Cost and Availability

Type S hydrated lime is quite widely available and costs about the same as bagged cement. Hydraulic lime is less common, but there are distributors throughout North America. Both kinds are starting to make a slow comeback because of their importance to the restoration of historical buildings. Do not use agricultural lime; make sure you are buying a lime that is created for plastering or mortaring purposes. Even among plastering limes, there are noticeable differences in quality, so ask people with experience or try some samples of several brands before buying a large quantity. Expect to encounter raised eyebrows and skepticism when you let it be known you are trying to mix a lime plaster! Don't let a cement guy talk you out of using lime.

Mixing and Application

Hydrated lime should first be made into a putty by soaking it in water for at least 24 hours. Some brands of Type S can work if mixed right out of the bag and into the plaster, but the longer it hydrates, the more workable it becomes and the better and slower it cures. Hydrated lime plaster hardens first by drying (which can happen too quickly if not adequately hydrated), then has a long period of chemical reaction absorbing large amounts of CO_2 to return to its natural state. It is slower to set into a hard surface than cement plaster, with a first coat taking two to ten days to harden to the touch. It is traditionally applied in successive thin coats, allowing each to have maximum exposure to the air. Modern additives — including portland cement and gypsum — have been used to speed up the curing process.

Hydraulic lime is not presoaked, since that would initiate its water-based curing process, causing it to harden. It is mixed directly into the plaster and used immediately, as with portland cement. Its curing process is longer than portland cement's, but shorter than hydrated lime's.

The highly pliable nature of both kinds of lime plaster makes them easy to work with; they stick well to the bales (even without the use of any reinforcing mesh) and are pleasurable to work with, offering longer working times than portland-based mixes.

Working with lime requires the same caution as cement. It is highly caustic to the skin, and correct breathing equipment must be used when you are mixing dry lime.

Code Compliance

Lime plasters are fairly rare in modern construction. This kind of plaster is unlikely to be covered by building codes, but familiarity with its historical precedent usually allows for its use.

Embodied Energy

The production of lime requires considerable energy to burn the limestone (although the temperatures are lower than required for making portland cement). The reason lime is seen as more environmentally sound than its portland cement cousin is that the CO_2 that is driven off the limestone is almost entirely reabsorbed by the lime plaster as it cures, resulting in no net gain of CO_2 in the atmosphere. Local small-scale lime production, now rare, is relatively sustainable (many homestead farms had a lime kiln in the back fifty).

Quality of Finish

Lime plasters have a softer feel than cement and are naturally a brighter white. Pigments will work well with lime. Any kind of finish — from a highly polished, glassy smoothness to a rough stipple — is possible to achieve with lime. It can also be mixed into a paint-like wash and applied in its natural white or with added pigments, making an easy color coat.

Other Factors

Lime is commercially packaged for many applications other than plaster making. Be sure to find a Type S lime that is meant specifically for plastering or masonry purposes — agricultural lime does not make good plaster. Hydrated lime putty can be mixed and stored indefinitely, since it will not cure as long as it's protected from exposure to air. This means you can always have some on hand for repairing cracks or creating additions. There are relatively few modern resources available to those who wish to use lime plasters, so expect to take some time finding the materials and experimenting with application.

Lime plasters, because of their high alkalinity, tend to discourage the growth of mold and mildew and can also repel many breeds of insects.

Clay- or Earth-based Plasters

Earth-based plasters are made with soils that have a naturally occurring balance of sand and clay. For centuries, such plasters have protected buildings from the elements, and they are an entirely feasible and practical option in a modern context.

The biggest strike against earth plasters is simply a cultural prejudice against using something so old-fashioned and unscientific as mud on something important like a house. But hundreds of bale structures have been plastered with earth, and the results are quite remarkable.

The only weakness of earth plasters is their susceptibility to erosion under repeated exposure to rain, which is typically addressed either by generous roof overhangs or a protective coating.

But there are so many positive aspects to using earthen plaster that it is certainly worth considering. Its sheer simplicity, beauty, ease of application, and environmental friendliness are all compelling reasons to choose an earthen plaster.

Durability

We know that earth is a durable substance; it has been around for a long while! Historically, earth-based plasters were repaired or resurfaced on a regular basis — a maintenance schedule that may not suit current builders or homeowners. However, modern buildings have better roofs that, if made to overhang generously, largely eliminate this concern. Natural stabilizers (like flour paste, linseed oil, blood, and dung) can also

The Case for Clay

Like many straw bale enthusiasts, I was first attracted to this building style by its potential to reduce the environmental impact of my project. As there were no local bale buildings standing at the time, I learned what I could from books and from good old-fashioned trial and error.

I certainly tried to pursue the best environmental practices and materials that I could. I did consider earth plasters and floors, but something about using earth scared me. Here I was trying all kinds of untested and "radical" building methods, and yet I couldn't bring myself to trust in dirt.

My appetite for earth plastering was whetted when a client agreed to earth plaster his small load-bearing place with us. Our engineer, equally uncertain of earth plasters, called for a percentage of cement in the mix, "just to be sure." I loved applying that stuff.

Then, at the 2002 International Straw Bale Building Conference (ISBBC) in Australia, I was introduced to real earth plastering. All the fears about test patches, mixes, clay content, and other nagging fears were quickly laid to rest. Earth plastering was intuitive as much as scientific. In fact, the same intuitive sense I'd been applying to building projects for years was exactly what I needed to apply to this abundant, free, and ecologically sound plastering material! The lights started flashing in my head .... I was hooked. ☞

add water resistance to an earth plaster. Most earth-plastered straw bale homes have shown that the plasters are very stable and that maintenance is not required on short cycles.

Cost and Availability

If suitable soils exist on your building site or in the local area, earth plasters can be free. Where local soils require modification in the amounts of sand and/or clay, costs rise, although nowhere near the price of lime or cement. It is possible to use commercially prepared clays to make earthen plasters, with per-bag costs similar to cement and lime, but this not commonly done. If your soil has any degree of clay content, it is worth considering earthen plaster.

Mixing and Application

Due to infinite variations in local soils, generic recipes cannot be used for mixing earth plasters.

You will have to experiment to ensure that your particular mix is the strongest it can be. Earth-based plasters bond very well with straw and are easy to apply by hand because they are not caustic.

Most builders using earth plasters do not use any form of wire reinforcement, rather, they use the natural bond between straw and earth to increase the strength of the plaster. Earth plasters are very forgiving, since the addition of more coats and the blending of one coat into another can be done very seamlessly.

Code Compliance

Earth plasters are more likely to be acceptable in areas where they have been used traditionally. Testing has established the suitability of earth plasters for load-bearing straw bale construction and demonstrated that, while earthen plasters

The more I learn about building, both mainstream style and natural, the more I realize that a large percentage of any building is intuition, experimentation, and the application of prior experience. Architects, engineers, and professional builders may sound scientific and logical, but in truth, almost every new building is an experiment, blending science, superstition, personal preferences and habits, budget, skill levels, and a host of other factors into a finished product.

In Australia, up to my knees and elbows in mud, I made a commitment to myself. I was only plastering with earth from now on. It has no greater level of unknowns and uncertainties than any other material I've ever worked with and so many advantages environmentally and aesthetically. I've trusted my intuition with straw bales and other natural materials .... of course I should trust it with that most trustworthy of natural elements, the earth under my feet!

—Chris Magwood. A version of this article appeared in no. 43 of The Last Straw, and is reprinted with permission. ■

19.3: The earth plaster dance is easy and infectious, requiring little instruction and lots of laughter.

may not have the ultimate strength of cement or lime plasters, they are still well within the range of strength to create code-approved, load-bearing walls.

Embodied Energy

Where site soil is used, the embodied energy for earth plasters will be extremely low. Even with the use of imported materials, earth plasters are much more environmentally friendly than any alternatives. Clay that has been processed and bagged will obviously have a higher embodied energy, but significantly less than cement or lime.

Quality of Finish

An earthen plaster dries with a softer feel than cement and has different acoustical properties. Color and texture will vary with soil type and

method of application, and its finish can be very beautiful and blend well with the curves and bumps of a straw bale wall. Pigments, lime washes, natural sealants, and paints can all be used to color earthen plasters. Some will have a tendency to "dust," especially if brushed by moving bodies. A hardener such as sodium silicate can be used to minimize this dusting, or additives like flour paste can be added directly to the plaster. You can blend natural elements like stones, pebbles, twigs, bark, and ceramics into earthen plasters and include sculpting and relief work.

19.4: Clay plasters can be applied by hand, simplifying the finishing skills required.

Other Factors

Your willingness to experiment will dictate whether or not earth plasters are for you. There are mines of information about earth plasters that provide information and inspiration, but the variability of soil will mean that, in the end, it's up to you and your dirt to come to an agreement. But it's an entirely pleasant process to undertake.

Gypsum Plasters

Gypsum plasters are often what comes to mind when the term plaster is used, since gypsum was the base for the old style lath and plaster walls common in many older homes in North America. Gypsum is also the main ingredient used in making modern drywall compound and sheets.

Durability

Use gypsum plasters only indoors, since exposure to rain will cause rapid deterioration. As an indoor plaster, it is can last the lifetime of your home with no maintenance required.

Cost and Availability

Gypsum plasters are manufactured by many large companies under different brand names — Structolite, Sheetrock 90, Durabond 90, and Red Top are common — and most building supply stores will be able to order gypsum products if they don't stock them. Gypsum plasters are fairly expensive as base coats, especially if they are used directly from the bag without the addition of any sand or other aggregate. Prices tend to vary several dollars per bag for the same products, so check several sources before you buy.

Mixing and Application

Gypsum plasters come ready to mix with water. This must be done in relatively small batches, since gypsum plasters set chemically (except premixed joint compound), and each batch has a short workable lifetime (15 to 60 minutes). Some gypsum plasters include perlite in the mixture to add volume and reduce weight for base-coat applications. Fine screened sand or other aggregate can also be added to base coats to give extra volume; most commercially available bags include ratios for its addition. It will take some experimentation to judge what volume to make for each batch.

Gypsum plasters are easy to apply, since they are quite sticky and pliable while wet, making application on difficult spots like the underside of window openings relatively easy. Sculpting and relief work is also very easy. The gypsum adheres well to bare straw or a base coat of any other plaster, and look good if allowed to take the shape of the bales underneath. If your aim is to achieve straight walls, you will have to master the techniques of the old-fashioned plasterers, which can take a lot of practice.

Code Compliance

Gypsum plaster is acceptable as an interior finish in most areas. It has a long history in home building, and the companies that manufacture modern varieties have testing data on strength and durability.

Embodied Energy

Gypsum must be mined and heated like cement and lime, but the process requires only about one third of the energy. Manufactured products include chemical stabilizers and agents to slow or speed the setting process.

Quality of Finish

Gypsum plasters provide a soft finish and are not prone to dusting or cracking. They create a more pleasant acoustical effect than do cement/lime finishes. Some varieties dry to quite a bright white finish without the addition of any paints or pigments. Gypsum plasters take regular paints very well, or any number of pigment solutions can provide color. It is easy to sand a gypsum plaster finish to remove high spots and achieve a smooth finish. Patching is simple, since small batches can be easily mixed, and successive layers bond well to one another.

Other Factors

You might want to purchase a single bag of several different gypsum plasters and experiment to see which gives you the qualities you most prefer. The carefully engineered mixtures and the consistency of the mixes allow for generally crack-free walls. Gypsum plasters can be used as a top coat over any base plaster, providing your interior with a softer, more pleasing finish. You must clean your tools and mixing equipment frequently, since curing occurs very quickly.

Combination Plasters

None of the four main types of plaster has to be used on its own. It is possible to combine ingredients to make hybrid plasters or to use different plasters for different coats. We have tried reducing the cement content in our cement/lime plasters to as little as 20 percent without affecting the curing time or the end results. It is also possible to make earth/lime plasters that have some desirable qualities. Although gypsum and earth can be combined, gypsum and cement will start to get rock-hard very quickly! Before you make any unorthodox combinations, it is best to do some research or try some experiments — before you are committed to covering your entire house!

Check Your Local Area

Depending on where you live, plaster finishes may still be common on frame-walled and block-walled buildings, and you may find many professional plasterers to hire or consult. Check out plastered buildings in your area and talk to homeowners and professionals for advice. Plaster finishes used to be much more widely used, so often the best advice will come from retired builders and plasterers. These people are usually glad to help revive their old practices and may be willing to help you out.

If plaster finishes are uncommon where you live, you will have to do some research to locate talent or the materials, tools, and advice you'll need to do the job. Look for areas with climate conditions similar to yours where plaster finishes are in use.

Take Plastering Advice with a Grain of ... Grain?

Plastering a straw bale wall is quite different from plastering a wooden or cement wall. The plaster bonds with the straw rather than creating a separate and thin layer. You will use a good deal more plaster to cover bale walls than same-size wood or block walls. Not realizing this, plasterers unfamiliar with straw bale walls will often underbid straw bale jobs. They will either starve themselves or ask for more money to compensate for the extra materials and time involved.

You may be steered away from plaster finishes by people who have seen plasters that cracked and peeled from wooden or concrete walls. Plasters on bale walls don't operate as a separate skin and so aren't affected by the same differential expansion and contraction that occurs on wooden or concrete walls. Even where cracks do appear, the plaster itself does not pull away from the wall. Often, peeling and cracking is caused by paint on the exterior surface acting as a vapor barrier to trap moisture inside the plaster; color for plaster is better achieved by tinting the plaster itself or by using breathable lime washes or stains.

The Plastering Process

It is standard practice to apply three coats of plaster to the interior and exterior walls, and in some jurisdictions the building code will enforce this. Three coats will provide more than adequate protection against the elements, as well as significant structural strength. The three coats together should create an average coverage depth of one inch over the entire wall. The actual thickness of the plaster will vary from point to point, but you don't want the thinnest spots to be any less than ½-inch thick. Since the first two coats often provide adequate thickness, many people are inclined to skip the troweled finish coat and just apply a wash or paint.

First Coat/Scratch Coat

The first coat of plaster, the scratch coat, is the most time-consuming and material-intensive coat to apply. It is forced into the straw to achieve a good bond and built up to fill the hollow spots and irregularities of the bales. Plasterers who are experienced at covering straight walls are invariably surprised at the amount of time and material it takes to build the scratch coat on a bale wall.

The scratch coat uses the strongest plaster mix with a higher amount of binder to aggregate. Plaster is applied thickly enough to cover most of the straw ends, on average ½ to 1 inch thick, with most of this material being pushed into the straw. It is called the scratch coat because you will literally scratch the surface of the plaster with horizontal strokes once the plaster has begun to set. These scratches will afford the next coat a mechanical grip and supplement any chemical bonds that are formed.

Brown Coat

The second coat, or the brown coat, will average ¼- to ½-inch thick and will define the overall shape of the wall. It can be applied as soon as the scratch coat has set (i.e., is hard to the touch). Much less material and time will be required to apply the brown coat. A light scratching with a broom will roughen its surface and help the finish coat to bond.

Color Coat or Finish Coat

The third coat creates the finished look of the wall. From heavily textured pebble coats to thinly brushed color washes, the mixture and application of this coat depends largely on the finish you are trying to achieve. If you are coloring with pigment, add it to this coat. Whiter plasters like lime, gypsum, and lime/white portland cement will allow colors to show up more brightly. A number of different application and finishing tools can be used to create the effect you want.

Wall Preparation

The preparation of the straw bale walls is the key to a good plastering job. A poorly detailed wall can defeat even the best plasterer and is more likely to crack. Well-trimmed straw, nicely manicured meshing, and well-stuffed holes are a must. Be clear about where you expect the plaster to stop when it meets doors, windows, foundation, and roof plate.

Sweep old bits of loose straw from the intersection of floors, walls, and window ledges, then cover the floors with plastic or drop cloths. Plastering is a messy business, and these coverings are not likely to be reusable. Tape the edges of the drop cloths at the base of the walls to create the desired seam between the floor and the plaster.

Apply masking to windows, doors, and any other elements you don't wish to have plastered. Be sure to cover up window sills, since plaster dropping from above can stain them permanently.

It can be helpful to precut a number of metal pins — for pegging down any wire mesh you find sitting too far from the straw you are plastering — and keep them handy. Sometimes, errant mesh can be persuaded to sit flat with a stab from a trowel. But it's better to have the walls properly prepared rather than count on such fixes while plastering. (See sidebar: Prepping a Bale House for Plastering, Chapter 18).

Preparing the Site

Plastering is hard, heavy work. You want to minimize the amount of effort you expend on anything other than plastering the wall, so prepare your site thoroughly. Clean up any obstacles inside and outside the house. You will need to walk without impediment and to deliver wheelbarrows of fresh mud to all points along the walls. Be sure to create wide, strong, well-braced ramps wherever wheelbarrows need to enter and exit the house, and bridge any holes or trenches on the site.

You need to assess the best place to situate your mixing equipment. Mixing is hard, hot work so try to find a naturally shaded area, preferably close to the building and near an interior entrance way. This area must have enough room to allow for a big sand pile, stacks of bagged material, the mixing equipment itself, and for several bodies to navigate around everything.

You will need a lot of water, so be sure you can get it to the mixing site. Pressurized water is best; if necessary, you may need to rent a storage tank and pump, which also require positioning close to the mixing station. Because a lot of water will hit the ground during mixing and cleanup, the mixing site must have good natural drainage. Don't mix in a hole!

You must also assess where difficulties may arise in reaching the tops of walls. For two-story buildings, scaffolding must reach the upper walls. Proper assembly and leveling of scaffolding (8 to 12 inches from the wall, ladders out except the top row) can be time-consuming, especially on uneven ground. Plan to have all this

19.5: *The plaster pumping station must be close to the building and have all of the elements close at hand.*

work done before you bring together your equipment and crew. If you've hired a plaster pumping crew, it is definitely in your interest to have the whole building scaffolded. This will allow the workers to avoid direct sun on the curing walls, increasing strength, reducing shrinkage cracks, and reducing the number of cold seams.

If you are plastering an upstairs wall inside the building, protect the stairs from the extreme wear and spills they are likely to receive. Plan for delivering plaster to the upper floor in the most practical and effortless way possible, maybe with a pulley or block and tackle to make lifting heavy buckets of plaster a bit less backbreaking. Alternatively, you could set up a smaller hand mixing station on the second floor. It's best to start by plastering the upper floor and do the hardest work first.

Put away any tools and construction materials you won't need, since everything left out is likely to get covered in plaster. Be sure you do have the tools and supplies you might need — staple gun, extra wire mesh, twine, and metal cutters — near at hand but out of the way of falling plaster.

Finally, set up a tarping system before you start plastering. While keeping the walls away from driving rain is important at this stage, the tarps will also be needed to keep out the sun and the wind, so the plaster cures or dries properly.

Plastering Equipment
Safety Equipment

You must take reasonable precautions when working with plaster. Anyone who is involved in mixing plaster should wear quality respiration equipment. Clouds of cement, lime, clay, and sand will be in the air. Don't invite the stuff into your lungs. Eye protection is likewise recommended for all mixers and plasterers. Splatters can occur at any time — keep them out of your eyes. Quality work gloves are a must, maybe two or three pairs per person, since they are bound to get soaked. Industrial-quality rubber gloves are another option. The mixing, moving, and application of plaster is hard physical work. Be aware of the onset of fatigue and take breaks as required. Injury is most likely to occur when you become exhausted. An eye washing kit should always be onsite during plastering.

Wheelbarrows

You will need at least two good construction-grade wheelbarrows for transporting plaster from the mixing site. The more plasterers you have, the more wheelbarrows you'll need. Some wheelbarrows are shaped specifically with a deep, narrow profile for dumping cement and plaster; cheap wheelbarrows will collapse under a heavy load of plaster. Wheelbarrows can be rented from most building supply or rental centers.

Shovels

It is best to have a different shovel for each ingredient you are adding to your plaster mix, and if you intend to use a shovel for mixing, keep it separate from the dry ingredients. If you do use multiple shovels, be sure they are of similar size, since most of your measuring will be done by the shovelful.

Mortarboards

A flat sheet of steel or wood can be mounted on a bucket or a milk crate to make a mortarboard. This can act as a transfer station between wheelbarrow and individual plasterer, allowing one wheelbarrow to deliver to multiple users.

Trowels

Quality plastering tools ease the effort required for this considerable job, so invest wisely. Trowels for applying and smoothing plasters come in a galaxy of shapes and sizes. Choose the ones that fit your application needs and are comfortable to use. All plasterers have a favorite trowels by

which they swear. Try to have a good selection of trowels on hand. Rounded-edge swimming pool trowels can be easier to use on wavy bale surfaces, since sharp-cornered ones will tend to dig in and scratch any lumps and bumps. Trowels of different lengths and widths will be handy, as will putty knives. A triangular brick trowel is good for reaching into tight spaces and can be used instead of a hawk to load a trowel with plaster.

Clean trowels are essential. Residue on the troweling surface makes it much more difficult to apply the plaster. Rinse your trowels frequently during use and clean them thoroughly with a brush every time you take a break.

JOANNE SOKOLOWSKI

Hawks

Any flat piece of wood or metal mounted on a handle can serve as a hawk to carry a load of plaster to the wall. From there, the plaster is cut from the hawk and applied to the wall with the trowel. You will be holding your hawk all day, and on it will be a remarkably heavy load of plaster. Be sure that the handle suits your grip

19.6: *Mixing is dusty, and water can splash out of the mixer so respirator, glasses and gloves are a must!*

and that the hawk is not too large for you to comfortably hold and maneuver. Some store-bought hawks come with a foam pad at the top of the handle — an idea you'll appreciate by the end of the day!

Sponges

Quality sponges can come in handy as finishing tools, especially for your top coat of plaster — sponged surfaces tend to crack less. Sponges are also useful for cleaning up spills.

Buckets

Five-gallon pails can be used to carry rinsing water for each plasterer, to move plaster around

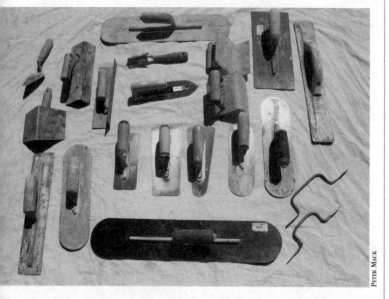

19.7: *An assortment of different sized and shaped trowels is an essential part of every troweller's tool kit.*

the site, to scoop sand or other ingredients, to hold up mortarboards. Try to have lots on hand! Restaurants often give them away.

Cleanup Tools

The best cleaning device for plaster-covered equipment is a plastic bristle brush, available from the masonry supply store, but any kind of stiff durable brush — including toilet brushes — will do. For stubborn cleanups, a stainless steel wire brush is ideal. Cleanup brushes will spend most of their day soaking in water, so plastic handles are better than wood. The more brushes you have, the more people can help with cleanup at the end of the day!

Water Barrels

Garden hoses do not deliver water fast enough to keep up with mixing demands. If you have several large barrels on hand, you can continuously fill the barrels and then use a bucket to add water to your mix in a faster, more measured way.

Water Storage Tank

If you do not have a reliable source of water at your site, you can rent a large storage tank and have it filled. The bigger the tank the better, so use at least the 1,000 - gallon size and expect to have it filled more than once. Be sure to check if water can be delivered on a weekend — there is nothing worse than to have a plastering crew on hand and no water left by Sunday!

Mix Formulas

Nothing is so sacred to plasterers as their particular mix formulas! Use the general recipes that follow as a starting place for your own custom formula. Be sure to talk to plasterers in your region or those who have experience with your particular kind of plaster before you settle on a formula. If you are making a unique mix, be sure to do some experimenting — on straw bales! — before starting to plaster your entire building.

A note on measurements: All the recipes below are volume-based ratios. The most common measurement is the shovelful. Of course, every shovel and every shoveler is going to produce a different amount, but as long as the same person is attempting to make the same-size shovelful every time, the system works!

Cement/Lime Plaster

1 part portland cement
1 part Type S lime (stucco lime)
6 to 7 parts fine screened sand
Or:
 1 part Type N masonry cement
3 to 3.5 parts fine screened sand

This mix is used with 6 parts sand for the scratch coat, 6.5 parts sand for the brown coat, and 7 parts sand for the top coat. If you are using a premixed cement/lime product (masonry cement), then mix 1 part of the premix to 3 parts sand.

Be sure that your cement, or premix is specified to be Type N, which is intended for above-grade applications. Type S products have admixtures for use below grade which will inhibit breathability. Natural or synthetic fibers can be added to this mix to provide extra binding strength.

Lime Plaster

1 part lime putty (hydrated lime) or 1 part hydraulic lime
3 parts sand

Lime putty can purchased ready made or is created by thoroughly mixing 1 bag (22.5 kg) of lime with approximately 20 liters of water — batches can be made in small buckets or large barrels. The mixture is allowed to soak for a period of at least 24 hours. As long as the top of the mixture is covered with water, it will last indefinitely.

Some hydrated limes are formulated to be used directly in powdered form. If you don't want to create a putty, be sure to find this kind of lime.

Lime water, a thin mixture of two to three percent lime to water, is sometimes sprayed onto the straw before the lime plaster is applied. The lime-dampened straw will bond better and make a stronger plaster.

Natural or synthetic fibers may also be added to lime plasters.

Earth Plaster

There is no precise formula guaranteed to be suitable for your particular soil conditions. The basic rule is that too much clay content in the plaster will cause cracking as the plaster dries, and too little clay will result in a weak crumbly plaster. As a rule of thumb, 65 to 85 percent of your mixture will be sand, and the remaining 15 to 35 percent will be clay. Chopped straw or other natural binders are often used at approximately the same volume as the clay content.

To test your soil conditions, dig through the topsoil, remove some root-free subsoil and half fill a jar with it. Top with water and shake the mixture vigorously. As the soil settles in the water, it will separate into three layers with sand on the bottom, silt in the middle, and clay on top. Take samples from several different areas of your site, since soil can vary dramatically in a matter of a pace or two and label them well. You'll be able to tell from your samples if you have to import sand or clay for your mix.

Only experimentation will lead you to the right mix formula. Start combining natural and/ or added ingredients with water and apply them to the sides of bales. When they dry, test them for crumbling and cracking: too much cracking and you've got too much clay; too crumbly, too much sand.

A good basic formula to begin with is:

2 to 3 parts clay (in creamy slip form)

2 to 3 parts sand (something approaching this ratio will exist in many site soils)

2 parts fiber (chopped straw, chopped hemp, cattail fluff, or any other natural fiber)

Apply this mixture about one inch thick to the face of a bale and allow it to dry thoroughly (out of the sun). Then adjust the mixture according to the results. The application of the plaster will tell you lots about whether the formula is correct; if it is so sticky you can't get it off your hands, there's too much clay, but if it won't stick to the bale at all, there's too much sand. Use your intuition: if it feels right when applying, chances are it is right.

CHRIS MAGWOOD

19.8: *Clay plasters include a high proportion of fibre in the mix, in this case, chopped hemp.*

Gypsum Plaster

Commercial gypsum products come with precise measuring formulas on the bag, including quantities for adding sand. Some hints for variations might come from plasterers experienced with the product — ask your supplier about such plasterers.

What About Water?

You may have noticed that none of the above formulas include measurements for water. It's impossible to know the exact amount of water required because of all the variables. The water content of the sand, the temperature and humidity, and the type of ingredients will all affect the amount of water required for a suitable mix. What we can say accurately is this: too much water will ruin your plaster. As any good bread maker will tell you, once you've overwatered a mix, it is very difficult to recover by adding more dry ingredients. So slowly increase the amount of water, and eventually you will get a feel for how much to add.

Mixing

In most plastering crews, one person will usually emerge as the Mix Master or Mix Mistress — the person most able to produce a good plaster with the least number of complaints from the plasterers. Mixing is a hard, and often thankless, job, but a good mixer will never let the crew run out of quality plaster.

Hand Mixing

Although mixing machines make better mud and save time and effort, sometimes it is appropriate to mix by hand. You can hand mix plaster in a wheelbarrow if small batches are all that's needed, or you can build a mixing box from plywood or sheet metal. A wide shallow shape will work best, and the box should be placed so the contents can be easily emptied into wheelbarrows. The best tool for mixing plaster is a mortar hoe. Masonry supply stores sell them, or you can make one by cutting holes in a standard garden hoe. You will also need a good shovel for sand and other bulk ingredients.

Thoroughly combine dry ingredients, push the dry mix to one side, and add water to the mix-free zone. The mortar hoe can then drag the dry mix into the water slowly. When the entire mix is damp, add more water until the desired consistency has been reached. It is very easy to overwater hand mixes, since it takes some vigorous action with the hoe to fully mix in the water.

Machine Mixing

We certainly recommend machine mixing. Barrel style cement mixers make lousy plaster mixers so don't plan to rent or use one. Mortar mixers are properly designed for the task and feature rotating, paddle like blades or a screw-type wheel. These mixers are usually gasoline powered, so be sure to have plenty of gas and oil on hand to keep your operation running. Mortar mixers come in different sizes, identified by the number of cubic feet of material they can handle. A six- or eight-cubic-foot capacity will enable you to create mixes using full bags of material rather than shovelfuls. Make sure your mixer is set up to allow easy dumping into a waiting wheelbarrow or plaster pump — you may have to raise the machine onto a platform or blocks.

With the machine in motion, add approximately one-half to three-quarters of the required water followed by half the sand. When the sand is thoroughly wet, add the lime or lime/cement, then any pigment or fibers. Continue to add the remainder of the sand followed by any required water until the desired consistency has been reached.

Measurement

Since your shovel acts as a large measuring spoon, be sure to add scoops of a similar size each time, but don't be excessively fussy about the size of each shovelful. If you are mixing bagged ingredients, you can determine how many of your particular shovelfuls are in a bag and then add the bags directly to the mix.

Consistency

The amount of added water will determine the stiffness of the finished mixture. Only with experience will you find the best consistency is

19.9a

19.9b

19.9a- b: The mixing station involves hard work and repetition as sand is shoveled into the mixer, followed by the bagged lime/cement.

for you. In general, the plaster should be stiff enough to maintain itself in a blob on your mortarboard or hawk, yet wet enough to be pliable under your trowel.

It's very easy to over-soak your mixture. Plaster mixtures will seem too dry until they hit their saturation point, and then they become too wet very quickly. Give your plaster enough time to thoroughly mix before adding more water, and then add water slowly, a bit at a time, allowing it time to mix again. If your mix is too dry, however, it is possible to jam up a mixer — a situation better to avoid! Unless you are dealing with bagged gypsum plaster, the quantity of water required will vary from batch to batch, so precise measuring is not possible. Using buckets rather than a hose for water will allow for accurate approximation, and you will very quickly get the hang of creating a desirable mix.

Preparing the Walls

Filling Holes in the Wall

Before getting into full-scale plastering, you may want to make a batch of plaster to use as fill for low spots in your walls or to smooth out highly irregular areas. This can speed up the actual application of the scratch coat by minimizing the number of heavy applications required. It's also a good time to practice measuring and making a mix and to try your hand at troweling before you face an entirely bare wall! Even if you are not plastering with earth, it's best to use a stiff, fiber-rich earthen mix (a cob mix) to fill the holes and low spots, since it can be applied by hand to fill in areas without using expensive materials.

Misting the Walls

After all the conscious effort you have made to keep your walls dry, you are now going to contradict your good bale training and turn a hose on them! Most plasters consume water in order to cure, and dry straw will wick away too much water to allow for proper curing. Plasters affixed to damp straw further strengthen the bond between the materials.

Avoid applying a direct stream of water at the bales; rather, apply a fine mist. Careful work with a garden hose and a spray attachment will suffice, but a back-pack sprayer as used by landscapers is also suited for the task. You can use straight water or lime water. Keep the walls damp as you proceed, since they will tend to dry out quite quickly.

Shading the Walls and Wind Protection

Direct sunlight or wind will cause the plaster to dry too quickly, hindering hydration, and causing cracking. Try to time your plastering to avoid direct sunlight on uncured plaster. If you plaster west walls in the morning, north walls at midday, and east and south walls in the afternoon and evening, you can avoid the sun. If this is not possible, hang tarps to provide shade and wind protection during application and curing.

Misting

Once a lime or lime/cement plaster has begun to set (i.e., become hard to the touch) it is necessary to keep it misted in order to achieve a proper cure. This misting should occur every 3 to 4 hours for at least the first 24 to 48 hours and continue less frequently for the next few days. This is a very important part of the process for these types of plasters and should not be forgotten or ignored.

Plaster and Frost

In northern climates, you will want to avoid plastering if temperatures are expected to dip below freezing within 24 to 48 hours of applying the plaster. The freezing of water within the plaster does all kinds of nasty things to the strength and durability of the finish. Do not plaster onto a coat that is below freezing. If you are plastering in questionable weather, when temperatures are flirting with the freezing point, you can hang tarps or blankets over your plastered wall. Heating the water and sand may help. In a pinch, a calcium-based accelerator (only available at masonry supply stores) may be added to the mix; however, accelerators have some negative effects on the plaster, including extra shrinkage and reduced strength.

Applying Plaster to the Walls
Hand Application of Plaster

By applying your own plaster by hand, you can drastically reduce labor costs for this time-consuming process. Mixing and applying plaster is a very basic, simple process, and the help of friends and family can be most welcome at this stage. If you spread the effort among a dozen people, it can speed up the work and make for a fun weekend of shared effort.

A natural division seems to exist in the human population: those who enjoy plastering and those who detest it. If you are among the former, you might actually have a good time putting in the effort that's required. If you are among the latter, it may be worth any price to have professionals do the work for you!

First-time plasterers are infamous for the creation of unintentional sidewalks of spilled plaster around the base of the wall. It's no easy feat to get a full trowel of plaster on a wall and have it stay in place! Still, with some practice, most people are able to get the hang of it and do a good job. The techniques are much easier

to demonstrate than to describe in written form, so getting a lesson from someone with experience is a definite plus. (It's even better if you can convince that person to join your crew!)

First of all, you should always start plastering at the top of the wall and work your way down. You not only get the harder stuff done first, but when you inevitably drop or roll some plaster down the wall, it doesn't ruin the nice job you've just finished on a lower section of the wall! From the top, you'll be able to rest the front edge of your hawk directly against the wall to take some weight off your arm without sticking it in fresh wet plaster.

If you are using a hawk, you can use the cut-and-swipe technique.

GREG MAGWOOD

Place a hawk full of plaster near or directly against the wall. Using the trowel, separate a hunk of plaster and smear it against the surface with a smooth curved swipe, lifting it onto the wall. Position the trowel so that you are using the trailing edge to push the plaster into the wall; the leading edge should be riding just above the surface. Apply lots of pressure to ensure that the plaster bonds well with the bare straw or the previous coat of plaster.

The most common mistake people make in plastering is to worry one small section of the wall at a time. The best technique is to quickly

19.10: *Misting the walls is very important; it helps the cement gain full strength and is essential to the adhesion of the next coat. On windy and/or sunny days, more misting is needed.*

19.11a

19.11b

19.11a - b: After getting a hawk filled up at the wheelbarrow, the troweller rests the hawk against the wall and starts to push plaster upwards.

smear plaster over an area of three to six square feet. This may take two, three, or several hawk loads of plaster. Then, once you have the plaster applied to the large area, start your trowel at the bottom-most edge and make one continuous stroke, applying lots of pressure to the trailing edge of the trowel until you run out of plaster to smear. Then, repeat with another long stroke right beside the previous one. Keep repeating until you've smoothed out the whole area. Then, if you have some ridges or hollows to be filled, go back over the surface you've just troweled, using less pressure. You may need to add a bit of plaster to low spots. Always make the longest trowel stroke possible; you'll never get things smooth by dabbing at the wall with the tip of the trowel! Wipe your trowel clean on the edge of your hawk to keep it from sticking to the plaster on the wall and dragging ridges into the finish. There is no point in visiting the same area of the wall more than three or four times, because you won't get it to look any better. On the first

and second coats, don't worry about it too much, there's still more plaster to go! Then, once you're happy with your area, repeat, over and over and over.

The hawk technique works well when you cannot work right next to a wheelbarrow or mortarboard full of plaster. The fully loaded hawk is very heavy, and your arm may quickly tire of holding it. A second technique, used by bricklayers and masons, involves a triangular brick trowel in one hand and your wall trowel in the other. Use the brick trowel to scoop some plaster and scrape it on the wall trowel. True professionals make this look easy as they throw perfect lumps of plaster onto their trowel in a seemingly fluid and endless motion! With some practice, anybody can get the hang of this technique and use a hawk only when necessary.

Applying the Scratch Coat

Applying the scratch coat is the hardest part of plastering. The bare straw will seem to swallow remarkable amounts of plaster, and you will require hawk fill-ups at an astounding rate. Avoid overworking the plaster by using as few strokes as possible to achieve your best result. The brown coat will offer lots of opportunity for straightening the walls, so concentrate mainly on even coverage and a good bond with the straw for the scratch coat. You should keep a pair of wire cutters in your pocket, to trim bits of string, straw, and wire that refuse to be buried beneath the plaster.

You will need to scratch the surface before it becomes too hard to do so. If the plaster is too soft, the scratching tool will leave lumps that will annoy you on the next coat, and cause that coat to be thicker than necessary. Be sure to score the plaster well, using horizontal motions.

We often use a trowel that has been cut with ridges to do this scratching. This allows us one last shot at working the plaster while also doing the scratching.

Applying the Brown Coat

Before applying any brown coat, it is very important that the wall be well misted. Applying fresh plaster on dry plaster will result in the dry layer sucking all the water out of the new one, ruining its chances of curing properly. Keep the wall well dampened ahead of yourself at all times.

It is best to apply the brown coat before the scratch coat is completely cured — hardened but still a bit damp. The brown coat should entirely cover the scratch coat, and pressure should be applied to each trowel stroke to press the plaster into the scratched grooves beneath. Use the brown coat to give the walls the shape you want. Add extra plaster in low areas; use less on high points. Corners can be shaped according to taste, using careful trowel work or special corner trowels. For the truly committed plasterer who really enjoys the work, the brown coat is where some real technique can be put to use!

As with the scratch coat, it is best to use long, even strokes with the trowel to cover the maximum area of the wall. Try to smooth large areas, rather than fussing over small ones. Keep your trowel wiped clean between strokes and learn to vary the pressure on the trowel as required.

Caulking Joints and Cracks

After the brown coat has fully cured (which can typically take one month), you will likely find that, due to the natural shrinkage of plaster, small openings will appear where plaster

PETER MACK

19.12: *Scratches for a mechanical bond between coats; make them horizontal to hold water for hydration and adhesion.*

meets door and window frames and posts and beams. Before applying the top coat, apply some quality caulking to these cracks — polyurethane is the most weather resistant — to prevent air infiltration. The top coat will cover the caulking, but you may want to choose a color to match it.

Finish Coats

Finish coats are a broad enough topic that you'll find the entire next chapter dedicated to choosing and applying them.

Excessive Cracking

Some minor surface cracking is not unusual in plaster

BARRY GRIFFITH

19.13: *The brown coat is scratched with a broom to roughen the surface.*

Tina Therrien

19.14: *This truth window was plastered in direct sunlight on a windy day, hence the appearance of many cracks in the plaster.*

finishes (and if you look at block and brick walls, you'll find the same cracks there, too). If you find that your scratch coat and your brown coat is cracking excessively, even when you adjust the mixtures and water content, you may want to hire a professional for some advice on how to solve the problem before you apply successive coats. Excessive cracking can result from too high a proportion of binder in your mix, too little water, too much water, or a curing that occurs too quickly. Applying too thick a coat may result in horizontal cracking, as the weight of the material can cause it to sag. You can fill cracks in scratch coats and brown coats with a

All About Cracks

Many different kinds of cracks can show themselves in plaster finishes. If you can identify the kind, this will help you determine its origin and the best strategy for dealing with it.

Sagging or Weight Cracks. When wet plaster is applied to a wall, the force of gravity is pulling downward on that heavy mass of plaster. If the plaster has not bonded well with either the straw or mesh, or if it has been applied too thickly, then it is common to see horizontal cracks open in the plaster as the material slides down the wall a bit before it can cure. This same kind of crack will occur if the plaster was applied too runny; the wetter the plaster the more likely these cracks are to occur. These cracks typically extend across the width of the heavy section (i.e., if you've filled in a deep hollow in the wall), and often have the shape of smiles or frowns. Check for too wet a mix, too thick an application, or too sandy a mix.

This kind of crack most commonly occurs during first-coat plastering, when the thickness of the plaster can vary dramatically. It is also not unusual to "see" the same kind on a second coat, if the second coat is being used to fill in low spots in the wall. Because they are typical of earlier coats, they are filled with the subsequent layer(s) of plaster and usually do not show through. When plastering over these cracks, ensure that new plaster is worked in deeply, filling them completely.

As long as they are not the result of excessively wet or sandy plasters (which will be weak, even when cured), these cracks are not problematic, as they are rare in finish-coat work. If you find them opening in your finish coat, rework the cracked area with a polishing trowel as frequently as required until the plaster is cured. If there are only a few of these cracks, they do not necessarily require repair, since they are usually only cracked through the one visible coat, not through the entire thickness of the plaster layer.

Cracks from Improper Curing. If your wall shows numerous, small, spidery cracks all over the surface, this is likely caused by improper curing. In these cases, the plaster cured too quickly or without sufficient hydrating during the process. ☞

soft wet mixture; rub it with a sponge until the crack is filled. The same can be done for the top coat, but not without affecting the finished look and causing discoloration. Always try to address the root cause of any cracking before undertaking repairs.

Cleanup

It is important to clean up your tools, equipment, and site before the plaster has hardened. Trowels, buckets, shovels, wheelbarrows, mixing equipment — anything that's touched plaster should be scraped and rinsed before it becomes impossible to clean. It's easy to lose expensive tools to hardened plaster, especially if you're using cement and gypsum. Pull tape off window and door frames and floors before the plaster sets. Otherwise, the tape will be hard to remove and will pull off chunks of plaster that should stay on the wall. Clean yourself well, too. Cement and lime will dry out your skin and cause painful rashes and cracking. Treat yourself to a good long bath and some lotion!

19.15: *These are trained professionals on a closed course; don't try this stunt at home folks!*

The most common causes of plasters curing too quickly are direct sunlight or constant winds striking the wall. When the water is sucked out of the plaster at an exaggerated rate, the normal shrinking happens too quickly, causing a big network of small, multidirectional cracks.

Prevent cracks by protecting your fresh plaster from exposure to direct sun and wind. Hang tarps or moistened burlap from the eaves or directly against the wall. Taking care to plaster the exterior of the building in such a way as to avoid the direct sun is also a valuable strategy.

This kind of cracking also occurs as a result of putting a new coat of plaster over an older one without sufficiently moistening the surface. It is imperative, with any kind of plaster, to moisten the existing plaster prior to adding fresh. Cured layers of plaster can be very thirsty; it is not uncommon to mist or hose down a wall repeatedly during plastering, especially when temperatures are high, or there is direct sunlight or wind. Keep a sprayer handy at all times during second- and third-coat work, ensuring that you are applying plaster onto a damp, darkened surface. Keeping the working surface moist also helps to establish the best possible bond between coats.

Cementitious and lime-based plasters also require hydration throughout their curing process, and the same network of small, spidery cracks can occur if they do not receive adequate moistening for at least a couple days after application.

Examine this kind of crack closely. If the cracks are widely spaced and very narrow, they are not likely problematic. But at their worst, they will be frequent and wide and indicate a coat that will be easy to delaminate from its substrate. If tapping and scraping at the wall does not cause plaster to fall off, then the cracks are only a visual blight and can be covered with another layer of plaster or a wash. If the plaster does fall off the wall when scratched, you will have to remove it and start again, moistening properly this time! ☞

Machine Application of Plaster

A spraying or pumping crew can do the job in less time than hand plasterers. Various machines allow you to spray plaster onto your walls without you having to carry and lift all the plaster. Troweling will still be required to create an appropriate finish, but it is much easier if the plaster is already on the wall.

Spraying machines are not very common, and rental units are few and far between. You will most likely have to hire a crew that has a machine and knows how to use it. A spraying crew may or may not be familiar with straw bale walls. If not, be sure they understand the extra amounts of plaster that will be required before you accept a quote. Some spraying outfits may be able to apply enough plaster in one coat to eliminate the need for a brown coat.

There are two kinds of machines for spraying plaster. Shotcrete machines pump mixed plaster through a hose and onto the wall. Gunnite machines pump dry mix that is combined with

These cracks in a finish coat do not require immediate attention, since they are not transmitted through the entire thickness of the plaster. They will, however, be susceptible to further cracking if they get wet and go through a freeze-thaw cycle.

Shrinkage Stress Cracks. These are the cracks most commonly found on plastered or masonry walls, usually running from the corner of a door or window opening to the top or bottom of the wall. They range in width from hairline to significant openings of 5/64 inch or more and are difficult to avoid. Most plaster surfaces (including clay, lime, and cement) will shrink as they cure, and the stress of this shrinkage will be relieved at the point of least resistance, where the sheet of plaster is at its narrowest.

At their thinnest (and most common) these do not require filling. Only if you can see into the crack (i.e., the width of a credit card or more) should filling them be a priority, especially if they are in a location exposed to direct rainfall.

Cracks Over Different Substrates. Some cracks appear where the plaster crosses from one substrate material to another, such as the seam between straw and wooden door or window frame. These cracks will follow the line of this transition, and vary from hairline to significant widths.

These cracks occur because the substrates withdrew moisture from the wet plaster at different rates, causing differential curing. They can be avoided by adequate reinforcing mesh across the transitions or by packing a thin layer of straw over the wood. Some plasterers also paint the wooden elements with a clay or lime slip prior to plastering to even out these transitions.

Structural Stress Cracks. Some cracks are the result of forces being applied through the plaster skins that overcome their strength. Often, wider cracks around windows and doors are the result of inadequate lintels causing high point loads on the plaster. Shifting foundations, twisting or racking due to wind forces or extreme events like earthquakes can cause this kind of crack. They can run in any direction and are usually quite long.

Examine these cracks carefully, trying to determine the forces that have caused them. If they remain static, they may not be problematic, but if they continue to widen or lengthen over time, you might want to consult an engineer.

Filling and Covering Cracks. Hairline cracks do not generally require attention or repair, unless they are continuously exposed to rain or window runoff. ☞

19.16a

19.16b

19.16a - b: This plaster pump is a Putzmeister, run by a putzmistress. It/she can keep a whole crew hopping.

Washes and breathable paints can often fill and close over these cracks. Often, plasterers leave their finish coat or the paint/wash until the two initial structural layers have had time to cure and crack. A finish coat properly applied after the cracking has happened is much less likely to telegraph these cracks.

When the cracks are wide, a mortar bag (similar to a chef's piping bag for icing cakes) can be used to squeeze new plaster deep into the crack. On interior surfaces (or well-protected exterior surfaces) using gypsum plasters or plaster of paris to fill cracks is preferable, since the former shrinks minimally, and the latter actually expands minimally when curing. The plaster for filling cracks should use the finest-possible aggregate.

If the crack is too narrow to fit the nozzle of a mortar bag, use a blunt knife or masonry blade to widen the crack so it can be properly filled.

Moisten the plaster on either side of the crack prior to filling. This will minimize the shrinking of the fill, and help to establish a bond between the new and old plaster. Force as much plaster as possible into the crack. If it can fill some voids behind the existing layer, it will hold better and be more effective.

Once it's filled, rub the cracked area with a trowel or damp sponge to even out the surface. Rinse the sponge and wipe the area one more time to remove excess granules from the surface.

Creative Cracking Repair. It can be difficult to match plaster colors and styles when repairing sections of a wall. Often, homeowners take the opportunity to re-plaster or repaint the whole building, or a particular well-defined section. But you can allow yourself to be creative when covering over cracks. Window and door areas can be given a raised treatment in a contrasting or complementary color, masking the cracks and adding a nice visual element to the home.

Those of us who promote bale building must be able to honestly inform clients about the near inevitability of cracking plaster, and owner-builders must educate themselves. In general, most of the typical cracking is not a concern from the structural or moisture control perspective. These are simply part of the natural look of the walls (nobody tries to seal up all the "checking" cracks in exposed logs!). But when cracks do allow moisture to penetrate the walls, they must be sealed well and properly.

Happy sealing!

— *Chris Magwood. A version of this article appeared in no. 45 of* The Last Straw *and is reprinted with permission.* ∎

The Birth of the Power Trowel

Very early on in our careers as straw bale builders, we realized that being able to pump plaster would be important if we were going to attempt multiple projects. Bodies and spirits just wouldn't be able to keep up with endless hand plastering. So we bought an ancient pump and started spraying.

Oh, how I remember the days of the sprayer nozzle! The comforting farting sound, the reassuring overspray sticking everywhere, plaster in our eyes, noses, lungs, hair, shirts, and sometimes even ending up on the new roof of the house we were plastering (do not trip while spraying!). The nozzle end was a tiny opening, just ½ to ⅝ inch, so if a tiny pebble made its way through the screening and into the nozzle, it could (and did sometimes, much to our chagrin!) jam up and create back pressure, even to the point of exploding the hose! Luckily no one has ever been in the way of the hose at the time, but what a sorry mess it makes!

We talked often about improving our lot in life. I had read about trowel ends for plaster pumps before, and this kind of fitting seemed like it would be cleaner and easier to use, but they seemed impossible to find. So as often happens in life, I set about to make my own. These are the steps I followed:

- Make a 30 degree (approximate) bend in the 1-inch pipe, leaving an 11-inch section of the pipe straight at one end. Use an acetylene or propane/oxygen torch and wind a coupler onto the threads, or they will get bent!
- Grind a flat face roughly ¾ inch across along the straight, 11-inch section. This is where the trowel will attach.
- Grind a slot through the pipe where you have ground it flat, ³/₈ inch wide by 5 inches long, centred 5 inches from the bend. This is where the plaster will exit.
- Place the flat face on the workbench with bend up and weld on 4 reinforcement bars flush with the face. Use the ³/₈-inch square bar. These are necessary to support the trowel attachment, as the trowel material is not strong enough by itself.
- Weld on the handle. Shape to taste from ³/₈-inch round bar, remembering that heavily gloved hands will be trying to hold the handle.
- Lay out the trowel face. An aluminum hawk makes decent material. Our trowel is 12 inches long by 6 inches wide, with a ³/₈-inch-by-4-½ inch slot. Bias the slot towards the end of the trowel by ½ to 1 inch to allow closer application to ceilings.
- Use a drill and saber(jig) saw to cut the trowel out. File off sharp edges.
- Fasten the aluminum to the steel pipe with polyurethane caulking and annealed steel wires twisted tight with pliers. Our earlier experiments using lexan for the trowel and held on by 20 machine screws failed, lasting only one or two homes.

The rest is basic plumbing. Use Teflon tape on all threads and heavy-duty hose clamps. As we're reducing the hose down to 1 inch, a full-size quick-connect is necessary at the upstream end of the 8-foot hose to allow for proper cleanouts.

Thus was the birth of the power trowel. It was a big success! It worked! No more overspray! We won't kid ☞

you .... we still make a mess when we plaster, but a least it's a bit more controlled now. The power trowel needs two operators (or one if that person is truly a power-power troweler): one is the hose holder, the other holds the trowel end up against the wall. The trowel can be moved either sideways across the wall, or more popularly, up the wall. There is quite a knack to this grueling job, and those who are quite talented at it actually seem to dance together as they pass the power trowel back and forth, weaving gracefully around scaffolding, rocks, and slow hand trowelers.

19.17a

Power trowel advantages:

- tends to fill hollows, somewhat self-flattening
- less clogging by far
- blow-off valve works
- less back pressure
- less loss of cement paste and water to atomization, resulting in longer working times
- no more overspray on windows, ceilings, and people (although we do still drop almost as much on the ground or floor)

Power trowel disadvantages:

- overhead areas are difficult
- does not quite reach ceiling, trowelers often have to push the mud up the last 3 or 4 inches
- occasional air pockets between coats
- somewhat more effort for the nozzleperson

19.17b

The power trowel has made life as plasterers easier, cleaner, and quieter.

— Peter Mack
A version of this article appeared in
The Last Straw, *no. 42.* ■

19.17a - b: *Pumping the plaster through the 'power trowel' takes about half the time of applying it by hand. Burt and Andrew both make it look easy.*

water at the nozzle. Both are suitable for straw bale walls although gunnite might be overkill.

Despite being faster than hand plastering, spraying is not necessarily less physical work. Feeding the hungry machine can take up to three dedicated mixers, and the person spraying will have to be followed by at least two trowelers.

You will need to prepare your site thoroughly for a machine application. Larger homes should have sand piles deposited on opposite corners ten feet away. The hoses are heavy and the machine is stationary, so make clear paths for moving the hose around the site. Scaffolding must be provided where necessary. It is critical to tape and cover elements you don't want plastered, since sprayers are less than completely accurate!

Plaster spraying outfits tend to be expensive to hire. If you are hand plastering with volunteer labor, your savings are significant. However, with a sprayer, the reduction in time and effort is equally significant, and a hired spraying crew will be cheaper than a hired hand-plastering crew.

19.18: *It's so easy your shadow could do it! The plaster should be stiff enough that it doesn't easily run off the hawk.*

You could hire a spraying outfit to apply only a base coat, which would take care of the most labor-intensive aspect of hand application. Or you could have a specialty top coat sprayed. You might hire a sprayer for the exterior and do the interior by hand. Any combination of options is possible.

Fun with Plaster

Plaster walls allow you to be very creative. Relief carving, artistic scratching, and sculpting are all possible. If you find the actual plastering process too exhausting to consider such artistic endeavors, you can always apply additional decorative plaster at a later time — as long as you haven't painted or otherwise sealed the plaster.

Every Plastering Job Is Unique

As with your bale house itself, plastered walls are highly individualized. For some, this lack of a standardized finish might be distressing, and professional plasterers can do a remarkably good job of minimizing it. For many people, however, the individuality of a plastered finish on bale walls is a large part of the building's charm and beauty.

The shapes and textures of a plastered bale wall can be pleasing to the eye — literally; our eyes respond better to textured surfaces than flat ones. The gentle play of shadow and light on an undulating wall changes the atmosphere of a room. Acoustically, too, plastered bale walls soften a space by eliminating the echoes found in square, straight rooms. You many find that people who visit your home have an uncontrollable urge to touch the walls. And why not? The warmth and subtlety of plaster walls are tactile and inviting!

Acrylic and Synthetic Stuccos: Never to Be Used on Bale Walls

The recent introduction of synthetic stuccos has caused no end of debate among plasterers. Synthetics are usually chosen as an exterior finish on non-straw bale buildings, but if you use an exterior synthetic, you will create a vapor barrier on the outside of your walls. This will cause problems with moisture buildup unless the interior is treated with a vapor retardant of at least equal value. This can come in the form of an interior coat of synthetic stucco or as vapor-retardant paint. Synthetic stuccos are the least environmentally friendly of all the finishing options and usually require the application of a bonding agent over the brown coat, making their application more labor-intensive than other plasters. We sincerely believe you should not use these stuccos on your bale walls, no matter what the guy behind the counter tries to tell you!

Plaster Magic

From shaggy bales to beautiful finished walls, the plastering process gives strength, shape, and definition to your building. It's long, hard work, but when you stand back and admire it, you won't notice your tired arms quite so much!

Other Options for Surfacing Bale Walls

Perhaps you live in a climate where plaster finishes are less than ideal, or maybe you need to conform to appearance requirements in an urban area. Or maybe you just don't like plaster finishes. Plaster of any form does not have to be the final wall finish for your straw bale building. In fact, it is possible to apply any kind of exterior or interior siding to bale walls. It is necessary to seal your bale walls with at least one coat before applying any other form of siding. This coat adds significant structural strength to the walls and acts as an excellent fire retardant and a barrier to insects and pests. The base coat of plaster can be applied by hand or by machine with no regard for finished appearance.

Unplastered bales exposed to moving air lose most of their insulation value, and fire may be able to spread along the loose ends of the straw even though the whole bales are likely to resist combustion.

Strategies for affixing other forms of siding typically use thin wooden strapping to act as attachment points. This can be run vertically between the wooden bale curb and the top plate, affixed at intervals that match building code requirements for the particular siding. Fill the spaces between the strapping with plaster. Wooden siding, plywood — as a base for cedar shakes — or even vinyl or aluminum siding can be attached to the strapping; for interior walls, drywall can be mounted.

Brick and stone can also be used to sheath bale walls. Again, a coat of plaster is recommended

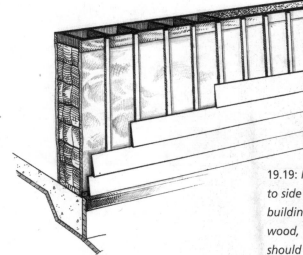

19.19: *If you wish to side your building with wood, the bales should still receive at least one coat of plaster. Then strapping can run from curb to top plate to support the siding. Brick or stone facing could also be tied to such strapping.*

first. This can be used to affix brick ties that stabilize the outer shell of brick or stone. Foundation design must be detailed to create a brick ledge. Your building code or a knowledgeable mason will outline applicable requirements. As with brick and stone facades over frame walls, a space must exist between the wall and the brick, and drainage must be provided at the bottom of the wall for any moisture that gets trapped. Your window and door buck design must also accommodate the requirements of brick and stone work.

References

Buxbaum, Tim. *Pargeting.* Shire Publications, Ltd., 1999. ISBN 0747804141.

Guelberth, Cedar Rose and D. Chiras. *The Natural Plaster Book.* New Society Publishers, 2003.

Holmes, S. and M. Wingate. *Building with Lime: A Practical Introduction.* ITDG Publishing, 2002. ISBN 1853393843.

Meagan, Keeley. *Earth Plasters for Straw Bale Homes.* 2000. ISBN 01615116485.

Portland Cement Association. *Portland Cement Plaster (Stucco) Manual.* Portland Cement Association, 1996. 1500 Don Mills Rd., Ste. 703, Toronto ON M3B 3K4

Stagg, W. D. and B. F. Pegg. *Plastering: A Craftsman's Encyclopedia.* BSP Professional Books, 1989. ISBN 0-632-02545-X.

Taylor, Charmaine. *All About Lime: A Basic Information Guide for Natural Building.* Taylor Pub., 1998. ISBN 0971558612.

Taylor, J.B. *Plastering.* Longman Scientific and Technical, 1990. ISBN 0-582-05634-9.

Van Den Branden, F. and Thomas Hartsell. *Plastering Skills.* American Technical Publishers, Inc., 1984. ISBN 0-8269-0657-5.

CHAPTER 20

Bale Wall Finishes

There are numerous ways of finishing your straw bale walls to provide long-lasting, beautiful surfaces. This is a field of endeavor that invites experimentation and creativity, as well as an eye toward healthy indoor air quality.

E ach type of plaster, wash or paint has many possible variations, and most can be applied over any kind of base coat. Here we describe a few of the more common ones.

Lime Plasters

Lime plasters can be used in many ways to create durable and beautiful surfaces. For finish coat work, they are often mixed a little richer than for the base coats, with less sand content: 2 parts sand to 1 part lime or lime putty is common. The sand needs to be very finely screened, since the lime finish coat needs to be applied quite thinly (¼ inch or less) in order to avoid cracking. Oxide pigments, colored clay, and universal paint tints can all be added to lime plaster for finish coats. Using marble or granite dust (available from many quarries) can give great results, as the very fine aggregate allows the surface to be buffed with a trowel until glassy.

Lime finish coats must be applied very evenly, as they tend to crack when the thickness varies too greatly. They must be applied to a moist surface and kept hydrated as they cure. Lime plasters are suitable for exterior and interior finishes.

Gypsum Plasters

We often use gypsum plasters as an interior finish coat. As thick or thin applications, they are easily textured and sanded, and don't crack. Sheetrock 90 is a common product to use, either by itself or sometimes cut with sand, colored marble, or granite aggregate. Gypsums are naturally white and take pigments very well.

20.1: *A final coat of venetian plaster is made from lime and marble dust. The act of burnishing it smooth makes it "venetian."*

Clay Plasters

Especially on a clay plaster base coat, troweled clay finishes are very beautiful and definitely the easiest to finish for trowelers with little or no experience. This is because the clay can be wet down and retroweled repeatedly until the desired finish is achieved, unlike the other chemically curing plasters. Often the natural color of the earth makes for the most appropriate color, but pigments can also be added. Naturally colored clays and colored aggregates can be used. Clay finish plasters do not always bond well to nonclay surfaces; some

preparation may need to be done if you are finishing over other plasters.

Lime Washes

Hydrated lime can be mixed directly with water (little or no sand or other aggregate) into a thick, paint-like consistency that you can tint easily or leave a natural bright white. Paint washes on with large brushes (whitewash brushes are ideal) or roll on with thick pile paint rollers. Lime washes make a very affordable, easy to apply finish, capable of filling most cracks in the substrate. Colors tend to be matte but can be very rich. Use lime washes indoors and out.

Silicate Mineral Paints

This kind of paint is made specifically for application on mineral-based plasters, including all the varieties discussed in the previous chapter. These paints create a layer of potassium carbonate that bonds to the surface through silification.

Their binder, water glass, petrifies on the plaster surface and minimizes the number of pores open to water penetration, while still allowing

20.2: *The top coat and relief work around this window seat are a gypsum and sand mix with a gypsum wash coat.*

20.3: *These tiles are set into a white clay top coat, and a hempcrete mixture forms the window sill.*

20.4: *A high quantity of chopped straw in a clay finish coat can add texture and color to the finish.*

moisture to transpire freely out of the wall. These paints are the most effective waterproofing available for plaster surfaces and make an ideal exterior coating. They are also manufactured in interior grades.

Milk Paints

Using casein (found in milk processing), traditional milk paints are easy to use and come in many colors. They are mixed thickly enough to fill cracks in the substrate, and provide a breathable, durable interior or exterior finish. Brushed or rolled, they can also be mixed with a lime wash for added durability.

Alis

Alis is a natural clay finish. The clay is mixed with water to the consistency of heavy cream and applied with brushes, sponges, or sheepskin. Lighter clays, including natural white clays, can be tinted, but often the natural color of the clay becomes the finish color.

Mica flakes and marble or granite dust are sometimes added for effect. Add a cooked flour paste to prevent the clay from dusting once dry. Although these finishes are ideal for interiors, they can be used on exteriors that are well protected by roof overhangs.

Waterproofing Cement

This is a manufactured product made to seal swimming

20.5: *Silicate paints, used on the exterior of this home, are ideally suited to plastered bale walls, as they are designed to bond with mineral surfaces to eliminate water penetration but still allow the walls to "breathe."*

20.6: *Window sills can be plastered, covered with a nice piece of wood, or artistically finished with a mosaic as pictured here.*

20.7: *Deep, rich colours can be achieved using clay-based tints in a clay paint. Coated with a clear silicate finish, this is a long-lasting colour.*

LAURA TAYLOR

20.8: *Make up a number of tint samples and apply them directly to the wall in question. The colors will change as they cure, and may not look like the tint color at all.*

PETER MACK

20.9: *Deliberate trowel strokes in the plaster follow the contours of the openings in the wall, creating movement and flow on the tall wall.*

pools and cisterns. It is mixed with water to a thick paint consistency for brushing or rolling onto the wall. The cement/lime and aggregate used to make this product are very finely ground, and the small pores make it shed most water while still allowing moisture to transpire out of the wall. It comes in either a gray or white base color; choose the white for best results with tints. Typically, this material is used as an exterior finish.

Latex or Oil-based Paints

These products should never be used on the exterior of a bale wall. They will create a moistureproof skin that will trap moisture in the walls and potentially cause rot to occur. Don't do this!

We also discourage their use indoors, although they are less likely to cause harm to the bale walls. They will, however, seal the interior walls and prevent them from absorbing excess moisture from inside the building. Painted bale homes are more likely to have condensation on the windows in the winter and higher overall humidity levels, since the walls cannot perform their sponge-like duties.

If you are going to use latex paints, be sure to source low-VOC (volatile organic compounds) versions that leave fewer toxins in the air you breathe.

Pigments and Tints

The nature of the pigment or tint you add to your finish will have an important effect on the quality of the color you achieve. You can find a wide variety of powdered tints at masonry and pottery supply outlets. These powders are typically oxide based or clay based. (You can also use naturally occurring clays if you live in an area that has interesting soils or rocks.) These powders are added to lime plasters, clay plasters, lime washes, milk paints, or used in making alis. Because the range of colors is quite remarkable, it can take some experimentation to get the desired finished color, but you will be rewarded with a natural, long-lasting color.

Artificial tints (such as those used in latex paints) are very concentrated and come in any hue and shade you desire. Add them to plasters, washes, and paints for brighter coloring. However, the colors won't turn out exactly like they do on the paint chip, since the material they are being mixed with will have an effect on the final appearance.

Texture

Plaster finishes can vary from glassy to roughly stippled. It will help if you can experiment to find which texture appeals to you. The same texture does not need to be applied throughout the entire building. You may have areas in which rounded trowel marks are suitable, and others which call for uninterrupted smoothness or a pattern. Different trowels will give you a range of effects; if you're frustrated by an inability to create the texture you want, you may have the wrong tool. Ask experienced plasterers how they achieve certain effects. Often, it's a combination of the right material, the right wall preparation, the right tool, and lots of practice.

Fresco

The Sistine Chapel was painted by rubbing pigment into a wet lime plaster. You can use the same technique by laying down a section of lime or clay plaster on a well-moistened surface and then using a brush or palette knife to rub in a concentrated pigment.

Mosaic

A wet bed of plaster is also ideal for tile and mosaic work for entire walls, small highlights, or trim. Simply press the pieces into the plaster and then rub plaster into the spaces between them.

Relief and Sculpture

Your plastered walls are ideal for carving relief work or for building sculpture. There is really no limit to what can be achieved with a palette knife

CHRIS MAGWOOD

20.10: *Pigments can be applied with a spatula directly into wet plaster, giving vibrant and permanent colors for painting or design.*

to carve into leathery plaster, or with some mesh and lots of plaster. From understated shadow lines to creatures leaping out from the walls, anything is possible.

The standardized nature of conventional building materials does not invite such experimentation with shape, color, or form. For this reason, we have largely forgotten to be playful and creative with our living spaces. Your plastered bale walls will invite you to engage in this kind of play and to create finishes that reflect your personality in a very direct way. We encourage you to take up that invitation.

Resources

Edwards, Lynn and Julia Lawless. *The Natural Paint Book*. Rodale, 2002 ISBN 0875969143

Guelberth, Cedar Rose and Dan Chiras. *The Natural Plaster Book*. New Society Publishers, 2003. ISBN 0-86571-449-5

PATRICK MARCOTTE

20.11: *This dragonfly mosaic was made by using broken pieces of beer bottles. Also note the relief plaster work cattail.*

20.12: *Tiles can be embedded in plaster.*

20.13: *Light and shadow love to play on plaster.*

20.14: *The human touch.*

20.15: *Workshop participants leave their marks.*

20.16: *Detailed relief and color work can create stunning effects.*

20.17: *A recess in the wall is prepared as a light sconce using chicken wire and clay plaster.*

20.18: *A Nicaraguan hotel room invites us to relax.*

CHAPTER 21

Common Mistakes

With a building style as new as straw bale, there are plenty of people out there making plenty of mistakes. Fortunately, they are sharing them with others, and we can all learn from one another's experiences.

This list of common mistakes is not meant to scare you or to make anybody feel bad who has made any of these mistakes. We've made most of them ourselves! Because they've been repeated often enough, we've listed them here for your edification and covered them in more detail elsewhere.

We Should Have ...

Considered passive solar. If we could change one rule in all the building codes, it would be that all building designs must account for the sun's interaction with the building. It is the ultimate source of energy on the planet, after all, and ignoring it wastes valuable resources. Almost every building can have a passive solar strategy that is cost neutral and effective.

Sited the house in a micro climate. Paying attention to existing site features, and in particular how the proposed building will alter them, results in buildings that are more comfortable and energy efficient.

Detailed the plans properly. Be sure that your plans adequately take into account all the requirements of a good bale building, including compression strategies, top plates, drip sills and flashings, adequate overhangs, and plaster stops. If you're not sure, hire somebody to review the plans. Simple mistakes caught at this stage are easy to fix; they're much worse once the building is underway.

Thought for ourselves. You will be given untold amounts of advice while planning and building (only pregnant mothers get more!). Especially when dealing with professionals, it is easy to be overwhelmed (or even bullied) into changing your mind against your better judgment. Don't be belligerent; do base your decisions on good research, but don't buckle if you believe you are right.

Insulated under and around a slab foundation. Many people think that insulating under a slab is a waste of time and money. Really, it's a waste of your heating energy. Common wisdom says the ground stays warm under the slab, so you won't lose much heat. Laws of physics say that your warm slab will try to heat the significantly cooler earth below it. When a slab wrestles the entire planet, the slab loses! Isolate that thermal mass for best performance.

Sealed air leaks caused by plaster shrinkage. The more intersections that exist between plaster and other building materials, the more air leaks there will be when the plaster inevitably shrinks away from these places as it cures. Even if you've properly installed vapor barriers behind such intersections, and especially if you haven't, make sure you properly caulk these areas.

Installed hydronic heat tubes in a slab. Whether the slab is concrete, earth, or any other material, it is a mistake not to directly heat such a thermal mass in the home. An insulated and heated floor will make a home so much more comfortable that it will be possible to lower the thermostat!

Protected against moisture due to rising damp. Whether it is rising through your foundation wall into your bales, through your slab floor into your home, or from the ground in a crawl space, rising damp is a powerful and destructive force. Be sure to stop it with appropriate vapor barriers.

Built appropriate curbs/toe-ups on the foundation. Placing bales directly on the foundation is an invitation to moisture damage that is easily avoided by stepping them up on a curb. The first time a bucket of cleaning water spills, not to mention small floods, you'll be glad for your curbs.

Done more research. The more alternative the building you are attempting to build, the more research needs to be done. There are hundreds of options to be considered. Don't just jump at the first thing that sounds good; find out how it has worked for others.

Had pressurized water onsite during plastering. Plastering uses a lot of water, quickly. Standing around and waiting for it to slowly arrive is frustrating and sometimes costly. It's so much easier to clean up properly with the force from a pressure pump.

Paid for consulting. Vast pools of knowledge are available to you in all facets of straw bale and natural building. But don't expect everybody to give their knowledge for free. Pay for books, journals, and consulting time (hint: it doesn't always have to be cash!). These will save you large amounts of time and money.

Matched the carpentry to the bales. For example, if you want rounded doorways, you'll have to cut properly beveled curb rails. If you want flared window openings, build the bucks accordingly. If you want flat window sills, build them with flat wood.

Had electricity onsite. We've worked on purist building sites where hand tools are the rule. That's okay, but expect things to take a lot longer.

Had better tarping strategies. Tarping the walls is often treated like an afterthought. It should be done according to a well-planned system. Taking the time to build a frame (which can be reused later in the project) will ensure dry walls and allow work even in the rain.

Formed a recess in the slab. Most exterior doors are pre-hung these days, and the sill is proud of the floor unless a space is cast into the slab.

Had the right tools for the job. Sometimes renting, borrowing, or buying a tool will be much more efficient than doing things the long, slow way with an inadequate tool.

Bought four ends of scaffolding. Most homes take long enough to build that renting scaffolding costs more than owning it. Buy four ends at the beginning and rent enough to wrap the house during the plastering phase.

Tied the vapor barriers into walls. The junction between the ceiling and wall is a prime spot for air leakage. A vapor barrier detailed into your top plate design effectively solves the problem without a lot of fussy work after the fact.

Sourced the right size of poly twine. Poly baling twine comes in many thicknesses. Some is so thick it's impossible to thread a needle or tie a knot. Some is so thin it can't be reefed or tied tightly, without breaking.

Managed the volunteers better. If you can't manage a group of volunteers, don't invite them. This means ensuring there are enough tools and safety equipment, enough knowledge, enough direction, enough food and drink.

We Shouldn't Have ...

Built it too big. So many homes are built much larger than they comfortably need to be. Remember when designing your home and your energy system that enough is all you need, and that your decisions don't just impact your own building project, they impact the whole planet.

Overbuilt it. Most modern buildings are overbuilt. The liability-driven nature of responsibility for buildings creates a culture in which vast resources are expended "just to be extra safe." In your building design, construction, and energy system, try to avoid this mindset as much as possible.

Underestimated electric utility hookup costs/Overestimated renewable costs. Many people interested in bale building are also interested in renewable energies, but sometimes the initial research into them scares people away. Don't forget to accurately establish the full cost of connecting to the electrical grid, including trenches, poles, service entrances, meters, inspections, fees, and ongoing bills. If this money went into a renewable system, it would provide a good start, if not a complete system. Remember that renewable energy is expandable; you can start small and add to your system later.

Used synthetic stucco. Traditional plasters, even of the cement based kind, are getting rarer all the time. Most stuccos are now synthetic and very inappropriate for bale buildings. They will create the same moisture problems as latex or oil paint (to which synthetic stucco is a close cousin). Don't let anybody talk you into this.

Rushed to build. We get a lot of calls in the spring from people who would like to build in the same season. Rushed plans are always more costly and problematic, and it's difficult to budget, finance, and get a project approved on a tight schedule. Custom buildings like straw bale take extra time to figure out properly; its best to give yourself plenty of time. Besides, with the growing popularity of straw bale building, it may be difficult to find a builder who can fit your project in if you leave it too late.

Underestimated costs. It's sad when a building project comes to a grinding halt due to lack of funds, especially when it leaves people in a difficult living situation. Take off the rose-colored glasses when budgeting. Even your best-researched, most realistic budget is likely to underestimate the actual costs. Know how much money you have and plan a home that's cheaper. (Add 10 to 15 percent to your projected budget for a more accurate idea of true cost).

Insulated a slab with bales. Below-grade, bales (or any other cellulose material) have no way to balance their moisture levels with the atmosphere. So, they rot. Bale-insulated slabs use lots of concrete, have many thermal bridges, and eventually won't have any straw bales left inside them.

Pinned the bales. Counterproductive regardless of the material used. If the wall won't stand until it is plastered, use temporary or permanent braces on the outside.

Rebar pins sticking out of the foundation. Would you invite your friends to a playground filled with sharp, rusty spears sticking out of the ground every foot or two? We didn't think so! Rebar pins wick moisture up into your walls.

Underestimated the amount of time required. As with your budget, assume that things will take longer than even your most pessimistic estimate. Doubling your worst case scenario is a decent rule of thumb.

Underestimated the time to properly prep bale walls for plastering. As much work is involved in preparing the walls once they are raised as there is in building them in the first place, sometimes even more. Don't wave all your volunteers or hired help goodbye once the last course is in place — this is when the real work starts! And be sure to schedule your plastering so that you allow for plenty of time to prepare the walls adequately.

Built on top of the unplastered walls. Large load-bearing walls should have at least one coat of plaster before the second floor or roof is installed.

Planned for compression wires in post and beam buildings. Compression wires and structural top plates belong in load-bearing buildings only.

Sized the building plans to bale modules. It is more economical and practical to size a building to lumber lengths and sheet material dimensions than it is to worry about bale lengths. Bale lengths will always vary and require adjustment anyway, but cutting a foot from every piece of lumber is expensive and time-consuming.

Rushed tasks onsite. As building projects progress, timelines go askew, and delays and holdups are inevitable. Never try to rush through a task just to keep things on time. Quality work at each phase will matter a lot more in the long run than a few weeks of time saved here or there.

Insufficiently scaffolded the site. It may seem expensive to rent lots of scaffolding, but it's more expensive to have to keep breaking down and reassembling scaffolding around the building. If the site is flat, renting a sky jack can be economical, especially when plastering.

Improperly designed the post and beam frame. We have seen some truly awkward fits between bales and frames. These scenarios cause air leaks and poor performance at worst, and long fiddly delays at best. If you're using a frame, plan it to integrate as smoothly as possible with the walls and plaster.

Used bales from more than one source. Different balers create different bales. Sounds straightforward enough, but it means you shouldn't try to mix and match bales in the same load-bearing wall. It will only cause you grief as you attempt to level your top plate.

Used vapor barriers between the bales and the plaster. Although conventional wisdom would tell you this is the right thing to do, don't. Your plaster needs to bond to the straw to create the wall system, and the wall doesn't need the "protection." And anyway, how are you going to attach it, by poking it full of holes?

Stored bales outdoors. A large stack of bales is very difficult to keep dry if it is outdoors for any length of time. Water comes from all sides: underneath, above, and the sides. Most tarps aren't strong enough to repel all this water, and wind and sun can quickly ruin even good quality tarps. The bales are best stored indoors or in a tractor trailer onsite until the day they're needed.

Plastered with poor quality sand. The quality of fine screened masonry sand differs at every quarry. Sand that is unwashed or unscreened is unpleasant to work with and can result in poor quality plaster. Inspect the sand before taking delivery or at least check it when it's delivered and reject any containing pebbles.

Placed plastering materials too far from the building. When your sand and plastering supplies are delivered far from your building site, you assign yourself the huge task of moving them all manually. Imagine taking a vast mound of sand and moving it one shovel at a time. That's what you're going to do, so make it easy on yourself.

Plastered with the wrong kind of lime. Don't use agricultural lime; it makes a terrible plaster. A proper hydrated or hydraulic lime intended for plastering is what you need.

Placed bales where they cannot be plastered. Sometimes bales are placed where plastering them will be difficult or impossible. Don't just leave the bare straw exposed. If faced with this situation, at least butter the straw with a light coat of plaster, or dip or spray it with clay slip. Unsealed straw does not perform as well thermally or in fire situations and is an invitation to critters.

Assumed bales in the attic are a good idea. Just because bales make great wall insulation, don't assume the same holds true for attics. Compared to lightweight, recycled insulations like cellulose and cotton, they require extra

framing, odd spacings, and a slip coat of plaster on the exposed side to be thermally efficient. In heavy roofing systems bales may work well, but in most residential situations they are unwieldy.

Been afraid of earth. Earth plasters and earth floors seem to scare a lot of people. Will they work? Will I get the mix right? Will they last? Yes, on all these counts. And you'll enjoy the process, too.

Used tar paper over wood. In several recently dismantled bale structures, mold was found only between the tar paper and the wood it was covering. The wood needs to transpire moisture too. Use slip coats or staple straw over wood rather than using sheet barriers, especially on the exterior. Air barriers also work.

Placed the composting toilet in a cold spot. Small composting toilets don't seem to work very well without some extra heat; an extra loop of hydronic tubing under the toilet might have helped.

Kerfed the slab. The unheated slab can conduct some heat to the next room, but it won't if the slab is kerfed too deep.

Trusted in the WWW. Most people do their research online these days. While there are fabulous resources on the Internet, there is also lots of bad information. Try to find out whose site you're looking at, what their qualifications are, and what experience they have. Sometimes, information on the Web, though well intentioned, is a bit like a giant version of the kid's game, telephone. Much can get lost in the translation from original source to an enthusiast's website.

Believed in products and services that sound too good to be true. We've heard many stories about homes that require zero energy, fuels that are free, building systems that are cheap. Treat these claims cautiously. We love innovation and new ideas, but nothing is perfect or free. If somebody tries to convince you there are no downsides or difficulties in what they are proposing, run the other way!

Had too many volunteers. It's great fun to have a volunteer bale raising. However, if there are way more bodies than useful tasks, less will happen than if there were only a few people. You can distinguish between hands-on helpers and friendly observers.

Shown up to volunteer, uninvited. If you are going to volunteer at somebody's work site, get permission first. Make contact with the owner-builder, arrange a time, and inform yourself about the process taking place beforehand, so you don't need as much coaching.

Dropped loose twine into the loose straw. Many people are proud that their building bales will create no landfill waste, just useful mulch. However, if your loose straw ends up full of pieces of poly twine, it's not so good as mulch and shouldn't be used for animal bedding. Keep garbage containers handy for bits of twine, and encourage people to use them.

Made a big fuss about our straw bale walls. Big bad wolf stories have penetrated the collective psyche deeply. Even if you love the idea of a straw house, not everybody will be thrilled. If this idea doesn't sit well with your family, friends, lenders, insurers, building officials, etc., refer to the bales as Structural Fiber Insulation (or SFI for short). Sounds more impressive, doesn't it?

Tried to lift it all by ourselves. Make sure you have adequate hands around for any physically challenging aspect of your project. The stacking of dipped bales can be particularly demanding, as you add several more pounds to an already hefty weight. And don't attempt the truly heavy lifting at the very end of the workday if you can avoid it. Many jobsite accidents occur at the end of the day, when people are already feeling tired.

Taken on more than we could chew. It's terrible to see people who have undertaken a building project and who don't really have the time or resources to complete it. Even if you really, really want that bale house, be realistic about your ability to get the job done.

CHAPTER 22

Constructing with Work Parties

Many potential straw bale builders are attracted to the idea of orchestrating a communal wall-rais-
ing. Work bees are a practical, inexpensive, and often fun way to build parts of a home. But it's not
as simple as calling up friends and relatives and watching the work get done for you.

All About Work Parties

What Is a Work Party?

Like the barn-raisings of earlier times, work parties are gatherings of friends, family, and
community members who will help with the
construction of a building. Many people are
attracted by an image of building with shared
effort and community spirit, and work parties
have certainly played a large part in the raising of
many straw bale structures. The potential exists for
you to develop rewarding, meaningful work experiences and relationships that will last as long as
the building itself.

Good Work Party Tasks

Certain phases of construction are better suited
to work parties than others. Bale wall-raising is
one good example, as is plastering. Digging for
foundations and erecting a post and beam framework can also be done with many hands. Other
phases of construction
may require specific skills
or specialized tools or
will progress too slowly
for work parties to be effective.

Work Parties versus Workshops

Many people use the terms
work party and workshop
interchangeably. But they
are two quite different arrangements, and it is
important to distinguish which you are pursuing.

Hands-on workshops are a popular and useful way to learn the basics of straw bale building.
Workshop participants pay an instructor for the
experience of raising a building. It is important
to recognize that paying participants in a workshop setting have very different expectations and
needs than do volunteers. Hosting a workshop

22.1: *Your family and friends will want to come and help. You can usually find jobs for just about any sized person!*

when what you really need are volunteers is a surefire way to disappoint yourself and the participants.

Workshop participants are paying for a learning opportunity, expecting a qualified teacher and a good teacher-to-student ratio. They will rightly expect that their learning be equally important to the speed and progress of the project. They will expect a timely schedule and a full learning experience. If you plan to erect your building with paying workshop participants, be sure their need for instruction, guidance, and discussion comes first.

Volunteer work bees, on the other hand, are organized to help the home owner. Volunteers will expect to learn from the experience, but their learning will take place as they assist with the needs of the owner.

Calling a Work Party

You must first decide how many people you want to attend and who you want to call. It may take only a few phone calls to nearby friends and family to round up a suitable crew, or you may have to make a more public call for help. There never seems to be a shortage of willing volunteers for straw bale projects, but only you can decide on the appropriate mix of friends, family, and strangers — and live with the interpersonal dynamics created therein!

Taking a Straw Bale Workshop

My mother introduced me to straw bale construction by inviting me to attend a weekend workshop at the Ecology Retreat Centre (Hockley Valley, Ontario, Canada) in May, 1998. We had no previous experience with construction, but my mom is interested in possibly building one day, and after that weekend, so am I.

At first I was apprehensive about going since I knew nothing about it. So the first thing I learned that weekend was the value of new learning experiences and how these can open doors for possibilities one might otherwise not have imagined — in fact you can even make your own doors!

22.2: *Proud workshop participants pose next to the shed they erected in a single day.*

What does this have to do with straw bale construction? It has to do with imagining what is possible, taking risks, and potentially being involved with a building project in a direct way: a way that encourages awareness of how and where one builds; a way that encourages recognition of lifestyle choices and their impact on, or compatibility with, one's surroundings.

Working along with others, learning something new, was primarily fun and grounding. There was a sense of accomplishment that weekend as a small group of people with ranging talents and abilities was successful in building a straw bale structure. The sense of community and camaraderie that formed in one short weekend gave other ☞

Too many people on a work site can be more of a problem than a help. Figure out how many people you think are ideal for the task at hand, and try to limit attendance to that number. Everybody who shows up will want to do something useful and meaningful, and you don't want people to leave frustrated at not having been able to participate. Maybe you could schedule people for shifts to avoid having too many hands at a time.

Timing

You need to prearrange dates and times for your volunteers, which puts you in the position of having to complete all required preliminary

22.3: *Many owners are amazed by the volunteers who will come forth and help build their house. These volunteers were contacted from an e-mail sign-up list.*

dimensions to construction than merely the nuts and bolts. It seemed to me that construction can bring people together; that a focused group can accomplish a lot in a short period of time, and in that time people's dreams and creativity are given a chance to develop and be realized.

My mother and I both enjoyed learning about what had brought people to the workshop and what people were hoping to build some day. There was such an interesting and varied array of project plans — cottages, studios, additions, and houses, to name a few. We were inspired by these projects, the questions that were asked, and shared information.

I learned that straw, which has limited uses, can be extremely purposeful, versatile, and malleable. These features of building with straw, along with the many other attributes of straw bale structures, strike me as a powerful inspiration to the imagination. For example, I particularly like the idea of incorporating rounded or curved forms into living spaces. With straw bale, these shapes are more easily attainable than with other building materials.

I liked the feel of the straw bale house we visited and in the small structure we built. The thick walls and insulation create a unique atmosphere in which sound is muffled. I felt a quietness and calmness in the way that sound was carried. There is an ironic strength to these structures that I did not anticipate from a material that, when less contained, could easily blow away in the wind.

During the workshop we learned some practical construction skills and that it's possible to be directly involved in building. But beyond the mechanics of construction there can also be other enlightening and rewarding experiences. I would encourage anyone to think of the benefits of straw bale construction and I will definitely be on-hand and onsite if and when my mom decides to build!

— *Laura Ponti-Sgargi lives and works in Toronto.* ∎

work by the appointed date. You'll need to strike a balance between setting dates early enough that volunteers can plan to attend but not so far in advance that the inevitable delays put you off track and cause repeated rescheduling. It's best to be pessimistic when setting dates. Estimate the timing of your project to the best of your ability and then add several weeks. It's better to be ready a week early and busy yourself with other project tasks than to have volunteers arrive before they can be most useful.

Have Everything Ready

The more prepared you are for your work bee, the more will get accomplished. A bale raising won't be as successful if one or two people are

22.4: *Good instruction combined with a bit of experience makes the project move ahead smoothly.*

hurriedly trying to build a curb for the bales to rest on or are frantically nailing together window bucks. A plastering party can grind to a halt if the mesh still needs to be hung. However, a buck-making or meshing party can be a great success, as long as that was your intention in the first place! You need to have all the necessary materials and

equipment on hand. Everybody's time is wasted if you have to drive to the building supply store for forgotten items.

Start Early

If possible, gather your volunteers the night before work is to commence. This will allow new people to get acquainted, and it will help to ensure an early start. A work party needs a fair bit of time to build serious momentum, and the later you start in the day, the less time you will have to reap the rewards of that momentum.

Instruction

Be sure your volunteers have an overall understanding of what is to be achieved. Instruct the entire group about the entire process. When that is clear, the role of each individual process and function is made more meaningful. Talk about the tasks and the number of people required to perform them. Explain each task thoroughly, from what to expect at the start of the task — that is, making sure the previous job has been done correctly — to what will be expected of the people working on the following stage. Let your volunteers know exactly what's expected and why. It helps to make photocopies of your task list and explanatory drawings for each person so they don't have to rely on memory or repeatedly ask for help.

Try to match people to tasks that suit their personalities, knowledge, and strengths. People with certain skills — especially carpentry skills — will gravitate to certain tasks. Don't forget that people may want to experiment with several tasks and try things outside their realm of experience. There is little in the construction of a bale wall — or almost any phase of construction — that is beyond the ability of most people to learn, so be flexible and allow people to choose tasks that interest them.

Supervision

As a work party supervisor, you should expect to spend most of your time acting as a supervisor and trouble-shooter and not plan to do much hands-on building. Ideally, each separate crew will have a knowledgeable leader, but since this is not always possible, be sure that you circulate around the work site and keep tabs on the progress of each phase and crew. Don't be afraid to correct people in their work, but do so positively. In the end, it is your building, and you should not settle for work below your standards. Always be willing to re-explain, to show by example, and to reassign people who are not enjoying their tasks. As a site supervisor you will be incredibly busy. Remember to take breaks, drink, and eat throughout the day and encourage your volunteers to do the same.

Tools

Three people sharing one hammer will work no faster than one person with one hammer. Anticipate the number of people performing each task and be sure they have adequate tools. Borrow or rent, ask volunteers to bring them, but don't fall short. Label tools well, since they will inevitably get mixed together and scattered over the site.

Food and Drink

Busy workers eat and drink a remarkable amount. Be sure there is enough food and liquid to keep everybody well fueled. For large crews, assign somebody the specific task of feeding the crew or else arrange for catered food. Plenty of water and juice is essential, as are hot beverages when temperatures are colder. Don't forget the caffeine addicts in your crew!

Resist the temptation to schedule big sit-down meals, especially midday. By bringing the entire site to a grinding halt, you are interrupting a flow of work that is difficult to re-establish. Focus on a constant supply of finger foods, sandwiches, and other items that can be eaten at any time.

Be clear with your volunteers about what will, and will not, be provided in the way of food and drink, especially if you cannot afford to provide for everybody's needs. It is also worthwhile to check for food allergies.

Be sure your site has provisions for all food-related amenities — running water or plenty of bottled water, refrigeration, storage, dishes, and cutlery. A well-fed crew is a happy crew, and one that will gladly return. A hungry and thirsty crew will be easily inspired to mutiny!

Accommodation

Construction is hard work, and a good sleep will keep strengths and spirits up. Let people know if they need to provide sleeping bags, pillows, bedding, tents, etc. Always be sure to have some spare sleeping gear on hand for extra people who show up or for those who forget their own. Work parties often extend into nighttime parties. This is half the fun of building with volunteer crews. But don't forget to sleep or to be courteous to others who need theirs!

22.5: *A shared meal is one of the best parts of any bale raising day.*

Safety

Work sites attended by large crews change rapidly. What was once a clear path can become an obstacle course in a matter of minutes. People will be moving large objects, using power tools, and focusing on their particular task. Everybody needs to be reminded to move slowly and carefully.

Be sure to have an adequate first aid kit, and let people know where it is located. Minor injuries will consume large numbers of Band-Aids and antiseptic creams. Serious injuries are a possibility, so have the right supplies available. Be sure that at least two people onsite know how and where to get help and how to give directions so ambulance crews or firefighters can locate the work site.

Sunstroke and dehydration are common on summer work sites. Keep hats on heads and

Hosting a Work Party

Our house was built over a period of ten months, and over that time at least 50 different sets of hands participated in its construction. People volunteered for everything from helping us pick out the site to tearing down an old barn for beams, to hoisting those beams in place, raising bales, plastering and interior finishing. Some of my strongest friendships were cemented (!) during this building process, and the tears and frustrations were shared by many a willing (and sometimes unsuspecting) shoulder. A lot of wonderful memories have been built into these walls. Every time I look at the beam that holds up our roof, I think of the ten bodies that hoisted that 27-foot beam up to the peak of the second floor when the crane couldn't come. A lot of sweat and hard work goes into building a house, and if that work is volunteer labor, one of the best ways to reward and thank people is by taking good care of them while they work.

When Chris and I started to build, we wanted to share all the tasks and do everything equally; I didn't envision cooking and hosting to be an important part of these activities, but I soon learned that it was. Many people have since commented to me that it was the food, drink, and camaraderie, as well as the learning process of building, that kept them coming back. So, here are some things I learned over the many, many work parties we held:

1) Assume that people need to be fed while they are onsite, and take an approach to providing food that you feel comfortable with. Hosting a party on a work site can be very difficult as running water, electricity, and adequate shelter can be in scarce supply. For our first work party I took on the task of cooking everything (from chili to salads to cookies) in our little trailer onsite and soon learned that some things can be better purchased. It may be cheaper to cook everything from scratch, but it's not always possible or probable. Some alternatives may be: have the meal catered, buy deli foods and other prepared goods, do a mix of some prepared foods and some grocery items, arrange for a pizza or other takeout meal.

2) Don't try to make work parties pot luck. People are providing enough of a service by offering their labor, without trying to transport and coordinate food as well. You could ask people to bring their own mug, and possibly some water, though plenty of water should also be supplied onsite.

3) Don't plan a sit down meal during the day. For groups of over six people, breaks should be divided to make it easier on the eating area and to allow tasks to keep flowing on the work site. If possible, put out some ☞

plenty of liquid flowing. If your site has no natural shade, put up a tent or an awning and encourage people to take breaks in the shade.

Smokers must be kept far from a straw bale work site. Provide them with distant chairs and sand filled buckets for butts. Fire extinguishers, a functioning hose, and/or large barrels of water should be placed strategically around the site.

Realistic Expectations

Raising half a wall can either be a victory or a letdown, depending on what you expected to accomplish. Try to set your expectations carefully and know that delays, problems, and oversights are inevitable. A good rule to follow is to estimate how long you think a task will take, then multiply that by a reality factor of two or even three!

food at a designated break hour and leave it out for a little while, so people can break and eat when it is convenient. Make sure that you, and all on site, do take a break and get something to eat and drink. Remember that people need to eat and drink at different times — aside from the main meals, make sure there is a supply of on-the-go food: muffins, water or juice, sandwiches, fruit, hard-boiled eggs, granola bars, etc.

4) If you can't take on the task of coordinating food yourself, make sure someone is designated to do it. It is an important job!

5) Please don't leave all the women on the work site to coordinate food, and dishes, etc., while the men do the heavy stuff! Find some people who need a break from the sun and assign them the job.

6) Is it a party or ... While it is called a work party, the main reason people are there is to work, and the food and drinks should only support that, not be so enticing as to drag people away from their jobs. As well, hold off on the beer or other refreshments until people need to wind down at the end of the day.

7) Do think about food safety. On a work site, refrigeration can be tricky, but safe food storage is very important. If you don't have refrigeration onsite, try to arrange some with a neighbor, or pack a lot of coolers and ice, and plan food that keeps well. Also, you'll need to think about washing dishes and how to do that safely and efficiently. A hand-washing station, or at the very least a supply of hand sanitizer, should be organized. Contact your local public health office if you want to pick up some information on food and water safety. After all, you don't want your crew coming down with salmonella!

8) Supply some shelter. It's a good idea to have a spot onsite where people can relax and get away from the sun and bugs. A screen tent or other shelter also provides a safe spot for the food and drinks.

9) Only invite the number of people your site can handle. Make sure that your facilities (food, washroom, shelter) can handle all these extra visitors and plan your volunteer list accordingly.

8) Don't forget to get in there and get your hands dirty and have fun!

— Julie Bowen has been responsible for more happy, well-fed bale workers than anybody on the planet. ∎

Try to plan useful secondary tasks that can be performed by people who are temporarily unemployed because of delays. Work parties can easily end up with a large group standing around a single trouble spot, offering advice and trying to help out. As supervisor, try to assign people to work out problems, and redirect others to useful jobs.

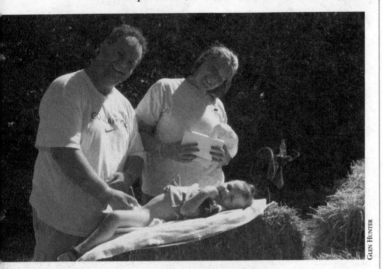

22.6: *These straw bales sure do come in handy! If only we could get someone to weave straw diapers ...*

GLEN HUNTER

You Are the "Cruise Director"

Your mood and attitude on the work site transfer directly into the general mood of the project and its participants, so try to stay positive and focused, even if your expectations are challenged and your patience stretched. Temper tantrums are a no-no. You are going to be taking the job more seriously than any of your volunteers, so don't expect them to have your level of commitment. Treat your volunteers with respect and do your best to make the day fun and enjoyable.

Thank-Yous

Don't let those new friends get away without finding out how to reach them. Many houses would never have been built without the dedication of volunteers. Come up with meaningful and creative ways to thank people for their help. This means having addresses and phone numbers for all your volunteers. A guest book onsite is an easy way to accomplish this, and it makes a great memento of the process.

Good food, good company, and rewarding work are often thanks enough for a volunteer, but a card or a phone call is a positive extension of goodwill. Have all your volunteers come out to a nonworking celebration of the project when it is finished. Hand out awards, enlarged photographs of crews and participants, or give a Thank-you speech. Of course, the best way to show your appreciation is to go out and volunteer on the projects your volunteers will undertake in the future. Share the knowledge and your time!

CHAPTER 23

Other Straw Bale Projects

Throughout this book, we've concentrated on the home-building applications of straw bale construction. Of course, these techniques are easily translatable into similar structures, such as additions, garages, sheds, guest cabins, greenhouses and larger commercial structures.

Industrial and Commercial Buildings

Individual homes are not the only buildings that benefit from increased insulation value and decreased embodied energy. Vast amounts of square footage are contained in thin-walled, poorly insulated structures, and the energy wasted in heating and cooling them is likewise vast. In the past five years, numerous bale builders have endeavored to bring their knowledge from the residential experience to the commercial. Many of these projects have been well realized and have created effective solutions for the owners of the buildings.

In many ways, commercial/industrial buildings are well suited to bale construction, perhaps even more so than residential. These buildings are most often modular, prefabricated structures requiring little glazing and detailing, and bale walls are easiest to build and plaster with fewer interruptions in the wall. Such structures are particularly well suited to the panelizing of bale walls (see sidebar, Chapter 8).

The types of commercial buildings which use bales have included residential-type structures like bed-and-breakfasts, wineries, and motorcycle shops. More and more of these structures have been built, and as with residential straw bale, the learning curve will be steep, as the best ways to integrate bales with commercial architecture are discovered and fine tuned.

In our experience with one commercial structure, we found that there were no real barriers to the use of straw bales as insulation in this setting. We were able to meet the project's budget expectations and timeline.

23.1: *It looks just like any other steel framed building ... 'til you go inside and see the 17 foot high, shapely bale infill walls, that is!*

Public Structures

Local municipalities and volunteer groups can and do use straw bale construction in creating many projects, including low-income housing, public washrooms, band shells, and schools. As die-hard northerners, it is our dream to one day build a straw bale hockey arena!

23.2: *The Pelican Eyes Hotel in Nicaragua is a beautiful example of how creative you can get when building with bales.*

23.3: *Robin's Nest Bed and Breakfast in Norwood, once claimed to be the largest load bearing building in North America.*

Churches, schools, community centers, and youth recreation centers have all been built of bales with the participation of the people who will use and benefit from the finished building. By encouraging public participation in construction and by lowering lifetime operating costs, straw bale buildings make possible any number of exciting projects!

The hospitality business has taken a real liking to straw bale building. Bed-and-breakfasts, camps, and hotels have all realized that customers love the warm, comfortable feeling of plastered bale walls.

Developing Nations

Numerous projects have been undertaken which combine the people-friendly nature of bale building with self-help housing initiatives in developing parts of the world. In Mexico, China, Mongolia, Iraq, and many other places, people have introduced straw bale building. Their goals are the same as ours: affordable housing built with local materials by people who need housing. The big difference in these cases is that a bale home is usually a bigger step up in thermal performance from the existing housing stock.

Many agencies have undertaken projects to help introduce bale building around the world. If you have an interest in joining their efforts, see the contact information below.

Yard and Garden Uses

Straw bales can be used to complement houses or other structures. Fences and privacy walls can be created with bales, as can garden and patio furniture. As long as you remember the basics of straw bale building, these projects can be tackled with creativity and inventiveness.

Resources

"European Straw Bale Scrapbook." *The Last Straw*, no. 26, 1999

"Going Commercial." *The Last Straw, no. 37, 2002.*

Kennedy, Joseph F. *Building Without Borders: Sustainable Construction for the Global Village* New Society Publishers, 2004. ISBN 0865714819. <http://builderswithoutborders.org/>.

"A World Tour of Straw bale." *The Last Straw*, no. 44, 2003.

TINA THERRIEN

23.4a: *Park furniture, garden walls, porch rails ... these are but a few of the other applications of bales in building projects. This bench was created at a workshop at the Ecology Garden in Peterborough, Ontario.*

MELINDA ZYTARUK

23.4b

CHAPTER 24

The Challenge

Stepping into the world of straw bale building has forever changed our lives. While we began look-
ing simply for higher efficiency and lower environmental impact and costs in our buildings, we have
ended up entering a new kind of life, where community, friendship, and a shared commitment to
the environment all meet. We invite you to remain open to this change too.

Straw Bale as a Lifestyle

Straw bale building has provided a window into a different way of living for many people. Although most don't approach their straw bale building project with the idea of a major life change in mind, it often does happen.

It's difficult to quantify the reasons why straw bale in particular has become such an open door invitation to a new way of thinking. But we have seen so many people who merely wanted a less expensive, do-it-yourself house become aware of social and environmental issues as a result of their building experience.

Perhaps it's as simple as taking responsibility for creating one's own shelter. When you buy or rent a house, the materials and labor that went into it can remain invisible, and since buying and renting is the most common experience, as a society, we are typically unaware of the design and materials considerations that go into our built

environment. But when you build for yourself, each of those decisions becomes a conscious choice, and you find yourself understanding more about the built world around you.

Perhaps the act of making a house is one of the few significant acts in which we feel we can make a meaningful difference to the environment. Our houses will likely outlast us; if we do a good job and choose the right materials and strategies, our buildings will go on having a positive impact after we are gone.

After working with many homeowners, and have building hundreds of others in workshops, we have found that even though these people come from diverse backgrounds, they have a common link between them all. Friendships form quickly, and connections last so that people end up helping one another on projects.

Straw bale building also lends itself to ideas like cohousing and shared living arrangements.

Used as interior walls, straw bales can provide the kind of privacy and comfort that make such shared living possible. Of course, all these choices involve you stepping away from what's considered normal. Your lifestyle will necessarily change. Think practically about what you really need and want from your living space, and plan accordingly.

The decision to stray from the wastefulness of mainstream construction can mean extra research, higher costs, or additional time as you create more sound solutions to your housing needs. From passive solar gain design to naturally based stains for finishing your walls, alternative choices are abundantly available and sometimes overwhelming in their variety. If you inform yourself before you start building, you'll know better what you want, what is available, and what you can afford.

24.1: *After all the craziness of building, you can nestle down, protected by your beautiful thick walls.*

Straw bale buildings make the adoption of renewable energy sources for both home heating and electricity viable. Fewer resources are needed to maintain a comfortable home, and with passive and active solar heating, the highly efficient straw bale house makes it possible to rely more on the sun's energy than ever before. That lowers the ongoing environmental impact of your home.

As more people make these positive choices, prices for the equipment will continue to fall. Already, many of these options are affordable by most people who are considering building a house.

For too long, we who live in northern climates have been pursuing an unsustainable lifestyle, based on the overconsumption of resources. We urge you to do your best to correct this trend with the choices you make in building, heating, and powering your home.

Conclusion

There are very few tasks as complex, meaningful, and rewarding as building a home. We hope we've provided options and solutions to many of the issues you will face when building with bales. We are certain, however, that we haven't answered them all. Each individual project is full of its own challenges, and it takes a great deal of resourcefulness and diligence to work out appropriate solutions. At each turn in the process, it is possible to find people with experience and advice to help you out. For first-time builders, the learning curve is very steep, and even the seasoned pros find new methods and procedures each time they build.

Straw bale building is still in its infancy. Practices and methodology will continue to improve. Some of the options outlined in this book will likely fade into disuse, while others will become predominant. Yet others are still to be invented and put to test. It is the openness to innovation and change that makes building with straw bales so exciting. We hope that the thinking we've encouraged you to do throughout this book serves as your best tool in ensuring that you are an active participant in the ongoing development of straw bale building.

Just as surely as bale building will grow and change, so too will awareness of the need to engage in more sustainable building practices in general. We've made an attempt in this book to provide some focus on the environmental issues that face builders and the choices that can be made. However, there is a lot to be improved before we can make any real claims to true sustainability for straw bale construction. Sadly, meeting building code requirements and building sustainably are often two opposing ideals. It is our hope that building officials and builders will begin to recognize more fully the need to improve practices to allow for greater sustainability. But such a change will only come about if individuals openly question and challenge prevailing trends and use their opinions and their building dollars to support more sustainable practices and products. We feel that using straw bales in construction puts an important foot in the door of the building profession, and may help bring about wider, deeper changes.

And for you, regardless of the methods or materials you've used, what can be more satisfying than to listen to the wind beat against the walls while sitting, feeling safe, secure, and warm in the house you planned and built? Good luck to you in your bale building projects, and may you thoroughly enjoy that first warm night surrounded by your straw bale walls.

The authors are always curious to know what people think of this book. Please send comments, suggestions, inquiries, project news, or resource additions to cmagwood@kos.net or strawbus@auracom.com.

Appendix: The California Building Code

At the time of publication of this book, the State of California is nearing completion of an ambitious testing program and revised building code legislation based on this testing. When this code is approved, it will represent the best working code for using straw bales as a building material.

Until that happens, the significant amendments made to the 2002 California code will stand, and still represents an important step forward from the earlier version. We reprint the 2002 code here, since it is the best in existence at the time of publication.

For those wishing to learn more about the new California code and the testing program it is based upon, please go the web site of the Ecological Building Network (EBNet) at <www.ecobuildingnetwork.org>. EBNet is a great resource, with postings of their latest testing results and initiatives, and deserving of your financial support as well as your casual viewing.

The new California code will be posted at this site as soon as it is available, and updates on its status can also be found here in the interim.

The people of the State of California do enact as follows:

SECTION 1. Section 18944.30 of the Health and Safety Code is amended to read:

18944.30. The Legislature finds and declares all of the following:

(a) There is an urgent need for low-cost, energy-efficient housing in California.

(b) The cost of conventional lumber-framed housing has risen due to a shortage of construction-grade lumber.

(c) Straw is an annually renewable source of cellulose that can be used as an energy-efficient substitute for stud-framed wall construction.

(d) The state has mandated that the burning of rice straw be greatly reduced.

(e) As a result of the mandated burning reduction, growers are experimenting with alternative straw management practices. Various methods of straw incorporation into the soil are the most widely used alternatives. The two most common methods are nonflood incorporation and winter flood incorporation. Economically viable off-farm uses for rice straw are not yet available.

(f) Winter flooding of rice fields encourages the natural decomposition of rice straw and provides valuable waterfowl habitat. According to the Central Valley Habitat Joint Venture component of the North American Waterfowl Management Plan, in California's Central Valley, over 400,000 acres of enhanced agricultural lands are needed to restore the depleted migratory waterfowl populations of the Pacific flyway. Flooded rice fields are a key and integral part of the successful restoration of historic waterfowl and shorebird populations.

(g) Winter flooding of rice fields provides significant waterfowl habitat benefits and should be especially encouraged in areas where there Ch. 31 - 3 - 94 is minimal potential to impact salmon as a result of surface water diversions.

(h) An economically viable market for rice straw bales could result from the use of rice straw bales in housing construction.

(i) Practicing architects and engineers have determined that the statutory guidelines established by Chapter 941 of the Statutes of 1995 contain specific requirements that they believe are either unnecessary or detrimental. Some of the requirements are considered costly and severely restrict the development of straw-bale housing.

(j) Statutory guidelines for the use of straw-bale housing would significantly benefit energy conservation, natural resources, low-cost housing, agriculture, and fisheries in California.

(k) Tests and experience with straw-bale construction demonstrate that it is a strong, durable, and thermally superior building system that deserves a larger role in modern construction.

SEC. 2. Section 18944.31 of the Health and Safety Code is amended to read:

18944.31. (a) Notwithstanding any other provision of law, the guidelines established by this chapter shall apply to the construction of all structures that use baled straw as a loadbearing or nonloadbearing material within any city or county that adopted the guidelines established by Chapter 941 of the Statutes of 1995 prior to January 1, 2002. This requirement shall not preclude the city or county from making changes or modifications to the guidelines pursuant to subdivision (b). Notwithstanding any other provision of law, the guidelines established by this chapter shall not become operative in a city or county that has not adopted the guidelines prior to January 1, 2002, unless and until the legislative body of the city or county makes an express finding that the application of these guidelines within the city or county is reasonably necessary because of local conditions and the city or county files a copy of that finding with the department.

(b) A city or county may, by ordinance or regulation, make any changes or modifications in the guidelines contained in this chapter as it determines are reasonably necessary because of local conditions, provided the city or county files a copy of the changes or modifications and the express findings for the changes or modifications with the department. No change or modification of that type shall become effective or operative for any purpose until the finding and the change or modification has been filed with the department.

(c) Nothing in this chapter shall be construed as increasing or decreasing the authority to approve or disapprove of alternative construction methods pursuant to the State Housing Law, Part 1.5 Ch. 31 - 4 - 94 (commencing with Section 17910) or the California Building Standards Code, Title 24 of the California Code of Regulations.

(d) It is the intent of the Legislature that the statutory guidelines of this chapter serve as an interim measure pending the evaluation of straw bales as a construction material through the normal processes used for the testing and listing of building materials, the determination of construction standards, and the adoption of those materials and construction standards into the California Building Standards Code.

SEC. 3. Section 18944.33 of the Health and Safety Code is amended to read:

18944.33. For the purposes of this chapter, the following terms are defined as follows:

(a) "Bales" means rectangular compressed blocks of straw, bound by strings or wire.

(b) "Department" means the Department of Housing and Community Development.

(c) "Flakes" means slabs of straw removed from an untied bale. Flakes are used to fill small gaps between the ends of stacked bales.

(d) "Laid flat" refers to stacking bales so that the sides with the largest cross-sectional area are horizontal and the longest dimension of this area is parallel with the wall plane.

(e) "Laid on edge" refers to stacking bales so that the sides with the largest cross-sectional area are vertical and the longest dimension of this area is horizontal and parallel with the wall plane.

(f) "Loadbearing" refers to plastered straw-bale walls that bear the dead and live loads of the roof and any upper floor.

(g) "Nonloadbearing" refers to plastered straw-bale walls that bear only their own weight, such as infill panels within some type of post and beam structure.

(h) "Plaster" means lime, gypsum, lime cement, or cement plasters, as defined by the California Building Standards Code, or earthen plaster with fiber reinforcing.

(i) "Straw" means the dry stems of cereal grains left after the seed heads have been substantially removed.

SEC. 4. Section 18944.35 of the Health and Safety Code is amended to read:

18944.35. (a) Bales shall be rectangular in shape.

(b) Bales used within a continuous wall shall be of consistent height and width to ensure even distribution of loads within wall systems.

(c) Bales shall be bound with ties of either polypropylene string or baling wire. Bales with broken or loose ties shall not be used unless the broken or loose ties are replaced with ties which restore the original degree of compaction of the bale. Ch. 31 - 5 - 94

(d) The moisture content of bales, at the time of installation, shall not exceed 20 percent of the total weight of the bale. Moisture content of bales shall be determined through the use of a suitable moisture meter, designed for use with baled rice straw or hay, equipped with a probe of sufficient length to reach the center of the bale, and used to determine the average moisture content of five bales randomly selected from the bales to be used.

(e) Bales in loadbearing walls shall have a minimum calculated dry density of 7.0 pounds per cubic foot. The calculated dry density shall be determined after reducing the actual bale weight by the weight of the moisture content.

(f) Where custom-made partial bales are used, they shall be of the same density, same string or wire tension, and, where possible, use the same number of ties as the standard size bales.

(g) Bales of various types of straw, including wheat, rice, rye, barley, oats, and similar plants, shall be acceptable if they meet the minimum requirements of this chapter for density, shape, moisture content, and ties.

SEC. 5. Section 18944.40 of the Health and Safety Code is amended to read:

18944.40. (a) Straw-bale walls, when covered with plaster, drywall, or stucco, shall be deemed to have the equivalent fire resistive rating as wood-frame construction with the same wall-finishing system.

(b) Minimum bale wall thickness shall be 13 inches.

(c) Buildings with loadbearing bale walls shall not exceed one story in height without substantiating calculations and design by a civil engineer or architect licensed by the state, and the bale portion of the loadbearing walls shall not exceed a height-to-width ratio of 5.6:1 (for example, the maximum height for a wall that is 23 inches thick would be 10 feet 8 inches).

(d) The ratio of unsupported wall length to thickness, for loadbearing walls, shall not exceed 15.7:1 (for example, for a wall that is 23 inches thick, the maximum unsupported length allowed is 30 feet).

(e) The allowable vertical load (live and dead load) on top of loadbearing bale walls plastered with cement or lime cement plaster on both sides shall not exceed 800 pounds per linear foot, and the resultant load shall act at the center of the wall. Straw-bale structures shall be designed to withstand all vertical and horizontal loads, and the resulting overturning and base shear, as specified in the latest edition of the California

Building Standards Code. Straw-bale walls plastered with cement or lime cement plaster on both sides shall be capable of resisting in-plane lateral forces from wind or earthquake of 360 pounds per linear foot. Ch. 31 - 6 - 94

(f) Foundations shall be designed in accordance with the California Building Standards Code to accommodate the load created by the bale wall plus superimposed live and dead loads. Supports for bale walls shall extend to an elevation of at least six inches above adjacent ground at all points, and at least one inch above floor surfaces.

(g) (1) Bale walls shall be anchored to supports to resist lateral forces, as approved by the civil engineer or architect. This may be accomplished with one-half inch reinforcing bars embedded in the foundation and penetrating the bales by at least 12 inches, located along the center line of the bale wall, spaced not more than two feet apart. Other methods as determined by the engineer or architect may also be used.

(2) Nonbale walls abutting bale walls shall be attached by means of one or more of the following methods or by means of an acceptable equivalent:

(A) Wooden dowels of ⅝ inch minimum diameter and of sufficient length to provide 12 inches of penetration into the bale, driven through holes bored in the abutting wall stud, and spaced to provide one dowel connection per bale.

(B) Pointed wooden stakes, a minimum of 12 inches in length and 1½ inches by 3½ inches at the exposed end, fully driven into each course of bales, as anchorage points.

(C) Bolted or threaded rod connection of the abutting wall, through the bale wall, to a steel nut and steel or plywood plate washer, a minimum of 6 inches square and a minimum thickness of 3/16 of an inch for steel and ½ inch for plywood, in a minimum of three locations.

(3) (A) Bale walls and roof bearing assemblies shall be anchored to the foundation where necessary, as determined by the civil engineer or architect, by means of methods that are adequate to resist uplift forces resulting from the design wind load. There shall be a minimum of two points of anchorage per wall, spaced not more than 6 feet apart, with one located within 36 inches of each end of each wall.

(B) With loadbearing bale walls, the dead load of the roof and ceiling systems will produce vertical compression of the walls. Regardless of the anchoring system used to attach the roof bearing assembly to the foundation, prior to installation of wall finish materials, the nuts, straps, or cables shall be retightened to compensate for this compression.

(h) (1) A moisture barrier shall be used between the top of the foundation and the bottom of the bale wall to prevent moisture from migrating through the foundation so as to come into contact with the bottom course of bales. This barrier shall consist of one of the following:

(A) Cementitious waterproof coating.

(B) Type 30 asphalt felt over an asphalt emulsion.

(C) Sheet metal flashing, sealed at joints.
Ch. 31 - 7 - 94

(D) Another building moisture barrier, as approved by the building official.

(2) All penetrations through the moisture barrier, as well as all joints in the barrier, shall be sealed with asphalt, caulking, or an approved sealant.

(3) There shall also be a drainage plane between the straw and the top of the foundation, such as a one inch layer of pea gravel.

(i) (1) For nonloadbearing walls, bales may be laid either flat or on edge. Bales in loadbearing bale walls shall be laid flat and be stacked in a running bond, where possible, with each bale overlapping the two bales beneath it. Overlaps shall be a minimum of 12 inches. Gaps between the ends of bales which are less than 6 inches in width may be filled by an untied flake inserted snugly into the gap.

(2) Bale wall assemblies shall be held securely together by rebar pins driven through bale centers as described in this chapter, or equivalent methods as approved by the civil engineer or architect.

(3) The first course of bales shall be laid by impaling the bales on the rebar verticals and threaded rods, if any, extending from the foundation.

When the fourth course has been laid, vertical #4 rebar pins, or an acceptable equivalent long enough to extend through all four courses, shall be driven down through the bales, two in each bale, located so that they do not pass through the space between the ends of any two bales.

The layout of these rebar pins shall approximate the layout of the rebar pins extending from the foundation. As each subsequent course is laid, two pins, long enough to extend through that course and the three courses immediately below it, shall be driven down through each bale. This pinning method shall be continued to the top of the wall. In walls seven or eight courses high, pinning at the fifth course may be eliminated.

(4) Alternative pinning method to the method described in paragraph

(3): when the third course has been laid, vertical #4 rebar pins, or an acceptable equivalent, long enough to extend through all three courses, shall be driven down through the bales, two in each bale, located so that they do not pass through the space between the ends of any two bales.

The layout of these rebar pins shall approximate the layout of the rebar pins extending from the foundation. As each subsequent course is laid, two pins, long enough to extend through that course and the two courses immediately below it, shall be driven down through each bale. This pinning method shall be continued to the top of the wall.

(5) Only full-length bales shall be used at corners of loadbearing bale walls.

(6) Vertical #4 rebar pins, or an acceptable alternative, shall be located within one foot of all corners or door openings.
Ch. 31 - 8 - 94

(7) Staples, made of #3 or larger rebar formed into a "U" shape, a minimum of 18 inches long with two 6-inch legs, shall be used at all corners of every course, driven with one leg into the top of each abutting corner bale.

(j) (1) All loadbearing bale walls shall have a roof bearing assembly at the top of the walls to bear the roof load and to provide the means of connecting the roof structure to the foundation. The roof bearing assembly shall be continuous along the tops of loadbearing bale walls.

(2) An acceptable roof bearing assembly option shall consist of two double 2-inch by 6-inch, or larger, horizontal top plates, one located at the inner edge of the wall and the other at the outer edge. Connecting the two doubled top plates, and located horizontally and perpendicular to the length of the wall, shall be 2-inch by 6-inch cross members, spaced no more than 72 inches center to center, and as required to align with the threaded rods extending from the anchor bolts in the foundation. The double 2-inch by 6-inch top plates shall be face-nailed with 16d nails staggered at 16-inch o.c., with laps and intersections face-nailed with four 16d nails. The crossmembers shall be face-nailed to the top plates with four 16d nails at each end. Corner connections shall include overlaps nailed as above or an acceptable equivalent, such as plywood gussets or metal plates. Alternatives to this roof bearing assembly option shall provide equal or greater vertical rigidity and provide horizontal rigidity equivalent to a continuous double 2 by 4 top plate.

(3) The connection of roof framing members to the roof plate shall comply with the appropriate sections of the California Building Standards Code.

(k) All openings in loadbearing bale walls shall be a minimum of one full bale length from any outside corner, unless exceptions are approved by an engineer or architect licensed by the state to practice. Wall or roof load present above any opening shall be carried, or transferred, to the bales below by one of the following:

(1) A frame, such as a structural window or door frame.

(2) A lintel, such as an angle-iron cradle, wooden beam, or wooden box beam. Lintels shall be at least twice as long as the opening is wide and extend a minimum of 24 inches beyond either side of the opening.

Lintels shall be centered over openings.

(3) A roof bearing assembly designed to act as a rigid beam over the opening.

(l) (1) All weather-exposed bale walls shall be protected from water damage. No vapor impermeable barrier may be used on bale walls, and the civil engineer or architect may design the bale walls without any membrane barriers between straw and plaster, except as specified in this Ch. 31-9-94

section, in order to allow natural transpiration of moisture from the bales and to secure a structural bond between plaster and straw.

(2) Bale walls shall have special moisture protection provided at all horizontal surfaces exposed to the weather. This moisture protection shall be installed in a manner that will prevent water from entering the wall system.

(m) (1) Interior and exterior surfaces of bale walls shall be protected from mechanical damage, flame, animals, and prolonged exposure to water. Bale walls adjacent to bath and shower enclosures shall be protected by a moisture barrier.

(2) Cement stucco shall be reinforced with galvanized woven wire stucco netting or an equivalent, as approved by the building official. The reinforcement shall be secured by attachment through the wall at a maximum spacing of 24 inches horizontally and 16 inches vertically, unless substantiated otherwise by a civil engineer or architect.

(3) Where bales abut other materials, the plaster or stucco shall be reinforced with galvanized expanded metal lath, or an acceptable equivalent, extending a minimum of 6 inches onto the bales.

(4) Earthen and lime-based plasters may be applied directly onto bale walls without reinforcement, except where applied over materials other than straw.

(n) (1) All wiring within or on bale walls shall meet all provisions of the California Electrical Code. Type "NM" or "UF" cable may be used, or wiring may be run in metallic or nonmetallic conduit systems.

(2) Electrical boxes shall be securely attached to wooden stakes driven a minimum of 12 inches into the bales, or an acceptable equivalent.

(o) Water or gas pipes within bale walls shall be encased in a continuous pipe sleeve to prevent leakage within the wall. Where pipes are mounted on bale walls, they shall be isolated from the bales by a moisture barrier.

(p) Bales shall be protected from rain and other moisture infiltration at all times until protected by the roof of the structure.

SEC. 6. Section 18944.41 is added to the Health and Safety Code, to read:

18944.41. Sections 18944.30, 18944.31, 18944.33, 18944.35, and 18944.40 shall become inoperative when building standards become effective after approval by the California Building Standards Commission pursuant to Chapter 4 (commencing with Section 18935) that permit the construction of structures that use baled straw as a loadbearing or nonloadbearing material and that are safe to the public.

SEC. 7. Notwithstanding Section 17610 of the Government Code, if the Commission on State Mandates determines that this act contains Ch. 31-10-94

costs mandated by the state, reimbursement to local agencies and school districts for those costs shall be made pursuant to Part 7 (commencing with Section 17500) of Division 4 of Title 2 of the Government Code.

If the statewide cost of the claim for reimbursement does not exceed one million dollars ($1,000,000), reimbursement shall be made from the State Mandates Claims Fund.

SEC. 8. This act is an urgency statute necessary for the immediate preservation of the public peace, health, or safety within the meaning of Article IV of the Constitution and shall go into immediate effect. The facts constituting the necessity are:

To ensure that recent improvements in the 1995 state guidelines governing design and engineering of structures constructed with baled straw are made available to the public at the earliest opportunity, and to expedite ongoing efforts by the California rice industry to develop alternative markets and uses for rice straw stubble, it is necessary that this act take effect immediately.

Index

acoustics, 11, 12-13, 238
active solar design, 105-107, 114, 115
adobe and earth bricks, 18
air leaks, 36-37, 248, 249
allergies, 36, 37, 176
anchor points, 130, 178
architects, 123-124, 145-146
asphalt shingle roofs, 95-96
ASTM236 Hot Box testing, 6
ASTME72, 32
ASTME-119, 32, 35

bale beater, 175, 193
baled waste, 20, 25
bale needle, 174, 175, 190-191, 196, 209
bales,
    availability, 24-26, 250
    characteristics, 26-28
    cost, 29, 173
    dipping, 208-209
    distributing, 190
    handling, 30
    plastered, 31-33, 34
    retying, 190-191
    storing, 29-30, 250
bale wall raising, 185-210, 253-260

shaping, 201-203, 204
sizing bales, 190-191
stacking 185-187, 191-199
steps, 187
stuffing, 192 , 200-201, 202, 204
See also corner guides; door and window bucks; electrical boxes and wiring
baling twine, 174, 249
Battle, Paul, 36-37
Belanger, Paul, 95-97
biodiesel, 107
Bowen, Julie, 258-259
brown coat, 221, 231
budgets, 159-168
    hidden costs, 161-162, 249
    preconstruction costs, 160-161
    samples, 165-168
    sustainable options, 175-176
    See also labor; materials
building code, 18, 27, 35, 40, 41, 69, 72, 76, 90, 108
    BC, 8-9
    California, 269-272
    compliance, 78, 117, 121, 125, 213, 215, 217-218, 219
    jurisdictions, 141-142

building industry, 14-15
building inspector, 142-144
building permit, 141-149
    documents, 147-148
    rejections and appeals, 148
building professionals, 152-153, 156-158
    See also architects; draftsperson; engineers
building size, 61-62, 78-79
building supplies, *See* materials; tools

California Building Code, 269-272
Canada Mortgage and Housing Corporation (CMHC), 7-9, 34, 40, 43, 98
cantilevered floors, 130
caulking, 178, 181, 203, 231
cedar shake roofs, 95
cement
    and concrete, 86-89
    plaster, 212-213
    lime plaster, 213-214
    waterproofing, 243-244
ceramic tile roofs, 96
cob, 17-18, 201, 202, 228
cold bridges, 8
composting toilet, 251

About the Authors

Chris Magwood fell into the straw bale void nine years ago, and has been immersed in all manner of sustainable building projects ever since. Currently the lead instructor for Fleming College's sustainable building program, Chris has also been the editor for *The Last Straw* journal, and has participated in the design and construction of over 35 really cool buildings, most with Camel's Back Construction. He lives in a house of straw with his family and various crazy animals. He always has good hair, often rivaling that of his co-authors.

Peter Mack and Tina Therrien met on a straw bale jobsite nine years ago, and haven't looked back since. They operate Camel's Back Construction from their home in Warsaw, Ontario. Peter Mack has been building and inventing for what seems like the greater part of his life. His commitment to building in a more sustainable and environmentally sound way sprouted with his first building project 11 years ago. In the subsequent years as a professional straw bale builder, Pete has helped refine bale building into a fine art and has provided guidance to other builders and homeowners on countless projects. An inventor, instrument maker, machinist, fitter welder, and avid mountain biker, Pete brings diverse skills and ideas to the straw bale community, as well as his esteemed Estonian mumbling. Combining her love of working with metal, making bread, and teaching, (even though she left her full-time elementary teaching job), Tina rounds out the Camel's Back Construction team with frequent homemade cookies, hand-forged bale needles, excellent plastering outfits and many other talents. Pete and Tina have worked on close to 100 straw bale projects in their collective experience, and in that time, have forged many lasting friendships with clients they have built for. Contact information: Peter Mack/Tina Therrien P.O. Box 61 Warsaw, Ontario K0L 3A0 strawbus@auracom.com www.strawhomes.ca   Chris Magwood R.R. #3 Madoc, Ontario K0L 2K0 cmagwood@kos.net

If you have enjoyed *More Straw Bale Building*, you might also enjoy other

BOOKS TO BUILD A NEW SOCIETY

Our books provide positive solutions for people who want to make a difference. We specialize in:

Sustainable Living ◆ Ecological Design and Planning ◆ Natural Building & Appropriate Technology

New Forestry ◆ Environment and Justice ◆ Conscientious Commerce ◆ Progressive Leadership

Educational and Parenting Resources ◆ Resistance and Community ◆ Nonviolence

For a full list of NS~~~~ ~~~~ur web site at:

Taylor Publishing
www.dirtcheapbuilder.com
707-441-1632
PO BOX 375
CUTTEN CA 95534

New Society Publishers

ENVIRONMENTAL BENEFITS STATEMENT

New Society Publishers has chosen to produce this book on recycled paper made with 100% post consumer waste, processed chlorine free, and old growth free.

For every 5,000 books printed, New Society saves the following resources:[1]

80	Trees
7,210	Pounds of Solid Waste
7,932	Gallons of Water
10,347	Kilowatt Hours of Electricity
13,106	Pounds of Greenhouse Gases
56	Pounds of HAPs, VOCs, and AOX Combined
20	Cubic Yards of Landfill Space

[1]Environmental benefits are calculated based on research done by the Environmental Defense Fund and other members of the Paper Task Force who study the environmental impacts of the paper industry.

NEW SOCIETY PUBLISHERS